D0760933

ALSO BY HOWARD BALL

The *Bakke* Case
Cancer Factories
Compromised Compliance
Controlling Regulatory Sprawl
Courts and Politics
A Defiant Life: Thurgood Marshall
Hugo L. Black
Judicial Craftsmanship or Fiat?
Justice Downwind
Murder in Mississippi
Of Power and Right
Prosecuting War Crimes and Genocide
The Supreme Court in the Intimate Lives of Americans
U.S. Homeland Security
The U.S. Supreme Court
USA Patriot Act of 2001
The Vision and the Dream of Hugo L. Black
War Crimes and Justice
The Warren Court's Perceptions of Democracy
"We Have a Duty"

Justice in Mississippi

The Murder Trial of Edgar Ray Killen

Howard Ball

UNIVERSITY PRESS OF KANSAS

Published by the University Press of Kansas (Lawrence, Kansas 66045),
which was organized by the Kansas Board of Regents and is operated
and funded by Emporia State University, Fort Hays State University,
Kansas State University, Pittsburg State University, the University of Kansas,
and Wichita State University

Library of Congress Cataloging-in-Publication Data
Ball, Howard, 1937–
Justice in Mississippi : the murder trial of Edgar Ray Killen /
Howard Ball.
p. cm.
Includes bibliographical references and index.
ISBN 0-7006-1461-3 (cloth : alk. paper)
1. Killen, Edgar Ray—Trials, litigation, etc. 2. Trials
(Murder)—Mississippi—Philadelphia. 3. Civil rights workers—Crimes
against—Mississippi—Neshoba County—History—20th century. I. Title.
KF224.K55B35   2004
364.152'309762685—dc22
2006010592

British Library Cataloguing-in-Publication Data is available.

Printed in the United States of America
10 9 8 7 6 5 4 3 2 1

The paper used in this publication meets the minimum requirements of
the American National Standard for Permanence of Paper for
Printed Library Materials Z39.48-1992.

Dedicated to a few of Mississippi's fine folk,
Stanley Dearman
Susan Glisson
Donna Ladd
Jerry Mitchell
Dick Molpus
Sid Salter
The members of the Philadelphia Coalition

To the blessed memory of
Mickey Schwerner
James Chaney
Andrew Goodman

And to
Rita Schwerner Bender
Carolyn Goodman
Fannie Lee Chaney

Contents

Acknowledgments

There are so many good people I am happy to thank for their help to me in the spring of 2005, as I set about to tell the story of the trial of Edgar Ray Killen, the "Preacher." My many weeks in Mississippi in 2005 meant my reconnecting with old friends in Starkville and Jackson. The visit was also the occasion for making new friends in Jackson and in Philadelphia, Mississippi.

Thanks to Bill Giles and Charles and Suzie Lowery, decades-old Starkville friends who gave me shelter and sustenance during a good part of the trip. I traveled more than 120 miles (from Starkville down to Philadelphia and back) each day, and returning to these friends was a nice end to long days spent in Neshoba County. I greatly valued the conversations and the dinners we enjoyed together and look forward to seeing them in the future.

I also appreciated the help I received from some former colleagues of mine in the political science and sociology departments at Mississippi State University, in particular, Steve Shaffer, Art Cosby, and Ed Clynch.

When I traveled to Jackson for a week of interviews and research, I rejoined another group of Mississippi friends, including Donna Ladd, a former student of mine at Mississippi State University and now the editor-in-chief of the exciting newsweekly the *Jackson Free Press*, and her companion Todd Stauffer, the publisher of the *Free Press*.

And, in Jackson and in Philadelphia, I touched base with another former student—and now a friend, Sid Salter, who is the features editor at the *Jackson Clarion-Ledger*. When we were sitting together in Philadelphia at the trial one day, it seemed that most Neshoba County residents were his friends, for many came over to shoot the breeze during recesses. These greeters included District Attorney Mark Duncan, Attorney General Jim Hood, even some of Killen's friends. Just about every Neshoba County Deputy Sheriff and Philadelphia police officer, as well as Judge Gordon, came over to shake hands and say hello to Sid—and to me. Thanks, Sid!

Through Donna's intercession, I met a delightful new friend, JoAnne Pritchard Morris, the widow of the wonderful Mississippi writer Willie Morris. I was thrilled to stay at her home and thank her for allowing me to take shelter there while I was in Jackson. Our conversational topics were wide-ranging and included Marcus DuPree, the fabulous high school football player Willie wrote about *(The Courting of Marcus Dupree)* and I saw in action when I officiated football games in the 1970s, and the differences between dogs and cats.

Donna also introduced me to one of the great staff members at the *Free Press,* the imaginative photographer Kate Medley. Kate, Donna, and I were seen together in Philadelphia as well; we saw almost too much of each other in that small town. Kate had the opportunity to shoot some excellent photographs of Edgar Ray Killen at his house. She also did fine work around the Neshoba County courthouse, and some of the photos used in this book are hers. Although she is now pursuing a graduate degree at Ole Miss, she still shoots for the *Free Press* and the AP when she can.

And, when one is in Jackson, there is the always-open Hal and Mal's, on Commerce Street, for lunch, dinner, good drinks, and great blues and jazz. While there I was able to meet and talk with Dick Molpus, another Mississippian I had the pleasure of renewing friendship with after some years—over some fine wine, of course.

I hadn't been to Philadelphia since I lived in Mississippi almost three decades ago. I visited the town then because I was a football official and had the pleasure of officiating the Philadelphia–Neshoba County football battle as well as working games at the Choctaw Reservation. I'll never forget those Choctaw games because the home team never had to huddle to call plays: They spoke their native language. (And I knew they were doing the before-the-game invocation because, while it was rendered in the native language, "Jesus Christ" came through loud and clear.)

And Neshoba County has changed a great deal—in many ways. I could not get over the huge casinos built and operated by the Mississippi Band of Choctaw Indians in Neshoba County. They provide entertainment and, more important, employment for many hundreds of residents of Neshoba County. There were new factories and a local infrastructure—as seen in the book—that is multicultural and diverse.

While in Philadelphia for the trial, I had the great pleasure to observe fine reporters at work—and to meet and become friends with a number of them. First of all, there was the ever-present Jerry Mitchell of the *Jackson Clarion-Ledger.* In this book, I call him a roving Sherlock Holmes, the epitome of the investigative reporter, who has been on top of these civil rights era tragedies for two decades. I appreciate the times we were able to break bread at the Coffee Bean eatery right off Courthouse Square and admire Jerry for his indefatigable spirit and courage in covering the Killen epoch—as well as his courage in dealing with his own family's medical demons.

Others I learned so much from are Shaila Dewan, of the *New York Times,* a very skilled reporter whose beat is the Southland. In addition, there is Emily Wagster Pettus, the AP staff writer out of Jackson, Mississippi, who did an excellent reporting job and whose words were read by millions across the United States. There is also Sophia Pearson, who covered the trial for *Bloomberg News;* Minna Skau, the U.S. bureau chief for the Danish newspaper *Politiken;* Debbie Burt Myers, who covered the story for the *Neshoba Democrat,* and that newspaper's photographer, Kyle Carter.

Thanks also go to Lisa Fisher and Marco Williams of Two-Tone Productions, in New York City, and to Ross Wilson, the senior producer-director at IWC Media out of Glasgow, Scotland. Both companies were producing documentaries about the trial, for the History Channel and for

Court TV, respectively, and I was fortunate enough to meet with them and chat about the substantive issues that are part of the trial's reality. Like all the other newspeople I met, these individuals were wonderful, very competent professionals who worked about fifteen hours a day and "played" for another five or so.

I also got to know John Suggs, a wonderful features reporter for *Truthout.* We had some good talks about the event taking place in that city in June 2005. In addition, Lena Jakobsson and Paul Hechinger of Court TV were people I worked with while covering the trial in Neshoba County.

I must acknowledge, too, the friendship I developed with Geoff Gevalt, the managing editor of the *Burlington Free Press.* Through his artful, often sardonic words of wisdom, I grew—almost instantly—to appreciate the reporting craft. It was Geoff who gave me the credentials that enabled me to mingle with the press corps down in Philadelphia.

While in Philadelphia, I met with and got to know a number of the members of the Philadelphia Coalition. One of them, Fenton DeWeese, is a gregarious lawyer who has from the beginning been one of those calling for justice in the "Mississippi Burning" tragedy. I know he took issue with some of my remarks about the trial, and I take this opportunity to apologize and wish him well.

Stanley Dearman, a dear man if ever there was one, is another coalition member I got to know and talk with during the trial. As noted in the book, he has seen change in Philadelphia since he moved there from Meridian, Mississippi, a few years after Schwerner, Chaney, and Goodman were murdered by the KKK in June 1964. He, like me, has lived long enough to see a murder trial take place in a state court in Mississippi.

I also want to thank Deborah Posey and Jewell McDonald, as well as Leroy Clemons, Jim Prince, and Deborah Owens, for their informative, and at times moving, conversations with me about life in Philadelphia and Neshoba County.

Still another person I met for the first time in Philadelphia was Susan Glisson, the executive director of the William Winter Institute for Racial

Reconciliation. She was a great help to me while I was in Mississippi and afterwards when, up here in the North Country, I needed answers to some questions. I appreciated and took up her invitation to attend the teacher workshop the WWIRR ran, with the Philadelphia Coalition, in June 2005. She is doing a great deal of work with leaders of towns and cities across Mississippi to guide these places through the truth and reconciliation process. This work is but one clear example of positive change in the state of Mississippi, and I take this opportunity to applaud her and the local leaders in these towns in their joint effort to move toward truth and reconciliation.

In Philadelphia, in Jackson, and over the telephone I got to know and respect a number of attorneys and investigators in the Mississippi Attorney General's Office: thank you's to Jim Gilliland, Jacob Ray, and their staff for providing me with needed documentation at the same time the office was preparing the *Killen* briefs for submission to the Mississippi Supreme Court.

I also need to thank the key participants in the Killen trial itself for allowing me the opportunity to meet with them and to ask them questions. These persons include the trial judge, Marcus D. Gordon; the prosecutors, Mark Duncan and Jim Hood; the defense attorneys and/or professional staff, Jim McIntyre and Wendy Moran (wife of Mitch Moran).

The commissioner of the Mississippi Department of Corrections, Chris Epps, provided me with much-needed data on how prisoners like Byron De La Beckwith, Sam Bowers, and Edgar Ray Killen were and are handled by prison authorities. I would also like to thank the friendly staff at Peggy's Restaurant. I appreciated their willingness to take time out from their hectic lives to speak with me about the Preacher and about justice.

Ann Amis Gilmer, the official court reporter for the Eighth Circuit Court District, Mississippi, did an outstanding job of preparing the trial transcript. Although faced with the terrible consequences of Hurricanes Katrina and Rita and her own personal battle with cancer, the venerable Ann came through with an outstanding piece of reporting. I appreciate the

care with which she did the work of transcribing the trial—and I appreciate her friendship as well. As she told me, she "feels like [she's] part of
this history." And indeed she is!

I want to take this opportunity to thank the editor-in-chief at the University Press of Kansas, Michael Briggs, for his friendship and his professional advice on this project. Thanks also to Susan Schott at the press and
to the reviewers of the manuscript.

Finally, I want to express my love and gratitude to my family: my
wife, Carol; my three daughters, Sue, Sheryl, and Melissa; my two sons,
Patrick and Jay; my three grandchildren, Lila, Nathan, and Sophie; and,
as ever, the four-legged family members: Maggie and Charlie, my therapy
dog Chessies; Candyman, my Missouri fox-trotter; Norman, Carol's quarter horse; and Dirty Harry, our mini-horse/magician/Houdini.

Inevitably, in any manuscript, there are errors. I take responsibility
for all of them.

Howard Ball
Richmond, Vermont
March 2006

Justice in Mississippi

Introduction

I'm glad I can't remember those old days. You hear so much about
"the good old days." The good old days weren't so good.
*Howard Armstrong, juror in the 1955 murder trial of two men
accused of murdering Emmett Till, a young black boy
from Chicago visiting Money, Mississippi* [1]

I'm looking for Justice.
Dr. Carolyn Goodman, 2004 [2]

It took Moses only forty years to lead the Jews to the Promised Land after
their hasty exodus from Egypt. And that period of time included the intercession of God to give Moses the Ten Commandments. [3] However, it took
the state of Mississippi forty-one years to bring murder charges against
only one of the seventeen men involved in the June 1964 murders of three
civil rights workers, Michael Schwerner, James Chaney, and Andrew
Goodman.

In 1967, eighteen Mississippi Klansmen were indicted for conspiracy
in the murders of the three young men. They were tried in U.S. District
Court in Meridian, Mississippi. Since felony murder at the time was solely
a state crime, the federal government could not try the Klansmen for the

1

murders of the three young men. Seven of the men were convicted of participation in the conspiracy to take the constitutional rights and liberties of the three men and received sentences ranging from six to ten years. There were three mistrials. The other eight defendants were acquitted.[4]

One of the three whose trial ended in a hung jury was forty-two-year-old Edgar Ray "Preacher" Killen, a logger and part-time Baptist minister at the County Line Baptist Church at the time of the murders. In his case, the jury voted eleven to one to convict. The lone holdout was a woman who firmly believed that a man of God could not have been part of the conspiracy. Years later, she ruefully admitted she had been wrong.

Ironically, the Preacher, according to the evidence presented by federal prosecutors in the 1967 conspiracy trial, was identified as the ringleader of the Klansmen. He was the man given the "elimination" order to kill Schwerner by Sam Bowers, leader of the Mississippi Klan at the time.

Killen, after being notified by Deputy Sheriff Cecil Price that the three young Congress of Racial Equality (CORE) workers were in the Philadelphia, Mississippi, jail, quickly gathered a group of Klansmen in a local eatery in Meridian and laid out the plan of attack once the young men were released from the jail later that evening. He gave out the deadly assignments at the meeting, including where the bodies were to be buried and who was to operate the backhoe to dig the graves. Yet because one juror refused to accept the evidence of Killen's participation in the executions, he walked out of the federal courthouse in Meridian a free man.

Forty years later, in December 2004, Mark Duncan, the newly elected district attorney of Neshoba County, Mississippi, convened a grand jury to review the evidence regarding the murders of the three men, with the goal of indicting one or more people for the crime. On January 6, 2005, the grand jury indicted Edgar Ray Killen on three counts of murder:

> On or about the 21st day of June 1964, in the county and state aforesaid, and within the jurisdiction of this Court, [Killen] did willfully,

unlawfully, and feloniously kill and murder Michael Schwerner [(Count One), and,] based on the same transactions and occurrences, [James Chaney (Count Two), and Andrew Goodman (Count Three)], human being[s], without the authority of law and with deliberate design to effect the death of Schwerner[, Chaney, and Goodman], in violation of Section 2215, Miss. Code of 1942 (recompiled as Section 97-3-19 (1) (a), Miss. Code of 1972, as amended).[5]

The indictment was the "first-ever state charges in a crime that came to be called 'Mississippi Burning.'"[6] That evening, the eighty-year-old Killen was arrested by Neshoba County deputies and was arraigned the next day at the Neshoba County Courthouse. When informed of the indictment, Andrew Goodman's mother, Dr. Carolyn Goodman, "gushed with joy: 'That's good news, very good news.'"[7]

In this book I will examine the trial of Edgar Ray Killen in an effort to understand the events that led to the decision to indict Killen before he died of old age. For forty-one years, state and county prosecutors had not acted to bring to justice the perpetrators of the 1964 triple murders.

Just as the biblical Moses had his challenges, moral tribulations that delayed the Israelites from reaching Eretz Yisrael for four decades (his followers bowing down to the gold idols, for one thing), so too did the blind goddess of justice have despairing times in Mississippi for an even longer period. For blacks in the Deep South, the short poem, "Justice," by Langston Hughes, expressed their views of the goddess:

> That Justice is a blind goddess
> Is a thing to which we black are wise:
> Her bandage hides two festering sores
> That once perhaps were eyes.[8]

There was in Mississippi and other Deep South states the very real existence of the centuries-old "culture of impunity." Until change occurred in Mississippi, this culture protected any white native of the Magnolia State who killed blacks or "outside agitators" from facing justice in a state court. Some Mississippians who grew up during the era of "Jim Crow" segregation and racial discrimination actually did not realize that murdering a black person or a civil rights "outside agitator" was a crime.

From the day the bodies of the three civil rights workers were found in August 1964 until 1989, most of the culture's bystanders, the residents of Neshoba County and Mississippi, were too frightened even to talk openly about the terrible crimes committed by the perpetrators, their neighbors. These murderers were free men, Klansmen walking the streets of Philadelphia and Neshoba County without a care in the world.

Although there was the 1967 trial in federal court, where a handful of the murderers were convicted of conspiracy and served brief terms in federal penitentiaries, there never was an effort, by either the State attorneys general or the district attorneys of Neshoba County to bring murder charges against these Klansmen until late 1999.

While events occurred between 1967 and the 1980s that suggested some molecular change in Mississippi,[9] the killers still walked with impunity in Philadelphia and Neshoba County. Evidently, none of them felt guilty or embarrassed enough to move from their homes, and from the scenes of their gruesome crime.

However, in 1989, a number of events occurred that began to shake the culture of impunity's foundation. Apologies by a state leader were rendered to the families of the murdered men, and a group of residents in Neshoba County—blacks, whites, and Choctaw Indians—banded together to demand that truths about the past be uncovered and reexamined and taught and that furthermore, justice must be sought in state courts for those who murdered the trio in 1964. For, these Mississippians argued, without truth and justice—even justice delayed—there can be no reconciliation of the races in Neshoba County and in Mississippi.

A 1988 Hollywood movie, *Mississippi Burning*, educated tens of millions, including young Mississippians who had no knowledge of the events, about the brutal 1964 murders. And a handful of investigative reporters began to search the old records in an effort to uncover the truth about these civil rights era murders and burnings.

By the 1990s, in Mississippi and seven other southern states, prosecutors began to open these "cold cases" from the 1960s and to indict dozens of elderly Klansmen for the murderous acts they committed three decades earlier. During this decade, top-notch investigative reporters found new information, new documents, and new informants and kept writing stories about the decades-old unpunished murderers.

By late 1999, the state attorney general, Mike Moore, and the Neshoba County district attorney, Ken Turner III, reopened the 1964 Neshoba County murders case. In the beginning, there was hope that indictments would be handed down against the nine defendants still alive and living in Neshoba County. However, when the leading witness for the prosecution—Deputy Sheriff Cecil Price—died in 2001, the effort to indict the murderers died a year later.

The story, however, does not end there. After the November 2003 elections, a new district attorney in Neshoba County, Mark Duncan, and a new state attorney general, Jim Hood, both forty-something men, took office. One was two years old, the other five at the time of the June 1964 murders.

In January 2004, when they found themselves with the untried 1964 murder case resting in their laps, they made the fateful decision to reexamine the case and, "once and for all," as the new attorney general said to me, come to some kind of closure. The following year, January 2005, the indictment was handed down by the Neshoba County grand jury.

In *Justice in Mississippi*, I will examine the cycles of events that led to the resurrection of this "cold case." I will look at the strategy of the prosecutors and of the defense counsel and examine the evidence that was

5

introduced by the prosecutors as well as evidence that could *not* be presented to the jury. I will explore the legal, social, political, and pseudo-religious roots of the crime and of the events that occurred in Mississippi in the decades after June 21, 1964. In so doing, I will assess the continuum of change in Mississippi that ultimately brought about, forty-one years later, the indictment and trial of Edgar Ray Killen.

In writing this book, I used the documents released by Mississippi Attorney General Jim Hood, papers that fully elaborate on Hood's efforts as well as those of his predecessor, Mike Moore, to bring the killers of Schwerner, Goodman, and Chaney to justice in a Mississippi courtroom.

In addition to original documents, the story I present incorporates new and important information that surfaced from my interviews with Jim Hood and some of his staff (notably Jim Gilliland); Neshoba County District Attorney Mark Duncan; the defense attorneys (more specifically, Wendy Moran, Mitch Moran's wife, and Jim McIntyre); the judge, Marcus Gordon; jurors; members of the Philadelphia Coalition; and others involved in the events leading up to the indictment and trial.

There are heroes in this story. There is a Neshoba County circuit Judge, Marcus Gordon, who is as forthright, courageous, and committed to justice as the fictional lawyer Atticus Finch in Harper Lee's *To Kill a Mockingbird*.

The prosecutors, too, are examples of "profiles in courage"; for both of them (Duncan and Hood) pushed forward with the indictment and then the trial itself even though they knew they could not present the best possible case because of the death of some key witnesses for the prosecution. As Duncan said to me, "it was not a perfect case." In the next election, these two prosecutors are sure to risk the censure of those who believe that there shouldn't have been an indictment and a trial.[10]

Beyond these key participants in the murder trial of Edgar Ray Killen, there are the other heroes of the story: the men and women of Neshoba County who willingly served as grand jurors and jurors; the local

6

press; and the members of the Philadelphia Coalition. The others in Philadelphia and Neshoba County—the schoolteachers, waitresses, retail clerks, and businesspeople—were able, for the first time since the 1960s, to talk about the past and to agree with many of their neighbors that it was time for justice in Philadelphia, Neshoba County, and the State of Mississippi.

1

Change in Mississippi: *Mississippi vs. Edgar Ray Killen* in Perspective

Leroy Clemons, the President of the local NAACP chapter and
Co-Chair of the Philadelphia Coalition, was stopped in front of the
courthouse by a white man who warned him to watch his back
because "you ain't no Martin Luther King." "I told him,
he was right. I told him I didn't believe in nonviolence."[1]

A [Mississippi] Senate committee chairman refused to take up a bill
Tuesday to honor the three men killed by the Klan in 1964
by renaming part of [Highway] 19 after them.[2]

Edgar Ray Killen, the Preacher, is an eighty-year-old unapologetic Mississippi Klansman. Until his June 21, 2005, conviction for manslaughter
in the June 21, 1964, slayings of three civil rights workers,[3] Killen had
lived his entire life in the hamlet of Union, Mississippi, at the southern-
most edge of Neshoba County, Mississippi. Until his incarceration, Killen
operated a small lumber mill on his property in Union and served as a
part-time Baptist preacher for a number of small congregations located in
isolated tiny villages in the county.

Until he was indicted for the 1964 murders by a Neshoba County
grand jury in January 2005, Killen walked freely in Neshoba County and

among its residents. Most residents, black and white, knew of his role in the Ku Klux Klan. Most had heard, through the town grapevine and after the 1967 trial of eighteen Klansmen in federal court[4] (he was freed because his case ended in an 11–1 hung jury/mistrial), of the major role he played in the killings of the three civil rights workers.

However, all but a handful of bystanders kept silent to avoid any "problems" with Killen and his like-minded friends. For the onlookers, remaining silent was the necessary predicate for their survival in an environment that reeked with the atmosphere of merciless violence against civil rights outsiders and all those in Mississippi who supported these "agitators." It was an environment that lacked simple justice for all.

The Old Mississippi: A Culture of Impunity

Buford Posey was a rarity in Mississippi in 1964. He was a white liberal Philadelphian who was intimidated into fleeing the state by "Preacher" Killen and the Klan in late June 1964. During the Killen trial he told a reporter about the prevailing view in Mississippi when he was growing up during Jim Crow time: "When I was coming up in Mississippi I never knew it was against the law to kill a black man. I learned that when I went in the army. I was 17 years old. When they told me, I thought they were joking."[5]

Marion Caples is a forty-four-year-old white homemaker who lives in Philadelphia. "When I was about 17 years old, the Ku Klux Klan still took up money at the red lights. It would scare anybody," she recalled while awaiting the start of the Killen murder trial.[6] Instead of volunteer firefighters at the traffic light, raising money for a new piece of equipment, hooded Klansmen stood there, buckets in hand.

John Walker's tale of horror and terrorism occurred while he was a seven-year-old riding with his mother and others to Yazoo City. The driver was Lee Andrew Ward, "one of the few black men in his area who owned a car—a shiny black Ford."

Just as they were nearing Yazoo City, a police officer pulled them over and said to Ward, "Where the hell you think you're goin', nigger? Who do you think you are?" Just then the officer pointed his revolver at Ward's head and "shot his brains out on the street," Walker said. [The boy and the other passengers in the car] were frozen in terror and sat in the car all day with the corpse until another black man from their area stopped and gave them a ride home. The officer was never charged with any crime.[7]

These three vignettes reflect the unvarnished reality of life in Mississippi in the middle of the twentieth century. There existed, in Neshoba County, and throughout Mississippi during that time, a culture of impunity. Mississippi and other Deep South states were places where killers of "outsider agitators" (read Jews, or Communists, or anti-Christs) were rarely indicted for their actions, much less found guilty by a jury of their peers. Their peers, after all, shared their malicious views of the hated outside agitator.

Killen "flourished in Mississippi's racist past."[8] Born in 1925, he grew up in the heyday of the twentieth century's "state's rights" segregationist movement. He went to segregated schools and preached in segregated churches, both hallmarks of a regional environment that blatantly and arrogantly flaunted Jim Crowism: official and unofficial racial discrimination.

Mississippi was a closed society, one in which its racist and discriminatory "folkways" and "stateways" remained unchanged for more than one hundred years.[9] It was a place where decent, and very privileged, white professionals—dentists, doctors, lawyers, bankers, farmers, businesspeople, Civitans and Rotary Club members, rabbis, and other Mississippi clergy—joined the local White Citizens' Council (WCC)[10] in order to defend these cherished southern values.[11]

If change was to occur in Mississippi, it "had to come from outside of this [tight] little society," said Mississippi State Senator Gloria Williamson.[12] And in the middle of the twentieth century it was civil rights groups, the "outside agitators," who sought to bring change to Mississippi by direct action and through litigation. Civil rights activism was one of the essential ingredients in the tragedies that led to the murders of individuals such as Michael Schwerner, James Chaney, and Andrew Goodman.

The other ingredient in this deadly clash between good and evil in America's southland were the wanton, lawless actions of the defenders of Mississippi's folkways. For five decades, Edgar Ray "Preacher" Killen "embodied Mississippi at its meanest and angriest: a county preacher with thick woodcutter's forearms, who ordered killings out of hate and who bragged about it."[13]

The battles the Preacher engaged in as a young man were between Mississippians and the always despised "outsiders," the ones who wanted to tell the natives what they must do and how they must behave. As one Neshoba County resident remarked during Killen's trial: "It was [like] when the North came into the South [after the Civil War] and told the South: 'You have to do this, this, and this.' [We] didn't want to be told what to do."[14]

Edgar Ray Killen was still in his thirties, a strong, grim man over 6 feet 2 inches tall, weighing probably around 165 pounds, all hard muscle, when the governor and the legislature created and funded the Mississippi State Sovereignty Commission (MSSC) in 1956. Its initial funding was $250,000. The MSSC consisted of twelve members appointed by the governor and the legislature. Its mission: "To protect the sovereignty of the state of Mississippi." In reality, the MSSC was a secret institution that spied on individuals and groups, mostly "outside agitators," and gave all its reports to White Citizens' Councils, the governor's office, and state legislators committed to preserving the Mississippi way of life.[15] It ceased operations in 1977.

In February 1964, an angry, segregationist Killen—and thousands of other Mississippians who shared his views about the need for absolute segregation of the races—joined in the third incarnation of the Ku Klux

Klan in Mississippi, led by the thirty-nine-year-old Imperial Wizard, Sam Bowers.

Like so many millions of Americans who grow up in small towns such as Union and Philadelphia, Mississippi, Killen didn't "move around that much and lots of people have been here [Neshoba County] their whole lives."[16] Because few people moved in and fewer still left Neshoba County, everybody knew everybody else. Dr. Andrew Sheldon, a jury consultant for the prosecutors in the Killen case, "marveled that 'everybody knows the Killens, and the Killens know everyone.'" "Philadelphia," another consultant noted, was "a place of cozy familiarities."[17]

Fraternity rather than liberty is the hallmark of life in these small, tightly knit towns. Whenever a crime occurs in such a setting, whether it occurs in Philadelphia, Mississippi, in 1964 or in Ulm, Germany, in 1938, there are the victims, the perpetrators, and the vast majority of "the others"—the bystanders. And when the crime is protected by the mantle of impunity that exists in the village or the county, the state or the nation, the perpetrator struts with an arrogance born of immunity and injustice.[18] And the bystanders stand by, mutely—fearfully.

Nettie Cox Moore, a sixty-four-year-old black Philadelphia resident, recalled "a time when men like Killen ran her town."

> Over the years, [she] would see Killen shopping downtown, near the courthouse square. . . . Like everyone, she knew . . . how he carefully orchestrated the burning of a black church and the beating of the worshippers there to lure [Schwerner, Chaney, and Goodman] to Philadelphia [, how Killen planned the murders of the three young men and how] the killers were never held accountable.[19]

However, in the old Mississippi, with its culture of impunity, until the 1990s nothing was done to the perpetrators. (Some still maintain that even in 2005, not very much has been accomplished to deconstruct the substantive systemic reality of white privilege in the state.[20]) For decades, except for the trial of the eighteen conspirators in 1967, no U.S. attorney sought to pursue justice in federal court. For decades, no Neshoba County prosecutor sought indictments from the grand jury. For decades, until the 1990s, no Mississippi attorney general sought indictments in state court against those who took the lives of resident black civil rights leaders as well as those outsiders who sought to affect the culture of racism in Mississippi and other Deep South states.

1989: A Turning Point in Mississippi's History

The year 1989 was a turning point for Mississippi. For the very first time in its history, an elected state government official, Mississippi Secretary of State Dick Molpus, born in Philadelphia, Neshoba County, Mississippi, publicly apologized to the families of the three dead civil rights workers. The venue was a memorial service held in Philadelphia on June 21, 1989, that marked the twenty-fifth anniversary of the murders. The family members attending the memorial service were Steve Schwerner and Rita Schwerner Bender (brother and widow of Michael Schwerner); Ben Chaney and Julia Chaney Moss (brother and daughter of James Chaney); and Dr. Carolyn Goodman and David Goodman (mother and brother of Andrew Goodman). For all of them, this was the first visit to Neshoba County since the three men were "eliminated" by the Klan in June 1964.

Molpus said, to them and to the others attending the ecumenical service at the rebuilt Mt. Zion United Methodist Church:

> We deeply regret what happened here 25 years ago. We wish we could undo it. We are profoundly sorry that they are gone. We wish we could bring them back. Every decent person in Philadelphia and Neshoba County and Mississippi feels that way. . . . Fundamentally, this was a human tragedy. Your presence here underscores that. Three mothers' sons died here on June 21, 1964. Sons, brothers, a

father, a husband—young men who had been nurtured by loving families, just as I was and my friends were as we grew up here in Philadelphia. Their loss cut deeply at the hearts of family and friends. It left an aching void. This is what Philadelphia, Mississippi has come to understand—that we are not talking about abstractions, but about human beings. . . . My heart is full today. It is full because I know the overwhelming majority of the people of Neshoba County are good and decent people. . . . My heart is full because I know that, for a long time, many of us have been searching for a way to ease the burden that this community has carried for 25 years, but we have never known quite what to say. But today we know one way. Today we pay tribute to those who died. We acknowledge that dark corner of our past. . . .

So to you, the families, I say: See what is around you. Draw strength and solace from it. Know that it is real. Black, white, and Choctaw Indian together have forged a new and strong bond and helped transform a community. *Fear has waned—fear of the unknown, fear of each other—and hope abides.* That is our story. And you and yours are part of it. God bless each of you. We are genuinely glad to have you here [my emphasis].[21]

Many years later, in an interview with me, Dick Molpus told me of Rita Schwerner Bender's poignant comment to him at the 2005 trial. "Thank you for what you said in 1989," she told him. "I've carried it [the graceful apology] with me ever since." The words touched him deeply.[22]

Molpus's 1989 apology pierced the veil of silence that enveloped Neshoba County and the entire state immediately after the buried bodies of the three civil rights workers were recovered in August 1964. Stanley Dearman, in 1989 the editor of the *Neshoba Democrat*, the county's weekly newspaper published in Philadelphia, Mississippi, said that Molpus's words immediately "resonated" with him and with other residents of the county. "A lot of people were opposed to it, but a lot of people were glad he said it."[23]

Dearman himself, as editor and reporter, has since the late 1960s played a continuing role in the effort to prod the state's law enforcement officials to formally, for the very first time, examine the events of June 1964 with a view to bringing criminal charges against the perpetrators still living in Neshoba County. Immediately after Molpus's speech, he published a lengthy interview he conducted with Dr. Carolyn Goodman in the *Neshoba Democrat* and periodically visited with her, both before and after her visit to the state in June 1989 to interview her for his Philadelphia readers.[24]

The Molpus apology did not lead to the state reopening the investigation of the three murders, but it "really started a healing process," said Fenton DeWeese, a Philadelphia lawyer and a member of the Philadelphia Coalition.[25] From that June 1989 day to the present, "the killings became a part of the public conversation. . . . In his newspaper, Dearman began calling in editorials for prosecution of [all those who participated in the] killings."[26]

Anne Pullin, a twenty-four-year-old waitress at Peggy's Restaurant, an always-crowded, serve-yourself Philadelphia gastronomic landmark, remarked to a group of us eating lunch: "For twenty or thirty years nobody really talked about [the murders], and then [in June 1989] boom. Now everybody talks about it."[27]

Ironically, the gracious apology was used against Molpus when, in 1995, he ran for governor against Republican opponent Kirk Fordice. Again and again during the campaign, the Republican rebuked Molpus for apologizing to the families. It was "no good" to drag up the state's past:

> I don't believe we need to keep running the state by "Mississippi Burning" and apologizing for 30 years ago. This is the nineties! This is now! We're on a roll. We've got the best race relations in America, and we need to speak positive Mississippi! We have the most black elected officials in the nation! This is Mississippi![28]

16

Although Molpus repeatedly replied angrily during the campaign: "I apologized then, and I make no apology to you about it," he lost the election to Fordice, winning only 40 percent of the vote to Fordice's 60 percent. (Since his 1995 defeat, Molpus has not run for office in Mississippi.)

Molpus's 1989 apology touched upon another new development, one that would have been impossible to realize in an earlier decade: The formation of an integrated group of Neshoba County residents, black, white, and Choctaw Indian, working together to address the reality of racism in their towns and county. While there were a brave handful of Neshoba County citizens who had spoken out against the Klan murders and against racism,[29] most of the county's citizens were silent bystanders—until the late 1980s. Slowly but inexorably, this small group began to look at ways in which they could make a difference in the lives of citizens of Neshoba County.

By 2004, the fortieth anniversary of the deaths of the three men, this Neshoba County coalition had a name and officers and a mission. It was now officially the Philadelphia Coalition. Its cochairs were Jim Prince III, the editor of the *Neshoba Democrat,* and Leroy Clemons, the president of the local chapter of the National Association for the Advancement of Colored People (NAACP). The coalition's goals were apparent in its motto: "Recognition, Resolution, Redemption: Uniting for Justice." (As will be seen in a later chapter, the group prodded and encouraged Mississippi and Neshoba County prosecutors to address the reality of "justice delayed is justice denied" in the murders of Schwerner, Chaney, and Goodman.)

In 1989, Hollywood also had an impact on the course of Mississippi history in a major way: *Mississippi Burning,* starring Gene Hackman and Willem Dafoe, was released toward the end of 1988. The movie included "powerful scenes depicting the racist terror that black people faced during this historic period—scenes rarely seen by a broad sector of the U.S. population."[30] While it was criticized by many for presenting a false picture of the role of the FBI during this era, for more astute observers the film was applauded for its educational value.

17

My initial screening of *Mississippi Burning* was in Seattle in late 1988. (I was there to participate in a celebration of the life of the late Associate Justice of the U.S. Supreme Court, William O. Douglas.) I saw the movie with Drew Days III, the U.S. Justice Department's Assistant Attorney General for Civil Rights during the Carter Administration, 1977–1981, and, in the Clinton Administration, 1993–2001, the U.S. Solicitor General. He is presently a distinguished law professor at Yale Law School. I hated the film for, among other things, its many fictions about the FBI and its depiction of blacks as passive onlookers.

Days, however, scolded me for my shortsightedness because I did not understand the educational power of the images the film presented. The "good guys," Days repeatedly pointed out, the FBI agents portrayed by Hackman and Dafoe, were battling for justice in an evil place and against really "bad guys." And they were confronted by the raw, unadulterated evil of white racists, the Klansmen, in Mississippi. We spent more than a few hours going around on the subject at a late-night yogurt establishment. Drew Days was absolutely correct in his assessment of the film's value.

By 1989, millions of young men and women across the nation, black and white, born years after the 1964 murders, watched the film's dramatic portrayal of the murders of the three young men by Mississippi Klansmen. They saw Klansmen full of venomous hatred of anyone who tried to change the customs and traditions of their "place."

While the film was largely a Hollywood treatment of real events, nevertheless the Manichean struggle between good and evil depicted in the film educated tens of millions of people, even Mississippians, about the culture of impunity that was rooted in the state and that accounted for such unrestrained violence and murder just over twenty years earlier. For example, during the June 2005 voir dire proceedings in the Killen trial, Neshoba County District Attorney Mark Duncan asked the group of almost 200 people in the juror pool: "How many of you have seen the movie *Mississippi Burning?*" Three-quarters of the potential jurors' hands went up.

Anne Pullin, the waitress who works at Peggy's and lives in Killen's small town of Union, Mississippi, attests to the continuing impact of the movie in the twenty-first century. She saw the film in late 2004 and spoke about its effect on her: "It just about tore my heart out. If he [Killen] did it, he deserves to be punished, that's only right."[31]

Another of the many tens of millions of people who "discovered" Mississippi's past by viewing the film was a young investigative news reporter with the *Jackson Clarion-Ledger*, Jerry Mitchell. He was, he told me while we were attending the Killen trial, initially informed about racism in Mississippi by the movie's graphic depiction of segregation. "The film was an epiphany for me," he said.

From 1989 to the present time, he has been investigating and reporting about past wrongs and about justice delayed in his state. "I've been probing the 1964 murders since *before* my fifteen-year-old son was born," he exclaimed to me over a very late lunch at the Coffee Bean eatery off the courthouse square while we were awaiting the Killen jury's verdict.

Clearly, 1989 was the starting point in the recent evolution of race relations in Neshoba County and in Mississippi itself. A public, very graceful, apology was given to the family members of the three civil rights workers; a newspaper reporter began an almost two-decade odyssey to discover the truths about the many civil rights killings that took place in his state in the 1960s; a multiracial group of Neshoba County residents formed a coalition; family members of the dead civil rights workers began a renewed effort to persuade prosecutors to reopen the case; millions of people were moved and educated by Hollywood's *Murder in Mississippi;* and residents of the rural county began to talk openly—for the first time in a quarter century—about the tragic, deadly events of June 1964.

A small group of them, from 1989 through 2004, went beyond talk to boldly demand that the state of Mississippi prosecute all those responsible for the deaths of Michael Schwerner, James Chaney, and Andrew Goodman. Justice, they said, must belatedly make its appearance in a Mississippi courtroom—even after many decades of inaction: To delay

19

justice is to deny justice. To deny justice is to perpetuate the culture of impunity in Mississippi. It was a new message heard in the state. It was a powerful message that eventually resonated with prosecutors in Mississippi—both federal and state attorneys.

The New Mississippi: Substantive Change, or the Old Mississippi but with a Smile?

Between 1989 and 2005, and including the recently concluded trial of Edgar Ray Killen, Mississippi prosecutors and state attorneys general in six other Deep South states have reexamined twenty-six murders from the 1950s–1960s era of the civil rights movement.[32] These reviews led to twenty-eight indictments and arrests and twenty-five trials. In addition to Killen's manslaughter conviction, twenty-one persons were convicted of murder, two were acquitted, and there was one mistrial. In the sixteen years since 1989, "Mississippi leads the nation in prosecuting civil rights-era killings that went unpunished in the 1960's. Killen's indictment marks the fifth case brought to court in the state."[33]

Underscoring the apparent nature of change in the State, within weeks of the Killen verdict and sentencing, the U.S. attorney in Mississippi, Dunn Lampton, announced that his office was reopening two murder cases connected with the 1960s era of the civil rights movement. One case Lampton is examining involves two young blacks whose bodies were found in the lower Mississippi River—almost in Louisiana—while FBI agents and others were looking for Schwerner, Chaney, and Goodman in July 1964. A second case involves the 1967 murder of a black man, the treasurer of the local NAACP, who was promoted to a job in a tire factory believed by Ku Klux Klan workers in that plant to be a job for whites only.[34]

In July 2005, shortly after Killen's conviction, Thomas Moore arrived in Jackson from his home in Colorado Springs, Colorado. Now sixty-two,

Moore is the brother of Charles E. Moore, a nineteen-year-old Alcorn A&M University student killed by the Ku Klux Klan in 1964. The bodies of Moore and his nineteen-year-old friend, Henry Dee, a sawmill worker, were found on the banks of the Mississippi River.

Thomas Moore was in Mississippi for two weeks to visit the area where his brother's body was found and to speak with the U.S. attorney for Mississippi, Dunn Lampton, as well as Mississippi Attorney General Jim Hood about indicting the Klansmen responsible for the deaths.[35] In November 1964, two Klansmen were arrested by Mississippi authorities and charged with the murders of the two young black men. Indeed, one of them confessed to involvement in the crime. However, the murder charges were dropped by the authorities. Both Klansmen, according to Thomas Moore, based on information he received from federal authorities, are still alive and living in Mississippi.[36]

At the same time, Lampton announced that his office was reopening a case involving the 1967 car-bombing death of Wharlest Jackson. The black man was killed as he drove home after being promoted to a "whites only" job at the Armstrong Tire and Rubber plant in Natchez, Mississippi. No arrests were ever made at the time of the murder.

Clearly, these most recent actions by federal and state authorities in Mississippi reflect serious, significant changes taking place in the state. Once-dormant murder cases are no longer being ignored by the U.S. Attorney's Office, the Mississippi Attorney General's Office, and by county district attorneys. Since 1989, there have been continuing efforts by prosecutors to bring to justice white racists who killed blacks and civil rights workers and who were either never indicted and tried or tried but not found guilty because of hung juries.

From 1989 until the Neshoba County grand jury met in January 2005 and indicted Killen, a small cohort of Neshoba County residents repeatedly called for the prosecution of the Klansmen who had murdered the three civil rights workers as well as other Klansmen who had killed blacks during the early years of the civil rights era. People such as Dick Molpus,

Stanley Dearman, Florence Mars, Jim Prince III (who became the editor of the *Neshoba Democrat* after Dearman retired from that position in 2000), and the multiracial, multiethnic cadre of men and women who were to become the Philadelphia Coalition in 2004 pestered and demanded that prosecutors bring to justice the perpetrators of the 1964 murders of Schwerner, Chaney, and Goodman as well as the perpetrators of other cold-blooded murders of the same era.

However, while the Philadelphia Coalition is a clear reflection of the changes occurring in Neshoba County and in Mississippi generally, there are still many people (a sizable minority) in the county and in the state who were against the Killen murder trial and other trials of accused men who allegedly murdered blacks and civil rights workers several decades ago.

In a 2004 opinion survey conducted by the Jackson-based Southern Research Group, when asked if the trials of those involved in the 1964 killings of the civil rights workers should begin now, 47 percent of 509 Neshoba County residents believed that they should. However, 35 percent of those polled believed that a trial should not be pursued by the county prosecutor. Another 16 percent were unsure, while 2 percent refused to answer the question. (Compare these figures with a poll taken by the Mississippi State University's political science department in 1994 regarding statewide Mississippi attitudes about retrying Byron De La Beckwith for the 1963 murder of NAACP leader Medgar Evers: 45 percent felt it was fair to retry De La Beckwith; 41 percent felt it was unfair, while 14 percent had no opinion about the matter.)[37]

For some opposed to trying Killen for the murders, the reasoning was: what's past is past, leave the old pitiful men alone. It does the state no good to continually bring up the events that occurred decades earlier. (For these natives, Faulkner's words about the past not being dead ring false.[38])

Many shared the views of everyone's favorite waitress at Peggy's, Anne Pullin, who tells diners:

I don't think they should have brought it [the murders of the three civil rights workers in 1964] back up. It is going to cause more problems in town. A lot has changed since [1964]. You didn't see blacks and whites mingle then. You do now. This is a new generation. This [trial] could cause more problems.[39]

For others, opposition to indicting and retrying Killen was based on their open friendship with him, and along with this, their lack of discomfort about his Ku Klux Klan membership. For them, there was no problem telling jurors during the trial that the Klan was a "peaceful organization that did good things." The former four-term mayor of Philadelphia, Harlan Majure, testifying for the defense in the Killen trial, uttered those words—to the dismay of most of us sitting in the courtroom.[40] He and others also said in open court that Killen was a man of "good character," or a man who "had a good side"; a "preacher," and therefore a man who could not have been the organizer of the murderous band of Klansmen who took three lives that June night in 1964.

For a small number of Neshoba County residents, not nearly as many as in the past, there is still the fear of violence. There are, even in 2005, at least six separate but very small Klan groups in Mississippi and an almost equal number of "white power" extremist neo-Nazi groups.[41] During the June 2005 trial of Killen, a black Neshoba County man spoke to a reporter anonymously, afraid to give his name. "'I got my job, my life down here to think about,' he said. 'Hell, I got a wife.'"[42] How many other Neshoba County residents feel this way is unknown. However, for those who harbor such a feeling, change has not affected them at all.

The Pace of Change

Change has taken place in Mississippi since the three young men were murdered in 1964. At times it has come molecularly. In the last decade, it seems to have moved faster. One of my tasks, in telling the story of the 2005 trial of Edgar Ray Killen for the murders of Schwerner, Chaney, and

Goodman, is to examine the nature of the change by looking at the individuals involved in the 2005 criminal proceedings in the Neshoba County Circuit Court: Edgar Ray Killen, the defendant; the lawyers on both sides; the judge; and the jurors.

I believe it is an important story, for it will try to uncover the true character and extent of change in a state and region that has, for centuries, been committed to a set of revered principles based on a fundamentally antidemocratic notion: racial and ethnic superiority of and privileges for the white Anglo-Saxon community.

Will the "outing" of the truth lead to reconciliation and the overcoming of Mississippi's antidemocratic belief? After all, it is the one value that has been axiomatic in Mississippi for centuries. Over 140 years ago, America's bloodiest, most costly war (in terms of human lives lost) took place between the North and the South. It occurred because of the South's insistence on the inviolability of its sacred beliefs about slavery and racial superiority.

And, in the years following the end of the Civil War, this regional allegiance to racism continued, oftentimes accompanied by public, community-style lynching parties,[43] economic intimidation, violence, and murder. Following the Civil War, the Ku Klux Klan was born and, at different times throughout the South's history, resurrected to help ensure the maintenance of white racial superiority as well as white economic and social and political privilege.[44]

The Killen trial's story is a prism though which to gauge the nature of change in a city, a county, and a state that have resisted change using not only economic and political strategies—but also violence and even murder—for hundreds of years.

Change through the Truth and Reconciliation Process in Mississippi?

Beyond the reopening of cold murder case files and the conviction of aging Klansmen for their actions almost a half century earlier, the Killen trial story is one that displays the regenerative energy of decent people who have come to recognize the value and the imperative of truth and reconciliation, of openness and freedom, in a democratic society.

Members of a committee from Atlanta, Georgia, called Truth and Reconciliation in the South attended the Killen trial. In addition, Susan M. Glisson, the executive director of the William Winter Institute for Racial Reconciliation,[45] located on the campus of the University of Mississippi, in Oxford, also attended the trial and, more importantly, has worked closely with the Philadelphia Coalition for a number of years, currently serving as special liaison.

The Philadelphia Coalition's actions have ranged from organized events dramatizing the importance of reopening the trial; to assisting the Coalition in planning and printing an important brochure providing visitors to the area with a history of civil rights struggles and a map of the important civil rights sites in Neshoba County; to organizing a three-day civil rights educational program for secondary school teachers in the region.[46]

Glisson's recent observations underscore the growing impact of the concept of a Truth and Reconciliation Commission (TRC)–style process in Mississippi.

We have come far in the South, but still there is pain associated with acknowledging those dark days. *Partly that pain exists because many of these issues remain unresolved and operational in current policies and daily interactions. So we must frankly confront that past for those wounds to heal,* so we can begin to understand the legacy of racism that continues to harm us today in education, health care, housing, and other indicators [my emphasis].[47]

Observing the goings-on and the statements of the Philadelphia Coalition and others, it is clear that the idea of a TRC process, expressed so well by Glisson and possibly modeled after South Africa's TRC, has become an operative one for many Mississippians and others.[48] As Susan told me, "the spirit of [Bishop Tutu's] work animates what the Winter Institute does."[49]

Again and again, from Rita Schwerner Bender's daily comments before, during, and after the Killen trial[50]; from statements issued by the Philadelphia Coalition; and from journalists such as Donna Ladd, the editor-in-chief of the *Jackson Free Press*, the idea of a TRC-type process in Mississippi is seen as the way to reconciliation and greater equality. This process has also been adopted by the Philadelphia Coalition.

In a statement issued immediately after the Killen guilty verdict was announced, the Philadelphia Coalition noted that the conviction of Killen was only the first step on the road to "seek the truth, to insure justice for all, and to nurture reconciliation" in Mississippi.

> Seeking justice for the brutal murders of James Chaney, Andrew Goodman, and Michael Schwerner was long overdue. But we have only begun our work here.
>
> These three brave young men were not murdered by a lone individual. While a vigilante group may have fired the gun, the state of Mississippi loaded and aimed the weapon. The Mississippi State Sovereignty Commission monitored and intimidated civil rights activists to prevent black voter representation. The White Citizens' Councils enforced white supremacy through economic oppression. And decent people remained silent while evil was done in their name. These shameful acts have been little understood by Mississippi citizens.

For the coalition members, much more had to be done to educate Mississippians about the systemic effects of past racial intolerance. "We must all understand how and why these murders and thousands of others occurred. We must understand the system that encouraged it to happen so that we can dismantle it. We must never allow it to happen again. We have the power now to fulfill the promise of democracy. Join us in that strug-

26

gle,"[51] was the Coalition's call to its neighbors in Neshoba County and across Mississippi.

The TRC process underscores the importance of telling the unvarnished truth about past events in order to move forward toward reconciliation between former "warring" enemies. Donna Ladd's comments totally parallel the TRC concept as it was understood in South Africa:

> *We believe it is time that Mississippi natives actively tell their own stories, no matter how difficult they are.* A new generation of Mississippians are ready to step up and demand honesty and justice [my emphasis].[52]

In a similar vein, Rita Schwerner Bender warned against putting to rest the "dead past" before the state of Mississippi and its residents are educated about the terrible crimes and the injustices committed in the "people's" name. In a letter written to Mississippi Governor Haley Barbour after Killen's sentencing, made public by her on July 7, 2005, she said, in part:

> I am writing this letter because of recent and past actions of yours which are impediments to racial justice in Mississippi and our nation. Recently, after the verdict and sentencing in the Edgar Ray Killen trial in Neshoba County, you indicated your belief that this closed the books on the crimes of the civil rights years, and that we all should now have "closure." . . . People in positions of public trust, such as you, must take the lead in opening the window upon the many years of criminal conduct in which the state, and its officials, engaged. Only with such acknowledgement will the present generation understand how these many terrible crimes occurred, and the responsibility which present officials, voters and, indeed, all citizens, have to each other to move forward. . . .
>
> [After talking about the symbiotic relationship among the state legislature, the state executive, the WCCs, the Ku Klux Klan, and

27

the State Sovereignty Commission, the letter concludes with the following comments:]

Certainly, as the present governor, you must be aware of this history. This history must be known and understood by everyone. I spoke with many people in Neshoba County who are striving to understand the truth, and who are burdened by the responsibility they carry with them for the actions of their community and their state. But, there are still too many people who see only what they are comfortable recognizing. . . . Until individuals and their government understand why they do have responsibility, they cannot ensure racial justice and equality. So, please do not assume that the book is closed. There is yet much work to be done.[53] As the governor of Mississippi, you have a unique opportunity to acknowledge the past and to participate in ensuring a meaningful future for your state. Please don't squander this moment by proclaiming that the past does not inform the present and the future.[54]

Bender's concerns about the impact of the Killen decision and the consequences of a TRC process are echoed by others in and out of Mississippi.

One example of public officials refusing to act to redress past inequities was the recent U.S. Senate resolution apologizing for past Senate inactions regarding antilynching legislation that passed in the U.S. House of Representatives.

In a recent nationally syndicated column, William Raspberry, who was born and raised in Mississippi, noted that Mississippi's two Republican U.S. senators, Thad Cochran and Trent Lott, did not sign a U.S. Senate Resolution of Apology for the body's failure to enact antilynching legislation. He wrote:

OK, maybe I wasn't too surprised by Lott's nonparticipation. After all, he is the guy who was stripped of his party leadership role three years ago for opining that America would have been better off if

Strom Thurmond had won his overtly segregationist 1948 presidential campaign. But Cochran, though conservative, is thought to be less wildly right-wing than Lott—what you might call a Mississippi moderate. So why was his name absent from the list of sponsors? "I'm not in the business of apologizing for what someone else did or didn't do," he told me. "I deplore and regret that lynchings occurred and that those committing them weren't punished, but I'm not culpable." The trouble with Cochran's explanation is that he did in fact sign on as a co-sponsor of bills apologizing for the government's treatment of Native Americans and for the World War II internment of Japanese-Americans. Why did he find it so difficult to apologize for the Senate's failure to deal with House-passed anti-lynching legislation? More than 4,700 lynchings took place in the years between 1882 and 1968, according to Tuskeegee Institute, with Mississippi leading the pack with 581. The resolution was symbolic, of course. So, in many ways, is the action that brought Killen to trial 41 years after the fact. But it is a powerful symbol of a desire to atone not just for the crime of murder but for the prevailing attitude that, for many white Mississippians, made lynching acceptable.[55]

These "Truth and Reconciliation" declarations by Neshoba County residents have already made an indelible impression on many residents of the state. The question still unanswered is whether the demands for truth and justice and reconciliation will have a significant impact on others in the state—especially on publicly elected officials such as Mississippi's Republican Governor, Haley Barbour, and its two U.S. Senators, Republicans Thad Cochran and Trent Lott.

If a majority of Mississippi's citizens ignore the message contained in such truth-telling events such as the Killen trial, then the politicians in Mississippi, like elected officials everywhere, will take their cues for future actions from these silences. And the remaining vestiges of centuries of racial discrimination, in housing, health, employment, and education, may remain largely unchanged.

If this is the consequence of the TRC process begun by the Philadel-phia Coalition, then South African Bishop Desmond Tutu's warning may become prophetic: "Unless the gap between the rich and the poor, which is very wide, is narrowed, *then you could just as well kiss reconciliation goodbye* [my emphasis]."[56]

2

The 1964 Murders, the 1967 Federal Conspiracy Trial, and the Long Silence, 1964–1989

You didn't leave me nothing but a nigger, but at least I killed me a nigger.
Klansman Jimmy Jordan, June 1964[1]

They [the convicted Klansmen in the 1967 trial] killed one nigger, one Jew, and a white man [*sic*]. I gave them all what I thought they deserved.
U.S. District Court Judge Harold Cox,
Southern District, Mississippi, December 1967[2]

We know that when evil is done it is a complicit sin to ignore it, to pretend it didn't happen.
Speech by Mississippi Governor Haley Barbour,
June 20, 2004, Philadelphia, Mississippi[3]

Father's Day in 1964 was Sunday, June 21. That day in Neshoba County, Mississippi was hot and airless, with a temperature in the 90s and with almost 100 percent humidity. Three young men, Michael ("Mickey") Schwerner, twenty-four, James ("J.E") Chaney, twenty-one, and Andrew ("Andy") Goodman, twenty, left Meridian, in Lauderdale County, in the morning to visit the Mt. Zion United Methodist Church in the Longdale community, a few miles due east, off highway 16, of the small town of Philadelphia, in Neshoba County.

The three men were civil rights activists working in Mississippi to help disfranchised blacks register to vote. Two of the young men, Chaney and Schwerner, were Congress of Racial Equality (CORE) workers. Mickey was one of the first paid CORE workers in Mississippi. (He received $9 a week.) He and his wife, Rita, driving a VW "bus," arrived in Meridian in late January 1964, from New York City.

J.E. was a black resident of Meridian who worked as a plasterer and volunteered to work with CORE in his city in February 1964. He was a hard worker, and Schwerner had asked the CORE leadership in New York City to hire Chaney as another paid CORE worker. In April, J.E. and other volunteers, wearing "Freedom Now" T-shirts, picketed the Meridian Woolworth's department store. He and the others were arrested by the Meridian police.

Andy Goodman was a civil rights volunteer from New York City. He was an anthropology major at Queens College in the city at the time of his death. Andy heard about the Mississippi Summer Project in April when liberal New York Congressman Allard Lowenstein visited the campus. Even though Lowenstein told the students that "there is a great danger in coming to Mississippi," Andy was not deterred. He decided to participate in the voter registration campaign in that state.

After all, he reasoned—successfully—with his mother and father, he'd already participated in one of the first Student Nonviolent Coordinating Committee (SNCC) sit-ins in Nashville, Tennessee, in 1961, and in 1963 he joined the Southern Christian Leadership Conference (SCLC) protesters in Birmingham, Alabama. He was one of almost 1,000 volunteers who joined the 1964 Mississippi Summer Project in the coordinated effort to register black voters and to establish "Freedom Schools" for black youngsters in Mississippi during the 1964 summer. Very quickly, the project became known nationwide as Freedom Summer.[4]

By March, Mickey was known to the Mississippi State Sovereignty Commission (MSSC). This secretive state agency, with ties to both the White Citizens' Council and the Ku Klux Klan, had already started a file on Mickey and Rita. The dossier listed their address, phone number, past addresses, tag number on their 1959 Volkswagen, and their driver's license numbers. Their phone was tapped. "Their purpose," wrote Andy Hopkins, an investigator for the MSSC, "is evidently to contact local Negroes for the purpose of encouraging them to register to vote." Hopkins sent all information collected by the MSSC to the police officers at the Lauderdale and Neshoba County sheriff's offices, as well as the Meridian police department. "Many of [these law enforcement officers] belong to a group known as the White Knights of the Ku Klux Klan."[5]

The blacks in Meridian instantly took to the goateed Jewish New Yorker and his wife. Margaret Black was one of the civil rights workers who got to know Mickey soon after his arrival. She told John Sugg when he asked her about Schwerner:

Do I remember Mickey Schwerner? He was the first Jewish friend I ever had. I didn't know what a matzoh ball was. He'd bring me Swiss cheese on rye. I'd never had that, and I told him that's not what we eat around Mississippi. We laughed at that. . . . I can still picture him. He had a smile that would melt you.[6]

Although many in the Meridian community saw Mickey as a "fun loving guy [who] didn't believe anyone would ever hurt [the civil rights workers],"[7] others in the area did not share such a view. Weeks before the fateful Father's Day, Schwerner and Chaney had visited the leaders of the Mt. Zion United Methodist Church as well as the Mt. Nebo Missionary Baptist Church. Their objective was to see if they could receive permission to use the facilities as meeting places for voter registration as well as freedom schools during Freedom Summer.

By this time, early June 1964, Schwerner had shown himself to be a masterly planner of activities in Meridian and Lauderdale County that challenged the status quo. He established a fully functioning community center for blacks in the city, led a successful boycott of a local merchant who sold goods to blacks but refused to hire blacks to work in the store, and was making an impact on the entire community in the months since he and Rita arrived in Meridian.

Mickey was so successful that, by early May 1964, the newly reconstructed White Knights of the Ku Klux Klan, with thirty-nine-year-old Sam Bowers the Imperial Wizard of this Mississippi Klan, targeted "goatee," "nigger lover," or "Jewboy" (as Schwerner was variously called by the KKK) for "elimination." A "Number 4" order was issued by Bowers to the Lauderdale and Neshoba County Klavern (that is, chapter) leaders. It was conveyed to the Kleagle of the Neshoba Klavern, Edgar Ray Killen. The terse message: Kill Schwerner.

Bowers told his compatriots in late May that the coming invasion of "commies, Jews, and anti-Christs," was the beginning of the war between white Christianity and its enemies: "The events which will occur in Mississippi this summer may well determine the fate of Christian civilization for centuries to come."

> We must roll with the mass punch which they will deliver in the streets during the day, and we must counterattack the individual leaders at night. . . . *These attacks against those selected individual targets should, of course, be as severe as circumstances and conditions will permit* [my emphasis].[8]

For the thousands of Klansmen and many other Mississippians, including all elected officials, the upcoming COFO (Council of Federated Organizations) Freedom Summer project was the greatest threat to their white protestant, Southern way of life.[9] Something had to be done to maintain their folkways; it was the KKK who took the initiative to defend, in Bower's words, "the fate of Christian civilization."[10]

The Killing of Schwerner, Chaney, and Goodman, June 21, 1964

The impending Freedom Summer project led to mounting tensions in the entire state, which only increased as the July 1 start-up of the civil rights program loomed. The *Jackson Clarion-Ledger* labeled the civil rights project as an "invasion" of civil rights workers, Communists, Jews, and anti-Christs.[11] "The state was a powder keg," noted Jim Prince, the editor of the *Neshoba Democrat.* "The KKK made its presence known and fears were heightened among both blacks and whites."

In April 1964 the Klan burned about one dozen crosses in Neshoba County.[12] (By the end of Freedom Summer, in September 1964, almost fifty churches had been burned to the ground and hundreds of crosses burned by the KKK. The FBI labeled its soon-to-be-massive [40,000 pages] file on the three murders and the other ancillary criminal acts against civil rights workers MIBURN, short for "Mississippi Burning.")

And on the evening of June 16, 1964, almost two months after Schwerner had been targeted for elimination, Klansmen visited the Mt. Zion United Methodist Church, burned it to the ground and severely beat three parishioners. At the same time, Schwerner and Chaney were in Oxford, Ohio, on the campus of the Western College for Women where the first 250 of almost 1,000 volunteers were training for their upcoming participation in Freedom Summer.

Four days later, on June 20, 1964, Schwerner and Chaney, accompanied by three volunteers, including Goodman, quickly drove nonstop from Ohio to Meridian, Mississippi. Mickey heard about the church-burning and wanted to visit with the deacons and the parishioners as soon as he

35

could to "investigate and to offer solace."[13] His response was what the KKK expected.

On the morning of June 21, Father's Day, he, Chaney, and Goodman drove to the church in Neshoba County. He told colleagues in the Meridian CORE office that they would be back about 4 p.m.

After their visit ended, about 1:30 in the afternoon, the trio started the nearly 50 mile drive back to Meridian. To get back to Meridian from the church, they had to get back on highway 16 going west for a few miles and, once in Philadelphia proper, turn onto highway 19 South for the 40 mile journey to Meridian. They never made it back.

Just outside Philadelphia, with J.E. driving, the car was pulled over by one of the two law enforcement officers in Neshoba County, Deputy Sheriff Cecil Price, a twenty-seven-year-old member of the Neshoba County Klavern. The three were brought to the Philadelphia city jail. Chaney was charged with speeding and Price held the others for "suspicion of setting the church on fire."

Of course this was a simple subterfuge. As soon as the trio was locked up (about 3 p.m.), Price asked Billy Posey, another Neshoba County Klansman, to have Killen call the sheriff. When the Preacher called, Price told him that Schwerner and two others had been picked up and were sitting in the city jail. For the next six hours, Killen crafted the elimination plan. It was carried out later that evening by at least seventeen Klansmen.

Since Schwerner was with two other civil rights workers, they, too, had to die. Killen called up almost two dozen Klansmen from Lauderdale and Neshoba Counties, traveled to Meridian for an early evening meeting with the coconspirators, gave out the various assignments to the other Klansmen,[14] and then, about 6 in the evening, returned to Philadelphia to preside over two wakes at the local funeral home.[15]

In the meantime, back at the Meridian CORE office, volunteer Louise Herney grew very concerned after 5 p.m. when the three men had failed to return at 4 p.m. Suspecting foul play, she called the COFO office in Jackson to report that the three had not returned from Neshoba County and then began to call area hospitals, jails, and people Mickey had worked with since his arrival. "At 5:30 p.m., Louise reache[d] the Neshoba County Jail [located in Philadelphia], where the jailer [falsely] insist[ed] Mickey and others [we]re not there."[16] All her increasingly worried calls were dead-ends. The three men were missing. That meant, every one involved with the project believed, that they had been beaten to a pulp and left in some desolate hidden place or, worse, that they had been murdered.

Schwerner, Chaney, and Goodman, however, from late afternoon until late at night, were ensconced in the Neshoba County Jail. They were unable to telephone anyone while in the jail and, when released, went directly to their car for the short drive to Meridian.

At about 10 p.m. on June 21, the three men were let out of jail after Chaney paid a $20 speeding ticket. Contrary to a cardinal rule of CORE procedures, they did not call in to their CORE contacts in either Meridian or Jackson, but instead got into their car and started off for Meridian.

Ominously, they were followed by Sheriff Price and two carloads of Klansmen. J.E. was driving; he sped up when he saw the bevy of cars behind their vehicle. However, Price flashed his lights and J.E. stopped the car. Price then ordered the three men into his car. The cars turned around and, less than two miles going north on highway 19 the police car and the others turned left onto Rock Cut Road where they stopped.

Klansmen Wayne Roberts, a dishonorably discharged U.S. Marine, pulled Schwerner from the car. "Are you that nigger lover?" Schwerner replied: "Sir, I know just how you feel." Roberts shot once into Mickey's chest, killing him instantly. Roberts then pulled Andy out and executed him without saying a word. Another Klansman, James Jordan, yelled to Roberts, "Hey, save one for me," and ran over to the car. Although J.E. ran for his life, he was not successful. Jordan killed Chaney, saying to his friends: "You didn't leave me nothing but a nigger, but at least I killed me a nigger."[17] The three bodies were transported to the preselected burial site, an earthen dam on the Old Jolly farm. They were buried beneath 15 feet of red Mississippi clay, not to be discovered for forty-four days.

Back in Ohio the next day, June 22, 1964, Bob Moses, the young COFO codirector, told the volunteers: "Yesterday morning, three of our people left Meridian, Mississippi, to investigate a church burning in Neshoba County. They haven't come back, and we haven't heard any word from them." Rita Schwerner, who had come to Ohio with Mickey and J.E. and remained there while they returned to visit the burned-out church, then stood up and wrote the three names on the large blackboard. Jane Adams, one of the many hundreds of students in attendance that sad day, then went up to the blackboard and, in large letters, wrote one word: "FEAR."[18] It captured the thoughts of all the volunteers in attendance.

The civil rights veterans attending the training sessions knew better. The trio were dead. Roscoe Jones, one of the CORE workers in Meridian, "still remembers the mysterious, disquieting feeling that overtook him. . . . 'I had this funny feeling inside of me that they were dead.'"[19] Civil rights activists outside Mississippi and Ohio just knew that the three men had died at the hands of Klansmen. Emmett Burns, traveling to ministerial school in Virginia at that time, voiced the view held by the old hands: "I knew they were dead, because that's the way things were in Mississippi."[20]

For some Mississippians, however, the disappearance was merely a hoax perpetrated by COFO to gain additional national publicity for their Freedom Summer project. Mississippi governor Paul B. Johnson claimed that the three men were enjoying the nightlife of Havana, Cuba. The disappearance was, according to the senior U.S. Senator from Mississippi, the powerful James Eastland, a "publicity stunt."[21]

This response was a tried and true one in Mississippi. During the 1955 trial of the two men accused of murdering fourteen-year-old Emmett Till, defense counsel made the same kind of argument in defense of their clients. John W. Whitten Jr., in his closing argument, maintained that outside agitators "would not be above putting a rotting, stinking body in the river in the hope that it would be identified as Emmett Till."[22] Roy Tibble, one of the jurors in the Till case probably voiced the views of all twelve white men sitting in the jury box when he said:

> The body fished out of the Tallahatchie River was not that of Emmett Till—who was [claimed the defense counsel] still very much alive and hiding out in Chicago or Detroit or somewhere else up North— but someone else's, a corpse planted there by the NAACP for the express purpose of stirring up a racial tornado that would tear through [the Mississippi town of] Sumner, and through all of Mississippi, and through the rest of the South for that matter.[23]

It took the twelve white men less than two hours to reach their verdict. The two accused men, Roy Bryant and his half-brother J. W. Milam, were acquitted. Two months later, in an article in *Look* magazine by William Bradford Huie, the two men confessed to murdering Till because the young black boy had allegedly whistled at Roy Bryant's wife, Carolyn, while Till was in Bryant's general store in Money, Mississippi.[24]

For federal officials in the U.S. Department of Justice, U.S. Attorney General Robert F. Kennedy, Deputy Attorney General Nicholas Katzenbach, and the director of the FBI, J. Edgar Hoover, however, a different view prevailed: The three young men were dead and the task of the federal agents in the field was not to search for them but to recover the three bodies. Finally, on August 4, 1964, forty-four days after Schwerner, Chaney, and Goodman disappeared, their bodies were unearthed by the FBI. By October, there would be the first legal actions to bring the Klansmen to trial for their conspiracy to deprive the three young civil rights workers of their constitutionally protected rights and liberties.

However, for most of the natives of Neshoba County there was the return to life as it was before the Freedom Summer violence. For them, the dog days of August meant the heralded, traditional Neshoba County Fair. The event brought all the state's politicians into the county to give political speeches to the residents living in the small, indeed tiny, bungalows that dotted the fair's landscape.

At the 1964 Neshoba County Fair, the politicians and the residents tried to erase the reality of the tragedy that was taking place that summer in Mississippi. They tried using political oratory, cotton candy, games, and down-home cooking. However, the Neshoba County Klansmen did not lose their focus. They plastered the fair with flyers that went to the very essence of the group's raison d'etre in 1964: "Schwerner, Chaney, and Goodman were not civil rights workers. They were Communist Revolutionaries, actively working to undermine and destroy Christian Civilization."[25]

The Federal Conspiracy Trial, December 1967

How the FBI found out where the three bodies were buried is still, in 2005, *officially* an unanswered question.[26] No name is mentioned in the 40,000 pages of the MIBURN files. The FBI, from J. Edgar Hoover and Al Rosen, the leaders of the organization at the time, to the Special Agent in Charge (SAC) in Mississippi, Joseph Sullivan, never disclosed the informant who gave them the location of the three men's burial site. Nor did the Department of Justice attorneys who were preparing the federal case against the Klansmen involved in the murders of the three men.

However, just as the Killen trial was in the voir dire (jury selection) phase in the Neshoba County Courthouse, a story appeared in the *Clarion-Ledger* of June 13, 2005, finally identifying the mysterious Mr. X.[27] Jerry Mitchell posed the question in the first paragraph of his story when he asked: "Who is the man who told the FBI where the bodies of James Chaney, Michael Schwerner and Andrew Goodman were buried in 1964?" The answer, according to a great deal of circumstantial evidence: Maynard King, a highway patrol officer from Philadelphia, whose barracks was in Meridian (King died of a heart attack on September 8, 1966). Mitchell wrote:

In this dark chapter of Mississippi history, where the governor called the trio's disappearances a hoax and where law enforcement played a role in the killings, Maynard King became "one of the unsung heroes of the time," Philip Dray, co-author of the 1988 book on the case, *We Are Not Afraid*, said. "He's a man who probably spent several hours figuring this out and wondering, 'What should I do?' The fact he chose to do the right thing shows he was very brave." King's family never knew of his role as Mr. X until informed by *The Clarion-Ledger*, but they say they're glad to know he played such a positive role. "It makes you proud of him," said King's grandson, John, who lives in Madison. "It gives you a lot of peace of mind to know he did the right thing. I'd like to think if it'd been me, I'd have done the same thing."[28]

"Despite the revelation of King's role," concluded Mitchell, "one secret remains—the name of the Neshoba County citizen who gave King the information on where the trio's bodies were buried. "That one . . . we'll never know."[29]

Schwerner, Chaney, and Goodman, however, were found in early August because Maynard King told SAC Sullivan where the bodies were. And King told Sullivan the whereabouts of the bodies without any thought of a reward. Nor did the Philadelphia resident who told King where the bodies were ever receive the FBI's reward. However, if one was a resident of Philadelphia or Neshoba County, the better part of valor—and caution—in August 1964 was not to buy a brand-new Cadillac or plaster money around the county.

This was so because, at the very moment the FBI had backhoes digging up the bodies of the three dead men, word was spread by the agency in Neshoba County that there was a $30,000 reward for information about the three missing men. As a former FBI agent, Jim Ingram, of Jackson, told a reporter in 2001: "We made everybody think money was going to be paid. That way it would create suspicion among Klan members that one of them was talking for money."[30]

41

Florence Mars, a lifelong resident of Philadelphia, was in 1964 a rarity in Mississippi: She was a harsh and open critic of the KKK and its violent actions. She authored an important book, *Witness in Philadelphia*, which described the culture of impunity and the fears of the many resident bystanders. She affirmed Ingram's observations about the behavior of her neighbors in light of the FBI's announcement: "Anybody who bought a new car or anything else was looked at suspiciously. . . . [In 2001], they're still trying to decide who [told the FBI where the bodies were buried]."[31]

Over the next few months there were jurisdictional clashes between the federal government and the State, specifically the Neshoba County prosecutor, the Mississippi attorney general, the Neshoba County grand jurors, and the Neshoba County Circuit Judge O. H. Barnett, 8th Judicial District, Mississippi (who was a relative of former Mississippi governor Ross Barnett, one of the South's leading segregationist politicians of that era). The controversy could be boiled down to the simple question of who, the United States or Neshoba County, would try the individuals allegedly responsible for the murders of the three men?

In 1964, there was no federal statute that would enable the federal prosecutors in the Department of Justice to ask a grand jury to indict persons for murdering Schwerner, Chaney, and Goodman. The best the federal government's lawyers in DOJ could do was to make use of an 1870 congressional statute, the Enforcement Act,[32] and ask a grand jury to indict the Klansmen for "conspiring" to take the constitutionally protected rights and liberties of Schwerner, Chaney, and Goodman. If found guilty, the maximum sentence provided for in the statute—in 1964—was ten years in prison.[33]

Murder indictments, in 1964, were solely the province of local and state grand jurors. In the U.S. federal system, punishment for capital crimes fell within the domain of a *state's* machinery of justice. By mid-October 1964, the FBI obtained a confession from James Jordan, one of the Klansmen involved in the murders of the three civil rights workers. After months of questioning by the FBI, he confessed and agreed to testify against the other Klansmen involved in the murder plot. And in November 1964 Jordan signed a confession. It was a twenty-seven-page document, describing in detail the plot and the role Killen played in planning the murders, and identifying who actually killed the young men and who were the Klansmen involved in the event.

With this document in hand, along with another confession by a Klansman not at the murder site, by December 1964 the justice department attorneys convened a federal grand jury in the southern district U.S. District Court to indict all the participants in the murder plot. On December 4, 1964, twenty-one Klansmen from Neshoba and Lauderdale Counties were arrested by the FBI and charged with violating Section 241, the "conspiracy" statute.

In September 1964, however, the district attorney for Neshoba County convened a county grand jury to "investigate" the events that led to the murders of the three men and to indict, as appropriate, those persons the grand jurors—led by the district attorney and his staff—believed were probably involved in the murders. In preparing for this event, both the county prosecutor and Judge Barnett requested *all* pertinent information from the FBI including testimony in the grand jury room from nine FBI agents who had been gathering information from witnesses about the murders.

The two leading federal government officials, Nicholas Katzenbach, the acting U.S. attorney general, and J. Edgar Hoover, the director of the FBI, steadfastly refused to turn over *any* evidence to the Neshoba County grand jurors or to allow FBI agents to testify before the county grand jury. The two men received telegrams from District Court Judge Barnett on September 24, 1964. The messages asked the federal leaders, in their official capacity, to "instruct those that have been subpoenaed to appear in person at the county courthouse in Philadelphia, Mississippi, at 9 am Monday, September 28, prepared to testify before the grand jury."

Judge Barnett almost instantly received replies from Katzenbach and Hoover rejecting the grand jury's request. Hoover's response was brief:

"FBI agents will be unable to testify before state grand jury at this time regarding death of three civil rights workers, as they have been instructed not to disclose any information relating to material or information contained in the files of the DOJ."

For everyone working the federal side of the murder case, there was an absolute distrust of Mississippi justice officials. This mistrust started at the very top of Mississippi's legal hierarchy, the state's attorney general, and included everyone else—from police officials, to the local district attorney, to the grand jurors themselves.

From the very first day the three men were reported missing, there was a visceral, palpable enmity between the federal authorities and the state's law enforcement agencies. From the point of view of the feds, as Joseph Sullivan, the FBI's SAC said at the time: "They [the KKK] owned the place. In spirit everyone in Neshoba County belonged to the Klan."[34] The federal government did not, for a second, believe that information handed over to a county grand jury would remain secret for too long.

In addition, in 1964 Mississippi, there had *never* been a conviction for anyone who killed a black person or a civil rights worker, whether black or white. Most of the time, there were never even indictments handed down by a grand jury for such criminal behavior. There was the omnipresent culture of impunity; the DOJ was quite aware of this Mississippi gestalt and adamantly refused to turn over information.

On October 1, 1964, after repeated DOJ and FBI rejections of requests to turn over the information the federal government had, the Neshoba County grand jury—with the assistance of the district attorney—issued what the *Neshoba Democrat* labeled a "scorching report [to District Court Judge Barnett] on the refusal of federal agencies to cooperate in its attempt to solve the murder of the three civil rights workers here this summer."[35] The grand jury subpoenaed at least nine FBI agents to appear before it and divulge information about the murders. Under orders from Washington, these agents did not appear before the grand jury. The report stated:

Our investigation has been curtailed, and in fact stymied by the failure and refusal of agents of the FBI and other federal officers to testify. . . . We respectfully state that subpoenas were duly issued for all federal agents known to have participated in the investigation of these homicides, but not one of said agents showed up before this grand jury to testify and no written reports or documentary evidence have been presented to this grand jury by the U.S. Department of Justice. . . . We are at a loss to understand this attitude on the part of the DOJ inasmuch as our investigation of this matter reveals that a number of people in Neshoba County have been unofficially accused by FBI agents as having taken part in the homicide of the three civil rights workers.[36]

After the report heaped "the highest praise for the investigative work done by the . . . local law enforcement officers of Neshoba County [Sheriff Rainey and Deputy Sheriff Price, both Klansmen and both subsequently indicted and tried in federal court on a conspiracy charge]," it concluded in the following manner:

[Rainey and Price] have done an *exceptional job* of maintaining law and order in this county, even in the face of drastic provocation by *outside agitators.* These agitators are not interested in the welfare of the colored race in Neshoba County, but are interested only in their own selfish purposes. . . . They seek to divide the races, stir up friction, breed hatred, and engender suspicion among peaceful citizens who have lived together in peace and harmony for generations [my emphasis].

With the conclusion of the Neshoba County's grand jury term on October 1, 1964, there was no further action taken by a Neshoba County grand jury until January 2005, almost forty-one years later.

The federal government's justice system, however, slowly moved on. After dismissal of indictments by a U.S. Commissioner, Esther Carter, in

December 1964[37] and by a U.S. District Court Judge, Harold Cox, in February 1965, and after the federal government successfully appealed his judgment to the U.S. Supreme Court in 1966,[38] the federal conspiracy trial of the eighteen Klansmen finally took place in October 1967 in the federal courthouse in Meridian before U.S. District Court Judge Cox.

On October 20, 1967, one day after Cox used the dynamite "Allen" charge[39] to try to get a deadlocked jury to reach substantive judgments in *Price,* the all-white jury found seven men guilty,[40] seven others were acquitted, charges were dropped against one defendant, and, in three instances, the jury deadlocked and mistrials were declared.[41]

In December 1967, Judge Cox sentenced the seven men found guilty to prison terms ranging from three to ten years in federal penitentiaries across the United States. After exhausting their appeals, the seven Klansmen found guilty by the jury began serving their prison sentences in March 1970. By the end of the decade all seven were free and living in Neshoba County.

The Long Silence of the Bystanders in Neshoba County, 1964–1989

In late July 1964, before the three bodies were found, Martin Luther King Jr. visited Philadelphia. He was, with others in his group, roughed up by locals—led by Neshoba County Sheriff Lawrence Rainey—who did not appreciate yet another group of "outside agitators" coming into their county. King's observation was one that all who visited the county at that time agreed with: "This is a terrible town. The worst I've seen. There is a complete reign of terror here."[42]

Evidence presented in the 1967 federal trial showed that the killings were committed by a mob of Klansmen and "sanctioned, tacitly, if not openly, by high-ranking state officials."

The state-funded Sovereignty Commission spied on civil rights workers across the state, accusing some of Communist ties. Then-Governor Paul B. Johnson referred to the workers as "professional visiting trouble makers," . . . and Killen [and the other Klansmen were] "foot soldiers" in the state's fierce effort to preserve segregation.[43]

How did the people living in Philadelphia and Neshoba County respond to the murders? For a generation, until 1989, they shared in a sort of collective guilt and steadfastly refused to talk about the events of Father's Day 1964. Not one word about the event was spoken openly in the white churches, and certainly not in the public schools. There was a conspiracy of silence in Neshoba County.

The 1964 deaths of the three young men cast Philadelphia, Neshoba County, and Mississippi in a horrible light, one that for more than four decades did not change a whit. Compounding the problem was the absolute unwillingness of the people to talk about what had happened or to teach their children in public school about the vitriolic racist beliefs, the raw violence, and deep-seated hatred that existed in the state and accounted for the way in which the "outside" world viewed Mississippi.

The silence of the bystanders was rooted in the fear of retaliation. Anne Pullin, the "everyperson" waitress at Peggy's Restaurant, summed up the climate when she told us that for thirty years no one spoke of the murders and then, in 1989, "boom"—everybody began talking about what happened a quarter of a century ago. It was as if everybody in Philadelphia and its environs had come out of a collective coma.

The people in the county knew the labels tacked onto Neshoba County outside the state. The few residents who traveled outside Mississippi always ran into the stereotyped views of their home county held by the outside world. Only those Neshoba County travelers knew that the stereotype was a valid one, that cold-blooded, premeditated murder took place in their home town and that the killers were walking around town freely and doing so with an arrogance that grew out of the state's culture of impunity.

Jim Prince III, the editor and publisher of the *Neshoba Democrat* and cochair of the Philadelphia Coalition, wrote about one of the reasons for the coalition's creation in a 2004 editorial: "If this community [continues to] remain silent [on the fortieth anniversary of the deaths of Schwerner, Chaney, and Goodman] we can expect others to set the tone and another series of national headlines that read: Nothing's changed in Mississippi or Neshoba County."

> Shadows linger over this community and there is a sense of collective guilt many more young people are apt to admit than older generations. We do need to move on, but there is some unfinished business that must be dealt with first, a sin, a stain on this community. . . . [We must take] actions, not [remain] silent, committing ourselves to educating future generations, as well as pursuing the truth and seeking justice. To simply insist this summer how good we are—absent redemption or atonement—would be a terrible mistake.[44]

The silence was shattered in 1989 because many people, especially the younger men and women of Neshoba County, believed that the established order, the culture of racism and impunity, was wrong. But deciding that the culture was wrong was not enough. Action had to follow this first step.

By 1989, there were men and women, black, white, and Choctaw Indian, who felt that the culture should change and that, with proactive action by them, it could change.[45] And changes did come, slowly but inexorably until, in January 2005, a Mississippi grand jury indicted Edgar Ray Killen for the murders of Schwerner, Chaney, and Goodman.

In a sharply worded editorial in the *Neshoba Democrat* when the indictment came down in January 2005, Jim Prince wrote about the upcoming trial and its impact on Neshoba County and its residents:

"We're never going to wipe away the bloodstains of that crime, and I don't expect the trial to do that. But regardless of the verdict, the horse is out of the barn. There is a dialogue started, and that is only going to grow and develop."[46]

3

From Silence to Dialogue: Initial Efforts to Reopen the 1964 Murders Case, 1989–2001

> Neshoba can be a pretty place. . . . So long as you don't break
> the local taboo against mentioning the civil rights murders,
> everyone gets along better than people elsewhere think.
> *Neely Tucker, writing in the* Washington Post[1]
>
> In the 60's, you didn't do a whole lotta talkin'.
> *Bob Stringer, testifying for the prosecution at the 1998 murder
> trial of Imperial Wizard Sam Bowers.*[2]

For twenty-five years, no one in Neshoba County spoke of the murders of Michael Schwerner, James Chaney, and Andrew Goodman. Although during that time, it seemed that the "entire state was living in the past, or if not in it, at least living with it,"[3] the taboo held sway. Generally there was silence among family members around meal time; there was silence among friends on the streets and in the shops in Neshoba County. Even the textbooks were silent about the 1964 murders.

Although most residents of the county were mortified that the three young men were killed in cold blood by the Klan, and that the killers were walking the streets of Philadelphia, they hardly ever talked about the deed, or about the men who did it. They respected the local taboo. And when Edgar Ray Killen walked into the barbershop in Philadelphia all conversation—however idle—stopped.[4] It was as if just talking about the weather in front of one of the killers was awkward, or inappropriate, and, for many, frightening. As a witness for the prosecution, Mike Hatcher, himself a Klansman in 1964, said during the 2005 Killen trial: "After I testified against the Preacher in 1967, I feared for my life because of the conditions in the state of Mississippi at that time."[5]

People remained silent and looked away from the killers, yet felt, as someone wrote, a sort of "corporate guilt" about the murders.[6] On a number of occasions over the four decades of silence in the county, however, the taboo would be broken by Killen himself. Neshoba bystanders "heard Killen brag about [the three murders, saying] that 'you [didn't] have any more trouble out of those people.'"[7] There was never any response to these comments from those who heard them, just a downward glance and a quick walk away.

Killen, according to those who meet him for the first time or who have known him for decades, is "a garrulous man given to long conversations that are sometimes disjointed and rambling. 'Even people who know him don't feel they really know him. He's got this certain look in his eye like you're really looking into something deeper, but you don't know what.'"[8]

Not convicted in 1967, Killen, Neshoba County's "jackleg"[9] preacher, continued to preach and operate his sawmill. Except for a short period of time in 1975, Edgar Ray was a free man until his 2005 conviction.

However, Killen was *already* a convicted felon when, in 2005, he went on trial for the murders of the three young men. Killen served a five-month prison term in Mississippi's maximum security Parchman prison in 1975, convicted for making death threats over the telephone. Evidently, an estranged husband hired a private detective to spy on his wife. She and the Preacher were having an affair and the detective, Marvin Ware, spotted them exiting a local motel room. After the duo left the motel, Killen followed Ware to the estranged husband's home where Ware reported what he had seen.

The following morning and evening Killen called the Ware household and spoke to Ware's wife, Mary, both times. During the evening conversation, Killen threatened Marvin Ware's life. Mary Ware taped the conversation, one that was introduced at trial months later:

> Folks die for things that he did, honey. Did you know that? I don't make no mistakes and get the wrong man. Your life is too sweet and precious to throw it away on one sorry son of a bitch like that. You hear? You tell him that he is exactly right, that he is dead. Tell him that's the first thing I would like for him to do if you get to see him again is prepare to meet his maker.[10]

Ironically, the district attorney of Neshoba County who successfully prosecuted the Preacher in 1975 was his neighbor and, in 2005, the presiding judge in Killen's murder trial, Marcus Gordon.

The seven men convicted in the 1967 federal conspiracy trial served their time in federal prisons across the nation. By 1980, all were again living in Neshoba County. Deputy Sheriff Cecil Price, after his prison time ended, returned to Philadelphia, where he worked as a watch repairman, joined the all-white Neshoba County country club, and, in 1996, was elected vice president of the Neshoba County Shriners organization.

Sam Bowers went back to his business, the Sambo Amusement Company, in Laurel, Mississippi, until he was convicted in 1998 for the 1966 murder of NAACP leader Vernon Dahmer Sr. And the local taboo remained inviolate until a number of things occurred in 1989, twenty-five years after the three men were killed by the Klan.

1989: The Watershed Year, Revisited

As already noted, 1989 was a watershed year in Mississippi's response to its bleak, terror-filled history of race relations. There was the unprecedented public apology given to the family members—and more than 1,000 onlookers from Neshoba County—of the three dead civil rights workers by Mississippi Secretary of State Dick Molpus. Many people, wrote Jim Prince, were "impacted profoundly" by Molpus's apology.[11]

In 1989, a news reporter, Jerry Mitchell, began an almost two-decade odyssey to uncover the facts about the killings in Mississippi in the 1960s.[12] Mitchell and millions of other people were moved and educated by the Hollywood film version of the 1964 murders, *Mississippi Burning.* Andrew Goodman's mother, Dr. Carolyn Goodman, said that, although largely fictional, the movie "had a strong impact on many people in terms of arousing their awareness to the fact that there were three young men killed in their efforts in 1964 to register black people to vote, and they were murdered by the Klan."[13] And residents of the rural county began to talk openly—for the first time in a quarter century—about the tragic, deadly events of June 1964.

Stanley Dearman, then the editor and publisher of the *Neshoba Democrat,* played an extremely important role in this transformative year. Dearman was born and raised in Meridian, the city in Lauderdale County that escaped the ill will that was heaped on Philadelphia and Neshoba County by the press. When he was thirty-four, in 1966, Dearman moved to Philadelphia to publish the *Neshoba Democrat.* He loved being editor and publisher of a weekly county newspaper. For him, it was practicing journalism "at its most grass-root basic."[14]

Always critical of the bloody actions of the Klan in Neshoba County, and the lack of action by officials in response to it, in 1989 Dearman "put a face on the civil rights workers with his interview with Carolyn Goodman, mother of slain civil rights worker Andrew Goodman."[15] After sitting down with Goodman in her New York City apartment in 1989, he told her "that for 25 years we [in Neshoba County] had known nothing but a name, Andrew Goodman. 'Tell us about Andy. What was he like?'"[16] And, he recalled, she told Dearman (and his readers) about her son in "beautifully expressed words."[17] Some of her thoughts follow:[18]

Andy was a young man who was an athlete, he was a great ball player. He played the clarinet beautifully. And he loved the dramatic arts. He was a person who was very well liked. He was very fair. If he happened to be in the middle of a disagreement and he was kind of the arbiter between the youngest and the oldest. You know what happens to the youngest, he gets the squeeze. And Andy was always there to kind of help out because he wanted everybody to have the opportunity to express themselves. . . .

He was really quite remarkable in his thoughtfulness. I can remember how he never forgot a birthday. . . .

And how baseball and the Brooklyn Dodgers was the greatest thing in his life at that time. . . . I took him out to Ebbets Field one spring evening. He must have been about 13 years old at the time. I had a tweed suit on that was very itchy and I'd keep getting up and stretching throughout the game. At one point he said, "Mom, I want to tell you, don't get up in the top of the seventh." . . .[19]

The spring before Andy left for Mississippi we had a little garden in the country and Andy helped me plant some corn. There's nothing more dead looking than a corn seed. . . . And after Andy was missing for several weeks we went up to the country and there was that corn coming up—green, beautiful. I thought about this young man planting it.[20]

The interview "had a profound effect," not only on Neshoba County readers in 1989 but also on a "younger generation" when it was reprinted in 2004.[21] Dearman was motivated to speak with members of the families of the three dead men because his fellow denizens of Philadelphia "have never come to grips with it, have never faced it. There's a lot of denial."[22]

The April 1989 interview and others that followed and were printed in the *Neshoba Democrat* gave Andrew Goodman and his friends a humanity and a warmth that had not been recognized by Mississippians for twenty-five years. Until the interview, the three murdered civil rights workers were abstractions, and often characterized in the ugliest terms: "a nigger, a white man, and a Jew," as the federal judge incorrectly described—and defined—them in 1967.

Clearly, the Goodman interview provided some Neshoba County residents with a more positive perception of the three young murdered men. On the flip side, however, it must be noted that the "Goodman" name that appeared on COFO's Freedom Summer volunteer lists in 1964 reaffirmed the Klan's view that the thousand or so volunteers were anti-Christ, Communist-Jews: outside agitators planning to attack the cradle of American civilization.

Andy Goodman's father, Robert Goodman, was the President of the Pacifica Foundation, an offshoot of Pacifica Broadcasting. The Klan had found this out, as had the state's White Citizens' Councils (WCC), from Mississippi State Sovereignty Commission (MSSC) reports sent to them and to the governor. And the MSSC had found out about Goodman *père* from the regular contacts its investigators had with the senior U.S. Senator from Mississippi, James Eastland, and his staff. Pacifica was a "progressive, alternative broadcasting network founded in 1949 by pacifists. . . . Only a year prior to Andrew Goodman's death, the U.S. House Un-American Activities Committee (HUAC) and the U.S. Senate Internal Security Subcommittee (SISS), chaired by Mississippi Senator James Eastland, completed a three year investigation of Pacifica's programming, looking for 'subversion' [by the broadcasters and/or by others associated with the FM radio network]."

In 1962 Pacifica radio station WBAI (in New York City) was the first station to publicly broadcast former FBI agent Jack Levine's expose of J. Edgar Hoover and the FBI. The program was followed by threats of arrests and bombings, as well as pressure from the FBI, the Justice Department, and the Federal Communications Commission (FCC). Also that year, Pacifica trained volunteers to travel into the South for coverage of the awakening civil rights movement. The station also took a strong anti-Vietnam war stance.[23]

For Senator Eastland, the MSSC, the WCC, and the KKK, the Good-man name was an un-American one; and Andrew Goodman, the son of the president of Pacifica Foundation, typified the white outside agitator who, in 1964, threatened the very existence of white Anglo-Saxon civilization.

While Dearman's Goodman interview "put a human face" on the three dead men for many readers, it had an ironic impact as well. The mere mention of the Goodman name reaffirmed the need, on the part of many Mississippians, to eliminate these Jewish, Communist, anti-Christ subversives or face the destruction of their sacred civilization.

Reopening Old Wounds:
The KKK Murder Trials of the 1990s

The 2005 Killen trial is the fifth of the expiation trials of Klansmen who murdered civil rights workers with impunity during the 1950s and 1960s. The first of these recent trials took place because of the events of 1989. Jerry Mitchell was a young reporter for the *Jackson Clarion-Ledger* in 1989. After being told by his own "Deep Throat" of the availability of some misfiled pages from the secret MSSC files, he began his still-ongoing quest to find out the truth about these ugly racial incidents in Mississippi's recent past.

In December 1989, his government mole gave Mitchell one dozen files containing almost 2,500 pages of MSSC documents. This led to a story by Mitchell showing that while the state attorney general was prose-cuting Byron De La Beckwith for the murder of NAACP Field Secretary Medgar Evers in 1963, another state agency, the MSSC, with the governor of the state sitting as an ex officio member, was secretly providing helpful information to De La Beckwith's defense attorneys.[24]

Mitchell's story very quickly "prompted Evers's widow, Myrlie Evers-Williams, to call for a new trial. The state re-opened the case."[25] And in 1990, De La Beckwith was indicted, once again (his earlier trials had all ended in mistrials because of deadlocked juries), by Mississippi. This time, in 1994, he was convicted for the murder of Evers and sentenced to life imprisonment. He died in prison in 2002.

The conviction showed prosecutors in the Mississippi Attorney General's Office that other cold cases could be successfully prosecuted. This truth was also perceived by the attorneys general in other southern states and, by the time of the 2005 Killen trial, more than two dozen inactive civil rights murder cases were reexamined. This opening of closed cases led to the arrests of dozens of Klansmen and to almost two dozen convictions since 1989.

In Mississippi, after De La Beckwith was convicted in 1994, Mississippi Ku Klux Klan Imperial Wizard Sam Bowers was convicted, in his fifth trial, in August 1998, for ordering the "elimination" of a local black civil rights leader, Vernon Dahmer Sr., in 1966. He was finally convicted because of one person's testimony. Bob Stringer was a teenager who worked in Bowers's Sambo Amusement Company, in tiny Laurel, Mississippi. He was a bystander when Bowers and other Klansmen planned the Dahmer murder. After some time passed, Stringer became an informant for the FBI. In his testimony at the trial, Stringer said: "In the 60's, you didn't do a whole lotta talkin'. Sam [Bowers] was real upset about the civil rights workers that was getting blacks registered to vote. . . . I went through a lot of changes in my life at the time. I felt like I had to undo some wrongs in the past."[26]

(In 2004, Attorney General Jim Hood was assuming that Bob Stringer would be an important new witness for the prosecution if the 1964 murder case went to grand jurors. Stringer, it turns out, was *also* present when Bowers and Killen met at a church and discussed the elimination of Michael Schwerner. However, nine months before the convening of the grand jury in January 2005, Bob Stringer committed suicide. As will be shown in Chapter Four, Stringer's death created serious problems for the prosecutors.)

In 1999, in a Mississippi county courtroom, three Klansmen from Humphrey County, Mississippi, were brought to trial and convicted of manslaughter in the 1970 murder of Rodney Pool, a black, one-armed sharecropper. And in 2003, Mississippi Klansman Ernest Avants was convicted for the killing of a black sharecropper, Ben Chester White, in 1966.

Add to this list of convictions the 2005 conviction of Killen for manslaughter and the opening of a number of other civil rights era murder cases by Mississippi and federal prosecutors in the state and one understands why Mississippi leads the nation in reopening these kinds of cases. And all these righteous events have occurred—and are occurring—since the watershed year of 1989.

However, the major civil rights murder incident, the murders of the three civil rights workers in June 1964, was not substantively addressed until the latter part of the 1990s. And, once again, the peripatetic news reporter for the *Jackson Clarion-Ledger*, Jerry Mitchell, was the person responsible for restarting the justice engine.

Sam Bowers's Interview about the Man Who Got Away with Murder, 1998

After Sam Bowers was convicted in 1998, an interview he gave to State Archivist Debra Spencer in the 1980s was published in the *Jackson Clarion-Ledger* under Mitchell's byline. Bowers agreed to the interview as long as it would remain under seal and not be opened until after his death. However, Mitchell, the one-person "Mississippi Bureau of Investigation," somehow got hold of the transcript and ran segments of it in the paper. During the course of the interview, Bowers said that he was "quite delighted to be convicted and have the main instigator of entire affair—Killen[27]—walk out of the courtroom a free man."[28]

In late December 1998, immediately after the interview was published, the families of the three dead civil rights workers demanded that the State reopen the long-closed case. Dr. Carolyn Goodman said: "It's like having something hanging over your head. There should be a closing.

59

There should be a trial. I'm not looking for blood, but I think some decision has to be made as to the guilt of whoever is left."[29]

Leading the demands for such action was Mickey Schwerner's widow, sixty-two-year-old Rita Schwerner Bender. She wrote letters to Mike Moore, the Mississippi attorney general, and to J. Kennedy (Ken) Turner III, the Neshoba County district attorney, calling for them to reopen the case.

Her message was a basic one, repeated at that time in several letters and since then whenever she met with reporters.

I think that, even after all these many years, there can be a form of justice if this spurs the opening up of the discussion as to how these violent acts came to happen. There really was state-sponsored violence, certainly in Mississippi and in many other places as well. That's what this was, state-sponsored violence. It goes far beyond the indictment of one old man.[30]

The Neshoba County district attorney in 1999 was Ken Turner III. For sixteen years he was the chief legal officer in Mississippi's 8th Judicial District, leaving in November 2003 to return to private law practice in Jackson.[31]

His reading of the Bowers interview was different than Bender's. And he told her so in one of their conversations about possibly reopening the case. "As far as *evidence* goes," he said to a reporter, "I didn't think that was very important. As I read it, it was basically just Bowers saying, 'I didn't do it, somebody else did.' You can get a lot of people in prison to say that."[32]

Turner said that the 1964 triple murder case has "been an albatross around our neck for 36 years. It'd be nice to get it off." However, he told a reporter, he would bring before the grand jury and then into court only a case that the state could win! "It's not fair to throw a weak case out there, and say, 'well, we tried.' . . . That would be more harmful. I'd take the heat for that."[33]

60

Although he was not moved by the interview, someone else was, the Mississippi attorney general, Mike Moore.

The Reopening of the Schwerner-Chaney-Goodman Murder Case, February 1999

Mississippi Attorney General Mike Moore was one of the new wave of Mississippi elected officials who came into office in 1988. Ray Mabus was elected governor that year. Mabus, thirty-seven at the time, was called the "yuppie governor" because of his age and his progressive ideas for a "New South."

Standing alongside him in the November 1987 victory celebrations were Mike Moore (attorney general) and Dick Molpus (secretary of state). The trio were seen by voters and reporters as Mississippi's young turks. They were "a ball of fires (*sic*)," recollected Alton Bankston, a southern Mississippi educator and active member of the state's Democratic Party. Ray Mabus, Mike Moore, and Dick Molpus were the Democratic Party's progressive "go-getters," labeled by the press as, alternatively, "the boys of summer" or "the three musketeers."[34]

They were committed to improving Mississippi's woeful public education system, to providing better health services, and to taking steps to overcome the state's miserable reputation nationally and internationally. For Mabus and his "boys of summer," an overarching problem for them and for the state was to break away from the tradition that, "in politics in Mississippi, as long as you were *right* on race, nothing else mattered." For the young governor, this obsession with race "had often caused [the state's politicians] to ignore vital issues such as education, health care, and other important social matters."[35]

In his effort to break with hidebound Mississippi traditions and administrators and begin to create a "New Mississippi," Mabus chose out-of-state persons—moderates and believers in the ideal of a New

61

South—to head many of Mississippi's state executive department agencies.[36] These actions rapidly led to voter perceptions that Mabus was "aloof." This view by the electorate led to his diminished popularity and loss in the next gubernatorial election. Although Mabus was defeated in his 1992 reelection bid,[37] Moore was reelected and remained in office until he left public service in January 2004. Jim Hood followed Moore in the General's office at that time.

In 1997 Moore was named Lawyer of the Year by the *National Law Review* for his leadership in the watershed multistate legal battle against the nation's major tobacco companies. In 1994, he filed the first Medicaid lawsuit[38] against the tobacco industry and flew around the country successfully convincing other state attorneys general to file suit against the companies. Moore was the primary negotiator in the deal struck with the industry and successfully led the push for the massive national tobacco settlement.[39]

That same year, however, Moore again refused to reopen the 1964 murder case. Ben Chaney, James Chaney's kid brother (he was eleven years old at the time of the 1964 murders) recalled that

> On September 24, 1997, I wrote Mississippi Attorney General Mike Moore urging him to reinvestigate the murders. His response through his assistant was that his "office does not have the authority to reopen the case." The Mississippi Constitution and the Mississippi Supreme Court afford Mississippi's attorney general all the authority and powers needed to convene a grand jury and prosecute the murderers of Schwerner, Chaney, and Goodman.[40]

In his talk to the New York Bar, Chaney also noted that eight years earlier Moore was given a report that recommended such action. In 1989, two of Moore's special assistant attorneys general, John R. Henry and Jack B. Lacy, submitted a report to him recommending "that his office prosecute the murderers of Michael Schwerner, James Chaney, and Andrew

Goodman. In their report, Henry and Lacy concluded that 'enough vital evidence existed' for a state prosecution."[41] Moore, without reviewing the "vital evidence," declined to take action in 1989 and again in 1997.

However, in 1999, with the reopening and successful prosecutions of long-sleeping Klan murder cases, and after his reading of the Bowers interview, Moore changed his mind. Unlike Ken Turner III, when Moore saw the Bowers story in the *Jackson Clarion-Ledger*, it "piqued his interest," said Jose Simo, special assistant to the attorney general. As Moore said afterwards, the 1964 triple murder was "just mean. . . . The way the kids were killed is as mean a crime as I know about—killing for no other purpose than to kill them."[42]

Critics of Moore, and there were many in Mississippi, angrily claimed that the Mississippi attorney general was grandstanding again, just like he did in the tobacco industry lawsuit. (It rankled many of his critics that Moore played himself in the Hollywood film version of the tobacco case, *The Informer*, with Russell Crowe cast as the tobacco executive who blew the whistle on his colleagues in the industry.) One of his critics was a lawyer from Philadelphia, Mississippi, Scott Johnson, who said:

> Not everyone in Philadelphia thinks the case is important. Opening the case is a political tool for politicians like Moore. In 2000 to date [2002], there are unsolved murders in Jackson, in Meridian. What makes one death more important than another death? What are their motives [for reopening the case]? Moore is using the case as a hot button to get media attention and a cameo role when the movie comes out.[43]

Nevertheless, on February 25, 1999, Moore took the initiative and the state reopened the investigation. At the same time the FBI turned over to the state more than 40,000 files pertaining to the case. And, in the same year, a federal judge ordered the state archivist to open the entire MSSC file *now* rather than waiting until 2027. Both files, containing tens of thousands of pages of documents and investigative reports about the activities of the Klan and other domestic terrorist organizations in the 1960s, proved to be a font of valuable data for the staff preparing for indictments and a trial of the still-living Klansmen involved in the 1964 murders.[44]

Attorney General Moore saw the value in retrieving the cold case: "Maybe by doing this old case, we'll change some of those old stereotypes [about Mississippi]." However, Moore was not sanguine about the obstacles both his office and Turner's office would face in bringing the case to the attention of a grand jury.

As he explained, "The problem with [the Mississippi Burning] case is that we didn't do anything—we didn't investigate it; we didn't prosecute it. One of the problems with bringing charges in the 36-year-old case is that all but eight of the key witnesses—the Klansmen themselves—are now dead." Both prosecutors and their staffs knew that a successful prosecution most likely required that the state be successful in convincing some of the conspirators to testify for the prosecution.

In May 2000, Dearman published another editorial in the *Neshoba Democrat*. Its title indicated its focus: "June 21, 1964: It's Time for an Accounting."

It's time for an accounting. . . . The office of the attorney general of Mississippi has been reviewing the massive files on the case that was obtained from the FBI. We hope that the attorney general and the district attorney conclude that the case can be effectively prosecuted. It's time. . . . This is a case that never goes away for the reason that it has never been dealt with in the way it should have been. It's time to bring a conclusion by applying the rule of law. Come hell or high water, it's time for an accounting.[45]

The editorial reflected the view of many, but not a majority of, Neshoba County residents. However, they had to await further announcements from the attorney general and from the Neshoba County district attorney, to see if there would be an accounting.

A Key Potential Witness for the Prosecution Dies in 2001, and the Case Returns to the "Cold Case" File in 2002

In October 2000, Attorney General Moore was interviewed by Richard Schlessinger, a *CBS Evening News* correspondent who was reporting on the state's investigation of the 1964 triple murder case:

> Mississippi Attorney General Mike Moore doesn't want it (criminal prosecutions of the Klansmen) to end there (the 1967 federal conspiracy trial and seven convictions).
>
> To him, the fact that the case remains unsolved is unacceptable. [Moore:] "This is a murder case. This is a mean case. I can't find any excuse why Mississippi didn't investigate this themselves and prosecute this case back in those days. . . . You can do something about the injustices of the past. If you can do it in Mississippi, you can do it anywhere."[46]

Jim Gilliland, the chief investigator in the attorney general's office for almost two decades, indicated that the office spent a number of years speaking, more than once, with the former Neshoba County deputy sheriff Cecil Price and other living members of the Neshoba and Lauderdale Klaverns about the 1964 murders. Except for Price's conversations, the other Klansmen, including Sam Bowers, repeatedly rebuffed Gilliland and others from the office.[47] Except for the information received from Price, and the possibility of acquiring information from Bob Stringer about the three murders, there weren't any new discoveries.

Cecil Price, one of the seven men convicted in the 1967 federal conspiracy trial, was the exception. In August 2005, the new Mississippi attorney general, Jim Hood, acknowledged that the conversations Price had with the attorney general's staff in 2000 *categorically* implicated Killen and others in the murders of the three civil rights workers. Price's conscience had gotten the better of him; he was willing to testify in open court about the grisly events of June 1964.[48]

The most frustrating thing about preparing the 1964 triple murder case, said Hood after the 2005 trial ended, was the fact that there was "so much very vital information that could not be used because key witnesses"—especially former deputy sheriff Price—had died.[49]

In a recent interview, Hood indicated that Price's conversations with the attorney general's office "precisely paralleled" the information contained in the confession Horace Barnett gave to the FBI in November 20, 1964.[50] In his 1964 signed confession, Barnett, one of the Klan participants in the murders of the three young civil rights workers, directly implicated Killen:

We arrived in Philadelphia about 9:30 pm, we met Killen and he got into my car and directed me where to park and wait for someone to tell us when the three civil rights workers were being released from jail. While we were talking, Killen stated that "we have a place to bury them, and a man to run the dozer to cover them up." This was the first time I realized that the three civil rights workers were to be killed.[51]

A review of the Mississippi attorney general's file on the former Neshoba County deputy sheriff indicates that Price, because of conscience, in 2000 had a change of heart and was cooperating with Moore and his staff investigators.[52]

The records in the Mississippi attorney general's office indicated that Price met with investigators a number of times and, in a signed statement, fully described the events of the day and night of June 21, 1964.

After Price finished his interviews with investigators in the attorney general's office, his lawyer, Max Kilpatrick, received a letter from Ken Turner III, the Neshoba County district attorney. Dated, November 17, 1999, Turner wrote that

> The State of Mississippi desires to take a [formal] statement from your client, Cecil Price, regarding any and all information he can provide concerning the deaths of Michael Schwerner, Andrew Goodman, and James Chaney. It is hereby agreed by the State of Mississippi that upon Mr. Price's full and truthful cooperation, nothing he says in this statement will be used against him in any state proceedings, either on direct or cross examination, or in any manner whatsoever.[53]

Price agreed to the conditions and, in early 2000, met with Mississippi attorney general investigators Tony Shelbourn and Jim Gilliland on two occasions. In a three-page, single-spaced statement signed by Price, "pursuant to a proffer,"[54] he told the two investigators what happened on June 21, 1964.[55]

After bringing the three young men to the Philadelphia city jail, Price met with a few of his friends on the city square by the old city hall. One of them suggested that "they needed to get a group together and give them boys a good whipping. Price stated that Edgar Ray Killen's name came up at this time as an individual that could get some men together to whip the 3 boys."

After leaving the small group, Price went to Billy Wayne Posey's gas station where he told Posey "of his desire to contact Killen to get the boys beat up."

> Killen called [me] up at the police station later that day and, after being briefed by [me] found out that one of the boys was Schwerner, to which Killen responded, "Oh good, we have been looking for Schwerner." Killen then requested Price to keep them locked up until he could get a group together and he would take care of it from

67

there. Price stated Killen called later that day advising Price that it was taking him longer than he thought to get a group together, . . . and advised Price not to release the boys. Price told Killen that he could not hold them much longer.

The next call from Killen came after dark, said Price. Killen asked the deputy sheriff to come to Jolly's car lot in Philadelphia and meet them. When Price arrived he saw that Killen had gathered six or seven individuals from Meridian "he did not know," as well as Hop Barnett and Grady Eakes, from Neshoba County. The plan was then laid out by Killen: free the three boys, Price would stop them on their way back to Meridian, and turn the young men over to the "Lauderdale group [Meridian Klansmen]." Price "assumed the boys were going to be beaten but nothing was really said about what was to be done to them." The three boys were then released from the jail and drove off to Meridian.

Price caught and pulled the boys over at a wide section of Highway 19. . . . The 3 boys were placed in the back seat of Price's county vehicle [with] James Jordan getting into the front seat of his county car. Price admitted to hitting Chaney as he, Chaney, got into the county vehicle.

Price and the two cars following him drove north on Highway 19 to a gravel road [Rock Cut Road]. Price stopped as did the other cars. And then the document described the murders:

After stopping on the gravel road Price stated that Wayne Roberts ran up and pulled Schwerner from the back seat of the patrol car and shot him once. According to Price, Roberts then removed Goodman from the back seat of Price's vehicle and shot him once. James Jordan then pulled Chaney from the back seat of the patrol car and shot him 2 or 3 times. . . . Price stated that he was standing besides Roberts when he shot Schwerner and Goodman. Price advised that he was scared, thinking he may also be shot by Roberts. Price stated to investigators he did not know the boys would be killed. . . . Price advised the investigators that Killen gave the order to release the boys, organized the group, and set up the car lot meeting. Price also stated that he remembered Killen stating that he was going to the funeral home to establish his alibi. . . . Price remembers Killen visiting the Sheriff's Department [afterwards] and stating, "hope they (FBI) don't look in any pond dam." Price stated he took this to mean Killen was aware of where the bodies were buried.

Price also "voluntarily submitted to a polygraph examination," carried out on August 17, 2000. The person who conducted the examination, Jim Gaines, "did not detect deception on the part of Cecil Ray Price."[56] Tony Shelbourn was the investigator from the attorney general's office present when the test was administered.

Ten questions were asked. The substantive ones follow:

Question 5 was: *"Did you lie when you said that Preacher Killen told you to keep those boys in jail until he could get a group together?"*

The answer, truthful in Gaines's judgment, was "no."

Question 7: *"Did you know of any plan to kill Chaney, Goodman, and Schwerner when you released them from jail on June 21, 1964?"*

The answer given by Price, "no," was determined to be truthful by the certified polygraph examiner.

Question 9 was also answered truthfully by Price. It asked: *"Did you and Billy Wayne Posey plan to lie to the investigators about any details related to this investigation?"*

His answer was "yes."

Bob Stringer was another potential witness for the prosecution. In 2000 and again in 2004, he was interviewed by the attorney general's investigators. Stringer was a teenager (seventeen to eighteen years of age) who worked for Sam Bowers. Bowers "employed [me] to hand out Klan literature in the mid-1960's," said Stringer.[57] In May 1964, Bowers asked

Stringer to take a ride with him to a church in Raleigh, Mississippi. It was the location of a large Klan meeting, so large that some of the Klansmen had to congregate outside the church doors.

In early June Stringer took another ride with his boss. The two again traveled to the church in Raleigh. There Bowers met with two white males sitting in another car,

> One of the white males was Preacher Killen. . . . Upon arriving at the church Killen and Bowers exited their vehicles and walked behind the church. [As the two cars were leaving, they pulled next to each other] driver side to driver side. Bowers told Killen that "Goatee (Schwerner) is like the queen bee in the beehive. You eliminate the queen bee and all the workers go away."

Conversations with Stringer and Price and the attorney general's investigators led Moore, as early as October 2000, to say to a newsman that indictments and a criminal trial were very near. "Well, there's a preacher over [in Neshoba County]," said Moore, "Preacher Killen, who we strongly believe was involved in the planning of this [crime]."[58]

By early 2001, then, the attorney general's office investigators were seeing light at the end of their tunnel. They had Stringer as a possible witness and an even more potent witness, Cecil Price.

However, fate intervened in a very negative way. In early May 2001, Price fell off a cherry picker while working in Philadelphia. On May 6, 2001, three days after his fall, Cecil Price died of head injuries in a Jackson hospital. Price's death was seen by Attorney General Moore as a major setback to the ongoing investigation of the 1964 case:

> If he had been a defendant, he would have been a principal defendant. *If he had been a witness, he would have been our best witness.* Either way, his death is a tragic blow to our case.

[However] we were going to get indictments against one defendant, if not more. *When Cecil Price died, it took a lot of wind out of our sails* [my emphasis].[59]

Cecil Price's passing turned out to be the death knell to the state's efforts to indict the Klansmen involved in the 1964 murders of the three young men. Although another witness, George Metz, surfaced in the summer of 2001 and was interviewed by Deputy Attorney General Jim Gilliland on August 2, 2001, his statement was useless to the state prosecutors.[60]

By mid-November 2002, Moore ruefully said to the press that the chances were "very slim" that murder charges would ever be brought by the state in the 1964 murders: "We are winding down our investigation at this point. We've still got the zeal to do it, but there's no sense in doing it if you can't make a strong case. It's getting tougher and tougher, but we're still working. We have something in the works that may pan out. We'll see."

The Neshoba County district attorney was much more emphatic about sending the case back to the cold case bin. Turner recalled that "we had gathered everything it appeared we could gather from anybody that was going to come forward. We reviewed it and made a determination at that point (2002) that it was just not sufficient information to try to seek an indictment."[61]

Supremely ironic was the fact that, by late 2002, Neshoba County inhabitants were finally prepared *emotionally* for a criminal trial of the murderers of Schwerner, Chaney, and Goodman. The events since 1989 as well as the possible "revival of the old case was bringing [these feelings] out of shadows. . . . The day's headlines were forcing people all over the state to confront their past."[62]

Neshoba County residents especially were either resigned or delighted "to be facing a sordid, tragic history [that would emerge during the trial] that many of its 7,500 residents tried hard to forget."[63] Said one white female resident of Philadelphia: "We were just children when this happened. We don't want to see us portrayed as barefoot, backward people. That's not who we are. We're not the people who were here 40 years ago."[64]

A black resident of the small town, Jewel McDonald, who was a little girl when the Mt. Zion United Methodist Church was burned down by the Klansmen in June 1964 and who saw her mother severely beaten by them, agreed with her white neighbor. She told journalist Brian MacQuarrie: "We're trying to get this big elephant out of our living room," and the expected indictments and trial will, she concluded, "lift the cloud from Neshoba County." [65]

After decades of silence and denial, of living with the stigma that all residents of the "evil" town of Philadelphia and the "Klan-infested" county were tagged with by outsiders, Neshoba County inhabitants were ready for the trial. It came as a surprise to them, then, when the prosecutors closed the investigation in 2002.

However, after Moore and Turner wound down their investigation, another set of events in Neshoba County occurred that led to the ratcheting up of new demands to reopen the 1964 triple murder case.

4

Toward the Indictment of Edgar Ray "Preacher" Killen, 2002–2005

[Attorney General] Jim Hood realized that if it [the murder trial]
wasn't done now, it would never be done.
Stanley Dearman[1]

We've been investigating the case for several years now. It just
finally got to the point where we felt like we had done all that we
can do. It was time to present whatever we had to the grand jury and
let them make a decision on the case.
—*Neshoba County District Attorney Mark Duncan*[2]

Can you believe that this town produced [both] Dick Molpus and
Edgar Ray Killen?
Stanley Dearman[3]

Why was the case against Edgar Ray Killen brought to the Neshoba
County grand jury in early January 2005 after Mississippi Attorney General
eral Moore and the Neshoba County district attorney, Ken Turner III,
dropped it three years earlier? Between 2002 and 2005, as will be seen in
this chapter, there weren't any smoking guns found by the new attorney
general, Jim Hood, or by the new district attorney, Mark Duncan, in the

tens of thousands of pages from the FBI's MIBURN files and in the reams of Mississippi State Sovereignty Commission (MSSC) documents.

There were no new witnesses who, because of a guilty conscience, confessed to the new prosecutors who the perpetrators were who planned and participated in the 1964 killings of the three young civil rights workers—and who were willing to say so in open court. Cecil Price was dead. Bob Stringer committed suicide. Another possible witness for the prosecution, George Metz, had also died.

After Killen was arrested in January 2005, Mark Duncan told a reporter: "It wasn't like there was any one thing that happened that said, 'Here's the magic bullet.' It really was that we had gotten to the end. *There was nothing left to do* [my emphasis]."[4]

In this chapter, I examine the reasons why, even though there was no "magic bullet," no "smoking gun," or no repentant Klansman, the two new prosecutors (both assumed their elected positions in January 2004)[5] brought the murder case to the grand jury when it convened in January 2005.[6]

The Key Participants and the Events Leading to the Indictment of Edgar Ray Killen for Murder

Although District Attorney Duncan said that he and Hood "decided to take the case to the grand jury when [they] determined they had run down all the leads and collected every bit of evidence they were likely to collect,"[7] there were some persons, organizations, and events in Neshoba County and in Mississippi that encouraged them to take that fateful action.

Dick Molpus, Susan Glisson, and the Philadelphia Coalition

From all accounts, former secretary of state Dick Molpus played a very significant role in continuing the pressure on public officials to address the question of reopening the 1964 murders case after Moore's and Turner's 2002 decision to not reopen the case. It was largely a behind-the-scenes role. It was one played out from his residence and his office in Jackson where, since his electoral defeat in 1995, he is in the business of managing Mississippi timberlands.[8]

Virginia "Jinksie" Durr was a rarity in Alabama at the time Molpus was growing up next door in Mississippi: a white liberal woman who lived in Birmingham, Alabama, most of the ninety-plus years of her life. Jinksie, with her husband, Clifford Durr (who was one of Martin Luther King Jr.'s lawyers),[9] championed the cause of civil rights for blacks during the height of Jim Crowism across the Deep South.

Durr was the sister-in-law of U.S. Supreme Court Justice Hugo L. Black. (Black, like so many other Alabamans of his era, joined the Birmingham Klavern and was a Klansman from 1923–1926.[10]) She was the keynote speaker at the 1988 Centennial Commemorative of Black's birth. It was held at the University of Alabama's law school, in Tuscaloosa, Alabama, where the late Justice took his law degree in 1902.

She stunned all of us participating in Justice Black's celebratory memorial program when she spoke her first words: "We were *all* sons-of-bitches growing up in Alabama," she said. Continuing, she said that Jim Crow values permeated the region and dictated the manners and mores of every Southerner. Some of these sons-of-bitches were malevolent ones—with an evil, cruel bent toward violence against innocent blacks. They knew there was no punishment for their beatings and killings of blacks.

"Most of us," she said, "were passive sons-of-bitches. We didn't beat or kill blacks, we just accepted" the insidious segregation and discrimination and inequality that were the inevitable results of Jim Crow.[11] Until she left for Wellesley College in New England and until her brother-in-law Hugo Black left for the U.S. Senate in 1925, both were reflexive racists. Her exposure to a very different set of values at college and his exposure to life beyond Mississippi changed both of them, quickly turning them into champions of equality and fairness for all persons.

Molpus, like "Jinksie" and Hugo Black, was a passive racist. He, too, grew up in a totally segregated society. His family, like most residents of Neshoba County, simply accepted the way of life. Philadelphia, Mississippi, was another of the hundreds of small towns across the South where Jim Crow segregation was the way of life. "Jim Crow," he recalled, "was the way things were. No one questioned it."

His father, the owner of a sawmill in Philadelphia, was one of the town's leading citizens. However, he was ever critical of the violence foisted upon blacks by the local Klansmen. And Dick remembered his dad's words to him when he was a small boy: "[He] taught me to call black people 'mister' and 'missus.'" Working as a youngster in his father's sawmill, Dick saw that the black laborers had "a lot more kindness, compassion, and decency than what was sitting in the First Baptist Church," he recalled in 2005.

And when Schwerner, Chaney, and Goodman were murdered in 1964, Molpus, then fourteen years old, was affected in a transformational way: "There was right and there was wrong," he said recently. "It wasn't always possible to reconcile what I knew to be right with what I'd been taught growing up."[12] He carried these changed values with him when he attended Ole Miss. There he was president of Sigma Chi fraternity, where he voted to integrate the fraternity. This proposal failed, and his vote, as Molpus recalled in 2005, "got me in a huge amount of trouble."[13] Molpus started in politics in Mississippi as an aide to Governor William Winter, 1980–1984, the first Democratic moderate to win a gubernatorial election without reliance on the traditional election strategy of "out-segging" the opponent.

I personally recall Winter's progressivism because I was the head of the Department of Political Science at Mississippi State University during the first two years of his term as governor. Our department, with the assistance of faculty members from the Political Science Department at predominantly black Jackson State University, drafted an internship bill that would, for the first time, provide public administration graduate students to state agencies and legislative committees as interns for a six-month period—with a stipend of $750 a month per student.

Governor Winter and his chief aides, including Molpus, supported the legislation and it went through the legislature with little difficulty—even though more than half of the interns were black and female. This was so because the only two programs in the state in 1980 with accredited master's programs in public administration were Jackson State and Mississippi State.[14]

The people Winter brought into state government, including Molpus "were all young. They called us the 'Boys of Spring,'" recalled Molpus recently.[15] Unlike generations of earlier Democratic administrations and legislatures—under the leadership of segregationists and with the support of the "uptown Klan, that is, the WCC's"—the Winter Administration staff had absolutely no difficulty supporting such a diverse (both racially and in terms of gender) internship program.

Dick Molpus met with me in one of the truly great bars and eateries in Jackson—Hal and Mal's, off Commerce Street—a week after the Killen trial ended. Since his public apology in 1989, he was doing all he could to provide justice for the three dead young men and their families and to push for actions that would lift the onus of racism off his city and his neighbors in Philadelphia. "I couldn't be happier," he told me. "You can't underestimate the importance of this trial for everyone."[16]

"Who is Dick Molpus" [17] and why did he play such an instrumental role in the decision to go to the grand jury in January 2005? For Stanley Dearman, Molpus is the "ever-evolving archetype of what's good in the Southland."[18] Fenton DeWeese, a lawyer and alleged by some to be one of the more radical members of the Philadelphia Coalition, said that "without the courage Dick showed in 1989, when, unscripted, he told the families of the murdered civil rights workers that 'I apologize' for what happened in his town and his state, well I'm not sure that all the rest would have happened."[19]

Molpus is the person credited by all with pushing for the creation of a multiracial citizens' movement, the Philadelphia Coalition, as early as 1989. He was encouraged by the responses—the good ones, that is—to his apology, especially because people in Philadelphia began to talk openly about the 1964 murders and about the absence of any state action to investigate and bring to justice the Klan perpetrators.

Molpus told me that in January 2004, he joined about 200 people from Neshoba County who were gathered at Lake Tia'Khatta, a Neshoba County private recreational facility, to talk about the past and the future of their home. He was the keynote speaker and spoke about the need for local citizens from the County and Philadelphia to "rewrite" Neshoba County history.[20]

Once again, his words were very well received and the group, still without a name, decided that their first tasks were (1) to plan for the fortieth anniversary memorial commemorative program that would honor Schwerner, Chaney, and Goodman, and (2) to publish a brochure, with the financial support of the Neshoba County Chamber of Commerce and other local community backers, about the county's terrible civil rights era past and how it has evolved since 1964.

Susan M. Glisson, a Georgia native, is the executive director of the William Winter Institute for Racial Reconciliation (WWIRR).[21] She is also an assistant professor of Southern Studies in the University of Mississippi's Department of History.[22] Glisson's leadership of the Institute "grows out of her academic work. After receiving bachelor's degrees in history and religion from Mercer University, she came to the Southern Studies Program [at Ole Miss] and earned her master's degree after writing her thesis on Clarence Jordan and the theological roots of radicalism in the Southern Baptist Convention. She went on to earn her doctorate from the College of William and Mary in 2000."[23]

In early February 2004, Glisson received a phone call from Molpus.[24] At the time he was a member of the board of directors of the WWIRR. His daughter, Nash Molpus, attended Ole Miss, and was a graduate assistant in the department of history assigned to Glisson. Molpus asked Susan if she and the WWIRR could help "his people" in Philadelphia create the civil rights era brochure agreed upon by them in January. She somewhat warily agreed to work with the group even though she didn't know anyone down in Philadelphia. In late February 2004 Susan visited the small city in Neshoba County for the first time.

She found a small group of men and women—black, white, and Native American—waiting for her on her arrival in Philadelphia. There was the president of the local NAACP chapter, Leroy Clemons, in attendance, as well as Stanley Dearman and Jim Prince, the former and present editors and publishers of the *Neshoba Democrat*. Also in attendance was Fenton DeWeese, a local attorney.

One of the first things they did with Susan's help was quickly come up with a name: the Philadelphia Coalition. Susan also noted that the coalition had to both add to and "replenish their numbers" by publicly seeking new members.[25] This was done by publishing stories about the aims of the Philadelphia Coalition in the *Neshoba Democrat* and through open invitations to join the diverse group.

This recruitment strategy was successful. By June 2004, the coalition had more than thirty members. Furthermore, these members reflected the depth and breadth of the county with regard to economic, racial, and educational parameters. Among them were lawyers, newspaper publishers and editors, nurses, ministers, housewives, and roulette wheel operators (who worked in the gambling casinos owned and run by the Choctaw Indian tribe). There were young professionals, cautious conservatives (Jim Prince),[26] 1960s-era liberals, and a seventy-something retiree (Stanley Dearman). As Dearman recalled in an interview he had with Sid Salter:

> I've enjoyed working on the coalition. . . . Many of the younger members are of a different generation from that of 1964. These young people are very socially aware and feel strongly about what they are

doing to observe the anniversary and honor the lives and work of Chaney, Schwerner, and Goodman. And furthermore, they don't care who knows it.[27]

Many of them had emerged from a long silence to join a group that was unafraid to call for the truth about the past, and to call upon the state's legal authorities to bring to the bar of justice those who took the lives of the three young men killed in their county. Deborah Posey, a white nurse who works on the Choctaw Indian Reservation, was one of the new members of the Coalition.

Posey, once married to the brother of one of the seven Klansmen charged and convicted in the 1967 federal conspiracy trial, Billy Wayne Posey,[28] was one of the new recruits. She told me that only once did her brother-in-law talk about the 1964 murders. He told her that the killings were "an accident, that they were long-haired hippie troublemakers."[29] Only years later, after she became interested in the event, did Deborah realize that Billy was lying. "When I saw a picture of the 'Missing' poster put out by the FBI, I saw that the missing civil righters were not long-haired hippies."

In our conversation, Posey told me about her life growing up in "Jim Crow" Mississippi.[30] "It was just the way it was," she told me. "Blacks went in the back door, whites went into the front door." She doesn't remember being fearful or frightened except when, in 1971, the Philadelphia public schools were integrated. "Only then was I scared, terrified," she said, although integration in the Neshoba County public schools went off without any problems. She married her high school sweetheart (divorcing him years later) and, after high school graduation, raised two children, both in their twenties in 2005.

Posey is a very religious person (she is a Southern Baptist) and prayer is one of her daily activities. "I believe in prayer, and [since my awareness of the injustices that occurred in Philadelphia], I've been praying for my city for years." In 2001, she attended a workshop held in her church. The focus of the session was the 1964 Mississippi Freedom Summer project.

That event was the first time she seriously examined the 1964 murders and the experience led to Posey's continuing education. She began to read books about the event and the era because, she told me, "I need knowledge of an event in order to be able to pray." When she read Florence Mars's book, *Witness in Philadelphia*, "I cried and cried."

Hearing about and discussing these mid-twentieth-century events "opened my eyes and still tears at me. This is my town, where I was raised and there was this mindset of some people in the town who were afraid to let go, afraid to change." As a devoutly religious person, Posey is still perplexed about the Preacher's behavior. "Killen knows God's rules. God is God of love, not a God of murder. I just don't understand the Preacher."

According to Posey, the murders of Schwerner, Chaney, and Goodman "showed the core beliefs of the generation that lived then. It was a racist, hate-filled, and a close-minded generation." Although she did not recall the event itself when she was growing up, her exposure to the murders and the values held by most Mississippians through workshops, readings, and prayer led her to respond to the public invitation to join the Philadelphia Coalition.

When she met the members of the coalition, "I found other people who cared about the city. They came from all walks of life, they were from different economic levels, and they were from different races." But, she perceived instantly, they had only one agenda: To tell and talk about what happened in Neshoba County in the 1960s and what had to be done to reconcile the clashing populations: "I believe that God touched all these people in order to heal all of us in Philadelphia and the county. The road back must follow from an admission of the terrible events and we're on that path." Since 2003, Posey regularly goes to the site of the three murders, Rock Cut Road, off Mississippi Road 519 (less than 2 miles from Killen's home in Union), and prays there.

For Glisson, the recruitment of people like Posey was a success in another way. People who joined the coalition after the invitations went out were men and women "who can pull things together, [who] can get things done," said Glisson.[31]

From her first meeting with the multiracial group, Susan was able to assist the Coalition on the two themes that interested them: writing and publishing the civil rights era brochure and planning the fortieth anniversary memorial tribute to Schwerner, Chaney, and Goodman. By May 2004, another project was added to the first two tasks of the coalition: convene an educational summit for Mississippi public school civics teachers with the focus on developing and implementing learning modules about the civil rights struggle in Mississippi. (Coincidentally, the very first Schwerner-Chaney-Goodman Summit conference occurred in Philadelphia the second week of the Killen trial.)

Furthermore, from that first meeting to the present, Glisson found herself playing two roles: cheerleading for the group and serving as a mediator among cliques within the group. (Her formal title on the Philadelphia Coalition masthead is Special Liaison.) At that very first meeting, Glisson observed a salient fact. Because the members did not know each other very well, "they didn't trust each other—but they trusted me. I became the 'neutral broker'!"

The strains were evident in the small group during the first year. Molpus recalls that "some of the white members wanted just to build a memorial. The black members just looked at them and said, 'Whoa, that's not enough.'"[32] Yet another decision by the coalition led to further anxiety and the flaring of tempers. After the group decided to invite Haley Barbour, the conservative Republican governor of the state to speak at the 2004 memorial service, some of the activists in the coalition split from the majority and established a second commemorative program. *Neshoba Democrat* editor Jim Prince feels Fenton DeWeese and many of the black members are "radical liberals." DeWeese says Prince's conservatism has alienated many.[33]

With Glisson's "neutral brokering," these clashes were resolved. The two memorial services, for example, were scheduled so that one did not overlap with the other and coalition members and others could attend both. And, with her assistance, the group committed itself to calling for the state to reopen the 1964 murder case. Guided by Glisson, the coalition reached agreement on a "Statement of Purpose" that appears on its Web site:

> Purpose of The Philadelphia Coalition: The broad-based, multiracial task force is charged with planning the public commemoration on June 20, 2004, planning an appropriate public memorial to the civil rights workers in Neshoba County and establishing a perpetual structure that will foster racial harmony and reconciliation.[34]

These illustrations underscore the reality that "the going hasn't always been smooth," says Jim Prince III, a somewhat cautious member and cochair of the coalition. And Dick Molpus echoed these views in his observation to me in June 2005: "There were 100 things that all came together to make the Philadelphia Coalition work."[35]

Glisson's February 2004 comments made sense to the group in another substantive way. She said at the time, pretty directly: "Justice is a prerequisite to reconciliation. You have to do that groundwork first, and that's what they did in Philadelphia."[36] On May 26, 2004, the coalition issued its first statement to the public. It was a resolution in the form of a "Statement Asking for Justice in the June 21, 1964 Murders of James Chaney, Andrew Goodman, and Michael Schwerner." Dearman was, as he recalled, "assigned the task of writing a resolution that the coalition approved unanimously."[37]

> The state of Mississippi has never brought criminal indictments against anyone for the murders of the three young men—an act of omission of historic significance. . . . With firm resolve and strong belief in the rule of law, we call on the Neshoba County District

Attorney, the state Attorney General and the U.S. Department of Justice to make every effort to seek justice in this case. We deplore the possibility that history will record that the state of Mississippi, and this community in particular, did not make a good faith effort to do its duty. We state candidly and with deep regret that some of our own citizens, including local and state law enforcement officers, were involved in the planning and execution of these murders. We are also cognizant of the shameful involvement and interference of state government, including actions of the State Sovereignty Commission, in thwarting justice in this case.[38]

After apologizing to the families of the three dead civil rights workers on behalf of the Philadelphia community, the resolution ended by calling "on those in authority to use every available resource and do all things necessary to bring about a just resolution to this case."

Within a few days, other organizations and state agencies responded to the resolution. Both Neshoba County District Attorney Mark Duncan and the state's attorney general, Jim Hood, sought out help from the U.S. Department of Justice in their reexamination of the 1964 closed case. These requests were seen, correctly as it would turn out, as "a move some believe could lead to new evidence in a case that has drawn worldwide attention and brought disrepute on Neshoba County for 40 years."[39]

The resolution also brought the national media into the fold. Many major newspapers, including the *New York Times,* the *Washington Post,* and the *Atlanta Journal-Constitution,* announced that they were sending news reporters to cover the fortieth anniversary commemorative program. National Public Radio aired an eight-minute segment about the coalition's agenda on its afternoon program *All Things Considered.* Mississippi television stations began plans for airing specials on the 1964 murders and on the activities of the Philadelphia Coalition.

Local organizations and city government also responded positively to the coalition's resolution. The Mississippi Band of Choctaw Indians issued a statement of support for the coalition and its goals. Philadelphia Mayor Rayburn Waddell sponsored a resolution, unanimously passed by the city commissioners. It called for justice in the 1964 murders case. Amazingly, similar resolutions were passed by the Neshoba County Board of Supervisors and the Neshoba County Community Development Partnership.

For the coalition, then, working for justice in the closed case was the first step. *Recognition* of the problem of racial violence in Neshoba County, through the instrument of a murder trial of those responsible for the 1964 murders, was needed.

That had to be followed by *resolution* of the dilemma of racism in Mississippi. That would come about only after Mississippians acknowledged the past brutal history of the state and took the necessary steps to remediate the vestiges of Jim Crowism—poverty, illiteracy, economic inequality—still present in the state of Mississippi. If there was recognition and resolution of the problems finally confronted by citizens and their political and religious leaders, then a kind of religious or humanistic "redemption" will naturally follow.

In my conversations with them, both Glisson and Molpus said, of the Philadelphia Coalition's future actions, that there is more work to be done: the group must confront today's issues of poverty, literacy, inadequate schools, and health care, and these issues must be addressed through the process of race reconciliation.

The Roving Sherlock Holmes, Jerry Mitchell

Jerry Mitchell was born in Texas almost fifty years ago. He received his master's degree in journalism from Ohio State University. In his early years, he was a reporter in Arkansas. He joined the *Clarion-Ledger* in 1986 and has been there for almost two decades. He has a wife, Karen, and two children and resides in Jackson, Mississippi.

Since 1989, this one-person "Mississippi Bureau of Investigation," in his role as reporter for the *Jackson Clarion-Ledger*, has focused attention on unpunished killers from the South's past and the secrets surrounding those crimes.

Dating from the 1989 Molpus public apology, Mitchell's hundreds of stories about the Neshoba County murders, including those of Medgar Evers, Emmett Till, and Vernon Dahmer Sr.—all committed by Klansmen—have informed Mississippians and the rest of the world. His writings have helped to convict four Klansmen: Byron De La Beckwith, Sam Bowers, Bobby Cherry (one of the Klansmen who blew up a Birmingham, Alabama, church in 1963, killing four young black girls), and, in 2005, Edgar Ray Killen.

He has gone everywhere to track down the truths and to uncover the furtive facts about these murderous events in Mississippi's recent past. He has won dozens of journalism awards and has been honored as an outstanding investigative journalist by a number of news associations and organizations.

As already noted, without his reporting in 1989 about the role of the MSSC and in 1998 about Bowers's earlier conversations with an archivist about the man (Killen) who got away with murder, one wonders whether justice in the 1964 triple murder case would have taken place the way it did.

Especially important and extremely valuable for citizens such as Deborah Posey, as well as historians and prosecutors, was a series of Mitchell stories about the murders of Schwerner, Chaney, and Goodman published in the *Jackson Clarion-Ledger* between May 7, 2000, and January 8, 2001. Entitled "44 Days That Changed Mississippi," the essays took the reader from the 1960s civil rights era in the state to the early years of the twenty-first century. It was absolutely brilliant reporting that I believe must have put Mitchell in serious contention for a Pulitzer Prize. Clearly, Mitchell's investigative reporting over the past two decades was and remains a clarion call for readers and activists such as the members of the Philadelphia Coalition.

It is obvious that Mitchell is one of the persons responsible for the continued pressure that finally led to the 2005 indictment for murder of

Edgar Ray Killen. In a conversation with me after the trial, one of Killen's defense lawyers, James McIntyre, had absolutely no good words for that "damned" Mitchell and that "damn" newspaper he worked for.

However, what few people knew until recently was that Mitchell and his two children faced a threat from an assassin that for almost the past two centuries has killed off many family members and continues to attack them in this century. The killer, unlike those he writes about in his civil rights legacy stories, is a rare genetic disease that has taken the lives of so many family members.[40] All the while Mitchell was hunting down clues to unmask the facts in Mississippi's and Alabama's decades-old civil rights murder cases, he was at the same time roving the country from Boston and New York to San Francisco and Texas to hunt down the "monster" that killed his grandparents, aunts, uncles, and cousins and threatened him and his children.

The monster turned out to be a deformed gene (inherited) that one of the doctors called a "genetic disaster." The disease initially attacks "the muscles and then ravages the brain and sometimes the bone, a monster who leaves his victims in crumpled heaps, eyes swirling, unable to focus. It is a monster with no name, a monster who came to be called the 'family disease,' a monster," wrote Mitchell in 2001, "who may live inside me [and my children]."

Mitchell found out that the family monster reveals itself in three forms—muscular dystrophy, Paget's disease (which causes the weight-bearing bones to bend, the skull to enlarge, and other bones to deform and grow), and dementia. The mutant gene struck Mitchell family members as young as forty-six. The average age of death of those killed by the malady in the Mitchell family was around fifty-nine. (Naturally, it was Jerry who did the math after researching the family's history.)

In his late forties in May 2001, Mitchell began to suffer sharp pain in his left leg below the knee. His first thought was the most fearful one anyone in his family could have: he had the family monster. Being the peripatetic investigator, for years Mitchell searched medical books and Web sites and visited research laboratories that study genetics and genetic defects. Through these Web sites, he tracked down a disease, inclusion body myositis,[41] that Mitchell believed was the family monster. Within the past two years, Mitchell has tracked down the villain that triggers the monster: ubiquitin, a small protein that marks certain proteins in the body's cells for destruction.

January 12, 2004, was one of the most important days in Mitchell's life. He found out that his father did not have the disease—and therefore neither did Jerry. "'And that my children [Katherine and Sam] can't possibly get the disease,' I say to the Doctor. She nods. I hug her and thank her. . . . For the first time in more than a century, my family has hope. . . . *I felt such a sense of relief when I heard the news, as if some great burden had been lifted from my soul* [my emphasis]."[42]

Ironically, Mitchell's observations about the monster in his family paralleled the observations of most of the citizens of Neshoba County. They dealt with their human monsters, the Klansmen who roamed the sidewalks of Philadelphia with impunity for over four decades, in much the same manner as Mitchell. His remark: *"In many ways the family disease represents our elephant in the living room—something everybody notices but hardly anyone talks about* [my emphasis]."[43]

Ben Chaney's Caravan Departs to Mississippi, June 10, 2004

Ben Chaney, the younger brother of James, created the James Earl Chaney Foundation, a civil rights organization.[44] The "defense of all constitutional and human rights are the focus of the James Earl Chaney Foundation's efforts. Through educational and legal defense programs, projects and special events, the Chaney foundation focuses on human and constitutional rights, particularly the rights of suffrage and equal protection under the law. By accomplishing our goals we fulfill the legacy of James Chaney."[45]

To commemorate the fortieth anniversary of his brother's murder and to honor the sacrifices of the other murdered civil rights workers, Chaney organized the Freedom Summer 2004 Ride for Justice. A caravan of buses and private vehicles left New York City on June 10, 2004 (with a planned arrival in Neshoba County in time to attend the fortieth anniversary memorial honoring the three civil rights workers on Sunday, June 20, 2004).

The plan was to visit a number of sites between New York City and Philadelphia, Mississippi; spots that are of historical significance in the struggle for civil rights in America. Hampton, Virginia (the site of the first student sit-in in 1960); Raleigh, North Carolina; Columbia, South Carolina; Atlanta, Georgia; Memphis, Tennessee (Martin Luther King Jr. was murdered here in April 1968); Birmingham, Montgomery, and Selma, Alabama; Meridian, Jackson, Money (Emmett Till was murdered here in 1955), and Philadelphia, Mississippi, on June 19, 2004, were some of the places the caravan visited.

The "freedom riders" were, for the most part, high school and college students; young volunteers who worked in the organization, primarily conducting voter registration drives. In addition, there were businesspeople, labor leaders, and clergy on the trip. At each of the almost two dozen stops, "voter jams" were held and the caravan's participants conducted door-to-door voter registration drives, "the same mission the three young men in 1964 [were planning to do when they were murdered]," said Ben Chaney. "We want to bring attention to the fact that there are several murders that occurred in Mississippi that have not been resolved. There are open wounds there." Chaney went on to say: "Forty years is a lot of time. Time has not stood still and there have been changes, and I've gotten old. I'm very optimistic this [a murder trial] can happen. I want this to happen in my mother's lifetime."[46]

The project kicked off the trip with a grand gospel jamboree, Gospel Fest 2004, the evening of June 9, in New York City. It was held in the Bethel Baptist Church in Brooklyn, the oldest African American church built from the ground up in New York City. The goal of the concert was to highlight the critically important role of the black churches in America's fight for civil rights.

The group, totaling close to 100 Riders, arrived in Philadelphia, Mississippi, in time to attend the memorial services sponsored by the two Philadelphia Coalition groups.

The Fortieth Anniversary Memorial Services, June 20, 2004

The first of the two memorial programs was held at 2 p.m. at the Neshoba County Coliseum. It was an hour-long program that publicly acknowledged the murders and the coalition's May 2004 call for a reopening of the investigation and to celebrate the lives of Schwerner, Chaney, and Goodman, who were killed forty years earlier. The Mississippi Band of Choctaw Indians provided a catfish lunch for the attendees. The second Coalition-sponsored program, a memorial service that began at 4 p.m., took place at the Mt. Zion United Methodist Church in the Longdale community, a section of Philadelphia.

Former governor William F. Winter was the keynote speaker at the first program, attended by citizens and community leaders of Philadelphia and Neshoba County. He told the audience that the public calls for the reopening of the 1964 murder case was a day that many feared would never come in Mississippi. "Forty years is a long time," he said. "It should not have taken that long but thank goodness it has come."[47] He praised the coalition for its call for justice, as well as the city and county governments and the Mississippi Band of Choctaw Indians for supporting the coalition's demand for justice in the 1964 murder case. Neshoba County can honor the slain civil rights workers "by seeking to achieve together what we cannot achieve separately."

In addition, state officials and U.S. congressmen from Mississippi, Bennie Thompson (D) and Chip Pickering (R), attended. Representative John Lewis (D-Ga.) also attended and participated in the program. (Lewis, one of the original college organizers of SNCC [Student Nonviolent Coordinating Committee] in 1960, was beaten and jailed because of his civil rights activities in the turbulent 1960s, and told the gathering about those times: "Some of us gave time, some of us, a little blood. These three citizens of the world [Schwerner, Chaney, and Goodman] gave all they had.")

In addition to Winter, Mississippi governor Haley Barbour, Dick Molpus, and author Alice Walker spoke to the audience of almost 2,000 people. James Young, a black member of the Philadelphia Coalition and the president of the Neshoba County Board of Supervisors, welcomed the audience:

> I can see the cloud moving today because we are admitting that we are wrong, the justice system was wrong, the politicians were wrong, the people were wrong. You are looking at a new Neshoba, a new Mississippi where the politicians are now saying "let's have justice," the lawyers are saying "let's have justice," the citizens are saying "let's have justice."

Molpus was the most popular of the speakers at the coliseum. Many in attendance said that his speech that day "went far beyond his historic 1989 speech in which he became the first public official to have apologized for the murders."[48]

He spoke directly to the Klansmen involved in the murders, the "witnesses among us," who were still alive:

> They need to be encouraged to come forward. They need to know that now is the time to liberate those dark secrets. When we have heard murderers brag about killings but we pretend these words were not spoken, when we know about evidence to help bring justice but refuse to step forward and tell authorities what they need to know, that is what makes us in 2004 guilty.

Beyond the call for justice in the Mississippi judicial system, Molpus's message went to the general theme of reconciliation:

> This is 2004, not 1964. Many of the demons we face today are similar to the ones forty years ago. True, African-Americans have the

91

right to vote, but too few of our citizens black, white, Indian, Asian or Hispanic use that right. Public schools were segregated in 1964. With the growth of segregation academies and white flight many remain that way now. Few politicians today use outright race baiting, but we see the symbols some use and the phrases they utter and everyone knows what the code is—what really is being said. In 1964 there was a dependence on low wage jobs in manufacturing plants. 40 years later most of the plants are gone, but too many still scrape by on dead end jobs to make ends meet. Black, white and Choctaw Indian communities here in Neshoba County and Mississippi struggle with the scourge of school dropouts, teen pregnancy and drug abuse that keep the cycle of poverty unbroken. To build a lasting monument to James Chaney, Michael Schwerner and Andrew Goodman we must face these issues with a clear, unblinking eye and say "no more." And finally, we Mississippians must announce to the world what we've learned in 40 years. We know today that our enemies are not each other. Our real enemies are ignorance, illiteracy, poverty, racism, disease, unemployment, crime, the high dropout rate, teen pregnancy and lack of support for the public schools. We can defeat all those enemies—not as divided people—black or white or Indian—but as a united force banded together by our common humanity—by our own desire to lift each other up. 40 years from now I want our children and grandchildren to look back on us and what we did and say that we had the courage, the wisdom and the strength to rise up, to take the responsibility to right historical wrongs . . . that we pledged to build a future together . . . we moved on . . . yes, we moved on as one people.

Dick Molpus received a prolonged standing ovation from the audience. Sitting just behind him was Haley Barbour, the conservative Republican governor of the state and a man who, in his successful 2003 gubernatorial campaign, used the kinds of words that Molpus talked about: "the symbols and the phrases" of latter-day race baiters.[49]

The retired Methodist bishop Clay F. Lee delivered a short sermon at the memorial service in the Mt. Zion United Methodist Church. Lee was the senior minister of the First United Methodist Church in 1964 and was one of the few residents of the county to openly condemn the murders from his lectern. "We have come this far by faith," he told the smaller group attending the memorial. "We've come this far because God is still with us, but God is not done with us yet."

Former U.S. attorney Doug Jones of Birmingham also spoke at the service. He had successfully prosecuted the last of the Klansmen responsible for the 1963 Birmingham church bombing, a terrorist attack that killed four young black girls. He told the group that "I can feel another rising tidal wave of justice. The seas are beginning to churn and the waves are beginning to mount."

In addition, family members of the three slain young men also spoke. Dr. Carolyn Goodman, then eighty-eight, attended and spoke at the memorial. "I never thought the day would come when I would say I was happy to be in Neshoba County," she said, "but today I am."[50]

The two memorial programs were a watershed for Neshoba County residents and for the members of the Philadelphia Coalition. Jim Prince spoke of the difficult days that Coalition members faced in the months prior to the call for justice (May 2004) and the June 20, 2004, commemorative programs.

> [We] spent the better part of the last two months immersed in what has been described by some as cathartic, or soul-cleansing, experiences as members have come to understand each other, the hurts and the fears, the guilt and the shame, as [our] mission evolved into a single-minded quest for justice and redemption. . . . As for the Philadelphia Coalition, the 40th anniversary commemoration is just the beginning, the start, we believe, of a quantum shift in thinking.[51]

On Sunday, June 20, 2004, the *Jackson Clarion-Ledger* editorialized about the two events in Philadelphia held that day.

> Efforts are under way today to revive the case and bring state murder charges and some justice for the horrible crime. That should be a priority of state and federal authorities. Only new indictments can bring closure on that level. But there is some healing needed at another level. Today, a diverse coalition of Neshoba County citizens gathers to remember the three civil rights workers. For the first time, government, civic and business leaders and local citizens are working together—to express grief, to show community sorrow and regret, to honor the work of the three young men who died for the sake of freedom. But the ultimate, long-term aim is even more important because it is aimed at racial reconciliation for the community and [to] show what Neshoba County and Mississippi is today.[52]

By the time of the June 20 memorials in Philadelphia, Attorney General Jim Hood was already hard at work in the investigation of the 1964 triple homicide. By June, he had interviewed a number of potential witnesses, including all of the still-living Klansmen from the Meridian and Philadelphia Klaverns.

Hood's Meeting with Dr. Carolyn Goodman, September 14, 2004

In mid-September, at the invitation of the Philadelphia Coalition, Attorney General Jim Hood paid a visit to Philadelphia, where he met with members of the Philadelphia Coalition.[53] The group also invited Dr. Carolyn Goodman and her son down to Neshoba County to meet with Hood. The participants met in the Family Life Center of Philadelphia's First United Methodist Church.

Although Hood declined to discuss the investigation's specifics or any new evidence that may have been found, he acknowledged that it was in the final stages and shortly he and District Attorney Duncan would make the fateful decision to go—or not to go—to the Neshoba County Grand Jury with what they had.

Stanley Dearman told me that the almost two-hour meeting was intense and occasionally emotional. Hood, said Dearman, was "very sincere, very attentive" throughout the evening, especially so in his exchanges with Dr. Goodman.[54] Although Hood spoke in general terms, about the fact that there was ongoing research by prosecutors, and gave no commitment that there would be further action, he did tell the group that "he realized that if nothing was done now, nothing would ever be done. 'It was now or never,' he told us."[55]

After the indictment came down in early January 2005, Hood confessed to Mitchell that his conversation with Andy Goodman's mother was an extremely important, and moving, moment in his decision to work with Duncan to bring the 1964 murders case to a grand jury. "I knew it was my duty as a prosecutor to present this case to a grand jury. I was not going to change my policy as attorney general. *It all boils down to having been a victim myself* [my emphasis]."[56]

By this time Duncan indicated that *if* the case went to the grand jury and *if* there was an indictment, he planned to reintroduce testimony from the 1967 federal conspiracy trial by reading from the 3,000-page transcript.[57] He indicated that he was especially interested in James Jordan, the Klansman who confessed to the FBI in late 1964[58] and who testified in open court in 1967 that Killen was the Klansman who orchestrated the plans for the murders of the three civil rights workers.

Finally, on December 20, 2004, the Mississippi Religious Leadership Conference announced that an anonymous benefactor donated $100,000 as reward for information that led to the arrest, prosecution, and conviction of the Klan killers of Schwerner, Chaney, and Goodman. However, by that time, Hood and Duncan had reached a decision about going to the grand jury.

The Grand Jury Indictment of Edgar Ray Killen, January 6, 2005

"It really was that we had gotten to the end. There was nothing left to do," said District Attorney Mark Duncan to me about the late December 2004 decision to take the case to the grand jury in January 2005. The journey to that decision began as soon as both men formally took office in January 2004. Duncan disagreed with his predecessor's cautious decision to drop the case before going to a grand jury; he also told me that he disagreed with Attorney General Mike Moore as well because Moore went along with Turner's decision to drop the case without any definitive closure.[59] After the indictment came down, Duncan's predecessor, Ken Turner III, told Mitchell that Duncan "is a good, solid prosecutor. There are not a lot of frills to Mark. It's not a surprise he's taking it on. I didn't think he would shy away from this case."[60]

The two prosecutors knew each other "a little bit," said Duncan; they talked about the case before Hood took office in January 2004. It was the first of many conversations, in Jackson and in Philadelphia, and on the telephone late at night, that the two men had during the entire year of 2004.[61]

In a conversation with me after the trial ended in late June 2005, Duncan told me that the case was the proverbial elephant in the living room. He was "pretty much familiar with what we had because I had been Assistant D.A. for 16 years. I knew it was something that was going to have to be dealt with one way or the other," he acknowledged.[62] Not too long after the two prosecutors formally took office in January 2004, Duncan said: "we spoke on the phone about the case one night for a long time."

Because I knew the facts in the case inside out, basically we then spent most of 2004 with Jim [Hood] getting familiar with the case.

We also went back and talked to everybody we could again, making sure that there wasn't anything left undone.

We basically decided that [the case] had to be dealt with one way or another and we need to go ahead and deal with it. If we could do it [seek an indictment and gain a conviction] we would and if we couldn't, we wouldn't—the evidence was our guide in reaching the decision.

Jim Hood's conversation with me took place after the trial ended. I was back in Vermont when I called him to ask some questions about the prosecutors' work-up to the grand jury. Initially, Hood told me that, like his predecessor, Mike Moore, "I thought the case was over, too." However, after speaking with Duncan, who was committed to bringing closure to the issue, he told me of his thinking at the time:

Heck, I'll just read the case and give it a final answer one way or another. I assumed [in January 2004] that it would be just what Mike [Moore] decided. Once I started reading the testimony [I realized] I've got enough here to really take a good look at it—and that's when I personally interviewed every living witness I could.[63]

The two prosecutors were hopeful that "somebody would agree to testify. We tried, but it never happened." For many months, Hood and Duncan, together and separately, brought the Klansmen into their offices, hoping that one of them would become a witness for the prosecution. The two prosecutors—and their staff—spoke at length with the Klansmen but no one agreed to tell what happened—and what role Killen played in the planning of the murders—on the night of June 21, 1964.

We approached the Klansmen with the idea of them testifying—however, they all turned us down flat. There was no hesitation. Most said: "I don't know anything about [the murders]." It was not unexpected.

We literally had some of them at the grand jury door and said, "look, you can come in as a witness or go out as a defendant." *Every one of them called our bluff.*[64]

Duncan speculated on the Klansmen's responses. "We knew [their responses] were not true."

I don't know if it's that they denied being involved for so long that they told family and friends all this time [40 years] that they weren't involved in it and they just got to the point that there was no way they could change that story. They're all likable people if you don't know what they did. They all have nice smiles.[65]

Over half a year, Hood spoke at length with the four Klansmen still alive who had been convicted on conspiracy charges in the 1967 federal trial: Jimmy Arledge,[66] Billy Wayne Posey,[67] Jimmy Snowden,[68] and Sam Bowers.[69] Although there were eight Klansmen indicted in 1967 who were still alive, the prosecutors focused on the quartet of convicted conspirators in the hope that one of them would testify against the Preacher.

Hood had two long conversations with Arledge and with Sam Bowers. The attorney general remarked that Arledge, even though he was there the night of the murders—and was convicted in 1967 for his part in the conspiracy—"could pass a polygraph test, because he truly believes he wasn't there [the night of the murders]."[70]

Hood's conversation with Bowers, the Imperial Wizard who issued the "elimination" order in 1964 and who was then in Parchman Prison because of his conviction and life-imprisonment sentence in 1998 for the murder of Vernon Dahmer Sr., was an interesting one. It took place in March 2004. Hood vividly recollected the final words he had with the Wizard:

Bowers looked out my window and marveled at the green scenery [he is in maximum security at the prison which means twenty-three hours a day in his isolation cell, with only one hour every weekday spent outside his cell, also in isolation]. I asked him if he wanted to set the record straight in the 1964 murder case, and, for some moments, I honestly thought he would do it. He sat for at least three minutes in silence, then he swallowed real big, raised his head, tightened his jaw, and then said: "I'm not goin' to help you."

And Bowers has remained silent.

Billy Wayne Posey, once related by marriage to Deborah Posey, one of the members of the Philadelphia Coalition, also had a lengthy conversation with the attorney general. Hood said that Posey "gave the Office a *proffer* of what he would testify to if he was given immunity [in 2000], but then he refused to sign it." Like the other two Klansmen, he simply refused to change his mind. And Snowden, the fourth Klansman convicted in 1967, categorically refused to testify in the Killen trial, saying that "he didn't know what I was talking about."

Hood and Duncan "cranked up the pressure on them, including polygraph tests for each of them" before the prosecutors went to the grand jury. However, as Duncan told me, the four Klansmen "called our bluff." The attorney general said, with disgust, that Posey and Snowden were weak, "decadent men; they would love to admit [their roles in the murders as well as the role played by the Preacher,] but they can't take the medicine for it."[71]

Hood told me that Cecil Price, the Neshoba County Deputy Sheriff who died from a fall in 2001, "would have been a very good witness. It was a damn shame he died." Another potential witness who had spoken with the prosecutors and had agreed to testify in the trial, Bob Stringer, committed suicide nine months before the grand jury indictment came down.

Were there any pressures on Hood and Duncan to bring *any* case to the grand jurors? Duncan's answer was candid and direct:

> I really don't want to hurt [the Coalition's] feelings but they didn't have any effect on what I did at all. They never pressured me to do anything or anything like that. I did sit down with Jim Prince and

Leroy Clemons one day and talked about the case in general terms, but they didn't walk in the door and demand I prosecute the case. They were more respectful.[72]

While Duncan greatly admires the coalition's efforts to do "good things for their community," their work "was something completely separate from prosecuting a case." He leaned over to emphasize that the "fact was that we would prosecute if we had enough evidence regardless of what the Philadelphia Coalition or any other group was demanding."

He believed that most residents of the county "would probably say they were not in favor of opening the trial." However, after the indictment came down, "the good calls to my office outnumbered the bad calls 100 to 1." It was also a very tense time in the county in the months immediately before and after the grand jury met in early January 2005. "Fear still exists today," Duncan told me. "Some people called to jury service told the judge they were afraid to serve—and they were excused."[73]

Jim Hood told me that he wished his predecessors had brought the case to the grand jurors decades ago. However, for whatever reasons, they did not. And, he confessed, he felt "it was my obligation to take it on."[74]

Hood, however, was primed to go to the grand jury regardless of the serious problems the prosecutors faced. And he told some of us why he was ready to act.

When Hood was only fourteen years old, he became a victim of a murder. His first cousin, Glen Ford, was brutally murdered in October 1976. Ford and his pregnant wife went to a restaurant in Tupelo, Mississippi. He got into an argument with another customer over, of all things, deer hunting. The man left. When Ford and his wife exited the eatery, the man, 30 feet away and armed with a 12-gauge shotgun, was waiting for him. He shot Glen in the back, killing him instantly. Hood said:

As a victim, you never forget. A murder is even worse because you want to be mad at somebody, and that's what drove this [Killen] case.

There are people who say this will tear up Neshoba County and Mississippi, but the whole reason for me presenting this case to the grand jury was driven by my experience as a victim. I feel like everybody has a right to a day in court.[75]

When they decided to bring the facts to the grand jury that convened on January 4, 2005, the two prosecutors knew that none of the Klansmen still alive would be a witness for the prosecution. Price was dead for almost four years; Stringer had committed suicide a year earlier. As Duncan said, "there was no magic bullet," there was no "smoking gun" document or testimony—other than the testimony of dead men who had testified in the 1967 conspiracy trial. By the end of 2004, "after we had done all that we could do, we decided to present the case to the grand jury," Duncan said.

On December 19, 2004, Jerry Mitchell's front-page story in the *Jackson Clarion-Ledger* broke the news; the story shocked and surprised its readers. The headline declared that "AG Organizing Grand Jury to Eye '64 Rights Slayings." Mitchell's first paragraph thrilled some people, in and out of Mississippi: "Mississippi will make history early next year when Attorney General Jim Hood convenes a grand jury to consider the first-ever murder charges in the 1964 killings of three civil rights workers that helped cement the state's image as a haven of hate and violence."[76]

Jim Hood was quoted by Mitchell in the story: "We should be able to conclude our investigation by the end of January [2005]. I can't comment on grand jury proceedings or when the grand jury will meet." Mitchell, however, pointed out that the grand jury was scheduled to meet on January 4, 2005, "to consider other criminal cases."

The story included observations from the families of the three victims, as well as observations from members of the Philadelphia Coalition. Most of these comments were euphoric ones. Leroy Clemons, the cochair of the Philadelphia Coalition, gushed: "That's the best Christmas present I could have gotten this year." Another Coalition member, Jewell McDonald, said "hopefully something can come out of this to bring us closure."

Dick Molpus praised the attorney general: "This is a bold, courageous move to finally bring to justice the murderers of these three young men. I have absolute confidence that what Jim Hood begins, he will finish."[77]

The Neshoba County grand jury of twenty-one citizens[78] of the county was "empaneled [*sic*], sworn, and charged" on December 10, 2004. It reconvened on January 4, 2005. Jacob Ray, an assistant attorney general in Hood's office, told Mitchell that the prosecutors "presented all the evidence to the grand jury and made them aware of all possible defendants to charge. From there, the grand jury—at their discretion—only voted on four of the possible defendants."[79]

Duncan presented the grand jurors with whatever evidence the two prosecutors had amassed over the past year. The grand juror book, available to the public, showed that the jurors considered indictments against Killen, Arledge, Snowden, and Posey, but, except for Killen, returned "no bills"[80] for the other three.

Attorney General Hood told Mitchell that the grand jurors had the opportunity to indict more men: "We presented everyone who was living . . . for potential indictment, and they came and indicted Edgar Ray Killen."[81] According to the grand juror book, the jurors did not consider Sam Bowers, Richard Willis, Olen Burrage, and Pete Harris. Bowers was serving a life sentence for the murder of Vernon Dahmer Sr., and the other three were acquitted in the 1967 federal trial.

On January 6, two days later, the grand jury indicted Edgar Ray Killen on three counts of murder for "willfully, unlawfully, and feloniously kill[ing] and murder[ing] Michael Schwerner [count one], James Chaney [count two], and Andrew Goodman [count three], human being[s], without the authority of law and with deliberate design to effect [their] death[s] in violation of Section 2215, Miss. Code of 1942 . . . as amended."

Within hours, Killen was taken into custody by the Neshoba County sheriff. His arraignment took place the following day, Friday, January 7, 2005, at 11 a.m. in the Neshoba County Courthouse. He pleaded not guilty to the three counts of murder. Presiding was circuit judge Marcus Gordon. Seconds after the arraignment ended, the courthouse had to be evacuated because of a bomb threat. It turned out to be a hoax.

For the Philadelphia Coalition members and others, the indictment was seen as a victory for justice. Stanley Dearman, the feisty retired newsman, told Mitchell: "This [indictment] does my heart good, me and my pacemaker. It feels like a weight has been lifted off this community." And Dick Molpus, quite pleased with the indictment, said that "this trial will be a historic turning point for Neshoba County and Mississippi. Decent people in our state are ready to work on real issues that transcend race." Dr. Carolyn Goodman, Andrew's mother, told reporters: "That's good news, very good news. This was something that was late in coming [but] that had to happen—there was no question—It was something that had to be."[82]

Michael Schwerner's widow, sixty-two-year-old Rita Schwerner Bender, in a press release after Killen's not guilty pleas were entered, said:

I believe this is an opportunity to understand the consequences of government-sponsored racism. If we can teach that by this case to the present generation, then justice will be served. Racism is the elephant in the living room of this country. And we pretend it does not exist. Until we acknowledge it, until we acknowledge the past, we are not moving forward.[83]

Some family members were less enthusiastic. Reached by telephone at her home in Willingboro, New Jersey, eighty-three-year-old Fannie Lee Chaney, James Chaney's mother, said, tersely: "Mighty long time. Most of them dead about now."[84] And her son Ben Chaney, who led the Freedom Summer Caravan to Philadelphia in June 2004, was downright angry at the single indictment issued by the grand jury. The indictment gave him "a small semblance of hope. I'm barely, partially optimistic because we're still a long ways from justice."

It's like there is a void, because not all of the murderers have been indicted. And I don't think it is going to be filled with just this prosecution. This is going to be a whitewash. They are going to use the most unrepentant racist as the scapegoat, leave the others alone because they are more powerful, more wealthy, and more influential—and then move on.[85]

For others, as well, the indictment was a sham, a political ploy that would further exacerbate tensions between the races. But they spoke from the other side of the values divide. Billy Wayne Posey, who was one of two former Klansmen subpoenaed to testify before the Grand Jury,[86] stood outside the grand jury room and complained to a reporter: "After 40 years to come back and do something like this is ridiculous . . . like a nightmare."[87]

Attorney James McIntyre, Arledge's counsel that day (and cocounsel for Killen afterwards), spoke instead, condemning the indictment, saying that "it will only help the feelings of a few," and adding, "I think this is a sad day for Mississippi. This is going to open up old wounds. People (across racial lines) will look at one another differently. I never thought [the case] would surface again."[88]

While the prosecutors' decision to bring the case to the grand jury was based on the evidence, the actions of the individuals and the organizations—and the news hawking of Jerry Mitchell—did have an effect on them. Both Duncan and Hood knew that if they did not move to the grand jury in 2005 and ask for indictments, there would in all probability be no "next time."

In September 2004, Hood told the Philadelphia Coalition and Mrs. Goodman that "it's now or never." Only eight of the Klansmen were still alive, and all of them were in their senior years. The youngest was sixty-two years old, but most of the others were in their seventies. Killen was nearly eighty years old when he was indicted. Duncan said to me that it was not, by far, a perfect case: More than half of the prosecution's case would be based on the reading of segments of the 3,000-page 1967 federal trial transcript. Key potential witnesses for the prosecution were dead. However, given the two prosecutors' view of the importance of the case in the context of recent Mississippi history, they sought indictments in early January 2005—and the grand jurors indicted Killen.

From Indictment to Trial, January–June 2005

The time between the January indictment and arraignment of Killen and the start of the trial was filled with defense motions and decisions by Judge Gordon. On January 11, 2005, Judge Gordon set Killen's bond at $250,000 (which was quickly met by his supporters) and announced the opening of Killen's murder trial: March 28, 2005. (Because of a conflict in his schedule, a month later Judge Gordon set a new trial date: April 18, 2005.)

Killen was dressed in a yellow Neshoba County Jail jumpsuit for the hearing. His lawyer was tall, lanky Mitch Moran from Carthage, Mississippi. (Moran was to be joined by James McIntyre shortly thereafter.) After the hearing Killen was returned to the nearby Philadelphia jail where he stayed until he made bail.

In the days and months prior to an actual trial, there are a lot of tactics at play by both sides in a murder case, especially one of such historic importance. The Killen trial was no exception. By early February 2005, Killen had given two television interviews to Jackson stations. In both of them, he denied any role in the deaths of the civil rights workers. Killen's lawyer, Moran, said that his client was talking because he wanted to share *his* story with the public. District Attorney Duncan had another take on these interviews: "I think it's fairly obvious they're trying to influence the jury pool [but] I think most people are smarter than that."[89]

A few days later, it was the prosecutors' turn to grab headlines. The two men issued a list of potential witnesses for the prosecution. Included on the list were the seven Klansmen still alive who participated, one way or another, in the 1964 murders. Beside the name of each of the seven Klansmen was the notation: "The witness is expected to testify as follows: as to his knowledge of the events of June 21, 1964, and related matters."

105

Even though the prosecutors knew that—at that time—none of the Klansmen would cooperate with them, there was the hope that such public announcements would trigger pressure that just might get one of the conspirators to actually become a witness for the prosecution. And when Hood was asked about the list, he replied that "authorities developed new information on the same day the Neshoba County grand jury met."[90] This statement, of course, was false; the hope on Hood's part was that the statement would prod someone into changing their mind about testifying. This tactic did not work.

Further enhancing the pretrial scene was J. J. Harper, of Cordele, Georgia, the Imperial Wizard of the American White Knights of the Ku Klux Klan. He requested permission from the Philadelphia sheriff's department to demonstrate in support of Killen on the very tiny lawn in front of the Neshoba County Courthouse—including permission to burn crosses.

Although he said his group was nonviolent and Christian, he said on his Web site: "Brother Killen is being charged with murdering a nigger and two Jews back in 1964. Personally, I'd ask, 'What's wrong with that?'"[91] On his Web site, Harper encouraged all Klansmen to attend the trial and gave them specific instructions: "Dress appropriately for court. Whether you believe it or not, first appearances make big differences in the attitudes of people. Please wear some nice dress pants and an ironed shirt—at least. Personally, I'd like to see every one of us there in a business suit."[92]

While the prosecutors secretly savored the idea of a gaggle of Klansmen attending the trial, the defense team was aghast at this possibility. By the time the trial started, the Klan's plans had changed. Harper and a Klan buddy attended the first day of the trial and then went back to Georgia. Other than some local Klansmen, there was no horde of White Knights descending on the courtroom and burning crosses on its front lawn.

The defense then asked Judge Gordon to dismiss the charges against Killen because of the forty-year delay in bringing criminal charges against him. Moran's petition claimed that the inordinate delay deprived Killen of his constitutional right to due process of law, including the requirement, in the Sixth Amendment, that the accused must have a speedy trial. On March 4, 2005, Gordon denied the request: "I find no evidence of intentional delay and no actual prejudice. Vague assertions of lost witnesses, faded memories, or misplaced documents are insufficient to establish a due process violation from pre-indictment delay."[93]

Less than one week later, another event delayed the opening of the murder trial. On March 10, 2005, a tree fell on Killen, breaking his bones in both thighs. He was rushed to the University of Mississippi Medical Center, where doctors inserted pins in order to repair the damage. The medical staff said that it would be three months before Killen might be able to get about without the aid of a wheelchair. Consequently, Judge Gordon reset the date of the trial to June 13, 2005.

Killen was released from the hospital in Union, Mississippi, in mid-April. A month later, McIntyre speculated in the press whether Killen was up to the task of assisting his counsel in preparing an adequate defense. On May 11, McIntyre filed another motion in the Neshoba County Circuit Court, challenging the indictment. The prosecution of Killen is "selective prosecution in violation of [the Fourteenth Amendment's] equal protection [clause]." In part, the motion read:

Crimes and more particularly crimes of violence are on the rampage in the state of Mississippi and have escalated dramatically in the past 40 years. The public is being threatened each and every day by new crimes, but the state of Mississippi has chosen to single out an old charge of murder against this defendant (who) is not a threat.

Judge Gordon denied this motion as well and the defense reluctantly hunkered down to prepare the defense's case for acquittal.

But, ten days before the trial was scheduled to begin, the two defense attorneys sought another delay from Judge Gordon. Their argument was that Killen was suffering from osteoarthritis and was still too ill to stand trial. On June 8, 2005, Judge Gordon heard arguments on the latest defense request to delay the start of the trial. That same day, after hearing the arguments, Gordon denied the defense's request. He said that there would be a private room set up with a bed so that Killen could rest between recesses in the trial. Gordon also told the lawyers that he instructed the clerk of the court to have a registered nurse during the trial in case Killen needed assistance. A comfortable chair was ordered from a local business; however, throughout the trial Killen sat in his wheelchair.

And so, after all the events since January 2005 had played out, the trial of Edgar Ray Killen was set to begin on Monday, June 13, 2005, in the Neshoba County Courthouse, before Circuit Judge Marcus Gordon.

The FBI's "missing" poster displaying the photographs of civil rights workers
Andrew Goodman, James Earl Chaney, and Michael Henry Schwerner. (Corbis)

The burned-out CORE station wagon used by the three civil rights workers, June 1964. (FBI photo, courtesy Attorney General's Office, State of Mississippi)

Earthen dam, Neshoba County, where the three civil rights workers were buried, August 1964. (FBI photo, courtesy Attorney General's Office, State of Mississippi)

Above: The bodies of Schwerner, Goodman, and Chaney unearthed, August 1964. (FBI photo, courtesy Attorney General's Office, State of Mississippi)

Left: Edgar Ray "Preacher" Killen, ca. 1966. (FBI photo, courtesy of Attorney General's Office, State of Mississippi)

Edgar Ray Killen on his way to his trial in the Neshoba County Courthouse, June 2005. (Photo by Kate Medley)

Killen's family leaving the Neshoba County Courthouse, June 2005. Left to right: Oscar (brother), Dorothy Dearing (sister), and Betty Jo Killen (wife). (Photo by Kate Medley)

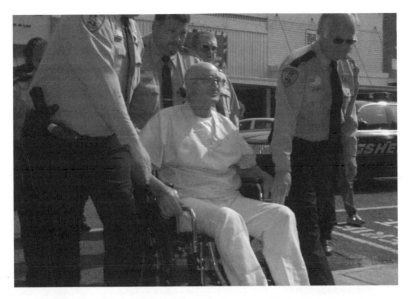

Killen being escorted to his sentencing hearing, June 2005. (Photo by Kate Medley)

Rita Schwerner Bender during Killen's trial. (Photo by Kate Medley)

Ben Chaney during Killen's trial. (Photo by Kate Medley)

Mississippi Attorney General Jim Hood with Rita Schwerner Bender during Killen's trial. (Photo by Kate Medley)

Fenton DeWeese and visitors during Killen's trial. (Photo by
Howard Ball)

Richard Molpus, Mississippi Secretary of State.
(Photo by Kate Medley)

Susan M. Glisson, director,
William Winter Institute for Racial
Reconciliation, University of
Mississippi. (Courtesy Susan M. Glisson)

Mississippi Attorney General Jim Hood and Neshoba County District Attorney
Mark Duncan during Killen's trial. (Photo by Kate Medley)

Mark Duncan, Neshoba County district attorney, in his office, June 2005. (Photo by Howard Ball)

Mitch Moran, one of Killen's defense attorneys, during the trial. (Photo by Kate Medley)

Jim McIntyre, one of Killen's defense attorneys, during the trial. (Photo by Kate Medley)

Judge Marcus Gordon in his chambers, Neshoba County Courthouse, June 2005. (Photo by Howard Ball)

Neshoba County Courtroom. (Photo by Howard Ball)

Shaila Dewan, national correspondent for the *New York Times* Southern Bureau. (Photo courtesy Shaila Dewan)

The author's press badge; Ball covered Killen's trial for the *Burlington* (Vermont) *Free Press.*

Donna Ladd, editor of the *Jackson Free Press,* conducting an interview during Killen's trial. (Photo by Kate Medley)

Jerry Mitchell, investigative reporter for the *Jackson Clarion-Ledger,* with Rita Schwerner Bender during Killen's trial. (Photo by Kate Medley)

Jerry Mitchell grimacing at one of Jim McIntyre's comments outside the Neshoba County Courthouse, June 2005. (Photo by Howard Ball)

Stanley Dearman, former publisher of the *Neshoba Democrat*, during Killen's trial. (Photo by Kate Medley)

Crowd in front of the Neshoba County Courthouse following the announcement of Killen's sentence. Note the Mississippi Highway patrolmen on the courthouse's rooftop. (Photo by Kate Medley)

Spectators observing the activities at the Neshoba County Courthouse, June 2005. (Photo by Kate Medley)

5

The Murder Trial of Edgar Ray Killen, June 13–21, 2005: Participants, Environment, and Jury Selection

Man, I just want to shake [Martin Luther King Jr.'s killer's] hand."
Edgar Ray Killen[1]

When it comes to racial matters, everyone's prejudiced. If you're not, then there's something wrong with you.
Mitch Moran, Killen's counsel[2]

The two prosecutors were frustrated as the June trial date approached. Duncan and Hood had hoped that at least one of the Klansmen who participated in the killings would develop a conscience and would testify for them. "They wanted to get Killen for murder, but they were undermined by a dearth of live witnesses decades after the killings," wrote one of the many dozens of reporters who covered the trial.[3]

As for the handful of living witnesses, the seven surviving Klansmen other than Killen, both men hoped that, as Hood put it to a reporter in 2004, someone would "'fess up. . . . There's somebody up there [in Neshoba County] sitting on that information thinking about meeting their maker. They need to do the right thing and tell law enforcement."[4] That, of course, did not happen.

Killen himself was surprised when, in January 2005, he was indicted and arrested. He believed that it would never happen to him. For more than forty years—with the one unrelated exception of his five-month sojourn in 1975 in Parchman State Prison for threatening to kill a private investigator—he went on with his ordinary life. And his life was fairly orderly for those four decades: preaching across the county and chopping wood and passing the days chatting up a storm with his neighbors in the small town of Union, Mississippi.

However, after the January 2005 indictment, time flew—even with all the events that occurred between indictment, arrest, and trial in mid-June. And, after Judge Gordon denied all defense motions for continuances, the trial began.

The Key Participants in the Murder Trial

Every criminal trial has a basic cast of characters: the defendant; the judge; the lawyers; the witnesses; and the jurors, and in this sense, *Mississippi vs. Killen* was no different than any other state criminal trial. There are the colorful advocates, and there are the ones who speak in monotone. There are a variety of witnesses, in this case, most living, although some have been dead for decades. These trial participants sometimes shock onlookers with their answers to questions.

There are the observers, the "crime junkies" who love to watch real-life "law and order" stories and have the time to watch. There are also those who come because a family member has been killed by the defendant or because they are the defendant's family. And, of course, there is the defendant, charged with one or more felonies, who must sit and observe and, at times, yawn, due to tiredness or tension.

In this criminal trial, there was a judge who controlled his courtroom at all times, a defendant who, at times, cursed prosecutors—albeit *sotto voce.* There were accusations from the grave and testimony about the "good things" the Klan did in the community. Above all, similar to a trial of a Nazi war criminal brought to the bar of justice many decades after the war ended, there were the questions associated with the passing of time since the crime was committed and the necessity of a trial of an old and frail defendant.

What follows are portraits of the leading characters in the 2005 felony murder trial of Edgar Ray Killen.

The Defendant: Edgar Ray Killen

The central figure in this felony murder trial was, of course, the Preacher. One story about this eighty-year-old unremorseful Klansman tells a lot about him. On April 4, 1968, in Memphis, Tennessee, an assassin murdered Martin Luther King Jr. King was in Memphis to support a local sanitation workers' union that was striking for higher pay and better working conditions. FBI agents across the country immediately began searching for clues that might lead law enforcement to King's killer.

Two agents visited Killen at his home in Union, Mississippi, but the Preacher refused to speak with them. Hours later, he telephoned one of them "wanting to know who killed King. 'Why do you want to know,' the agent asked. 'Man, I just want to shake his hand,' Killen replied."[5] The reporter Killen spoke to about the incident noted that the Preacher had a broad smile on his face as he recounted that story.

In 2004, Killen gave an interview to Richard Barrett, a native New Yorker who moved to Mississippi decades ago. Barrett is a rabid anti-Communist, a Klan supporter, and president of the tiny white supremacist Nationalist Movement, whose headquarters are in Laurel, Mississippi—and he is a lawyer. One of the books he authored was handed out before the trial began. Its title: *From Southern to American.* In it, Barrett writes that all blacks should be sent by air back to Africa. His view of Schwerner, Chaney, and Goodman matches Killen's view: "[The three] were not civil and they weren't right. They were communists and they were wrong."[6]

Posted on Barrett's Web site was the interview, one that provides further insight into the personality of Edgar Ray Killen, the Preacher.

Barrett: *What about your background?*

Killen: I have pastored churches all through Neshoba County for over 50 years. I am well thought of by most everyone. I have taken part in many political campaigns, especially for Ross Barnett,[7] and "Big Jim" Eastland,[8] who is someone I most admire. . . .

Barrett: *You were put on trial, once, over trying to keep Communists out of Mississippi.*

Killen: Old John Doar[9] kept staring at me, like he was trying to look right through me. I stared right back at him and sent him a signal that made him mad. He was really mad when he could not convict me. . . .

Barrett: *Any chance you will change your beliefs and turn against your own people, the way George Wallace did?*

Killen: No, I sure will never do that. People come up to me, all the time, and hug my neck. . . . We're poor folks, but we love our freedom and are against Communism. "Little Dick" Molpus came out against the [Mississippi "stars and bars"] flag. Neshoba County usually takes care of its own, but we turned him down soundly. . . .

Barrett: *What would you say are the prospects for defeating Communism and integration?*

Killen: R. G. Lee, the preacher up in Memphis, summed it all up in the title to a sermon he gave, his best sermon: *Payday's Coming.*[10]

To his neighbors in Union, Killen is a "quick-witted and friendly story teller who can outwork men half his age."

[He] would start his days cutting wood about 10 a.m. and work until dark or later. Killen lives deep in rural, southern Neshoba County in a wooden home surrounded by 20 acres. Junked cars and old work trucks can be seen in the yard. So can a placard listing the Ten Commandments, including the Sixth, "Thou shalt not kill."

"He is a talker," said [a neighbor]. "He came up one day when I was going to take my grandson fishing. We had to miss the trip because Edgar Ray was talking."[11]

The Trial Judge: Marcus D. Gordon

Judge Marcus D. Gordon grew up in Union, Killen's home hamlet. He is the youngest of three brothers; his father, Brenton, was a barber in Union. Gordon's mother, Flossie, worked in a local factory. When I asked the judge what prepared him for judging, he said: "My good parents. They taught me to recognize the difference between right and wrong and then to make decisions. A judge must be fair and impartial. Just like a Christian, if he goes to church he probably becomes a better Christian. Once a person starts to talk about fairness and equality, you start feeling it and you become more fair."[12]

After high school, which included an outstanding basketball career (which earned Gordon all-state honors in the sport), Gordon attended East Central Community College just 9 miles away from his home. Although he received athletic scholarship offers from Ole Miss and other major universities, he chose to attend the community college because he wanted to be near his sweetheart, a local Union resident.[13]

During his brief time at East Central, Gordon played football and basketball. The lovesick young athlete, however, found himself flunking out of the local college and, after one forlorn semester, in 1951 he enlisted in the U.S. Air Force where, he told me, he "grew up": "It was one of the best things I ever did. I learned the importance of studying. I learned how to study. And I figured out what I wanted to do with my life. . . . I was poor in math, but I always had the ability to talk. That's when I decided I wanted to go to law school."[14]

After serving four years in the air force as an airplane mechanic,[15] he returned to Mississippi and eventually received his bachelor's degree and, in 1959, his law degree from Ole Miss. Gordon entered private legal practice with his brother, Rex Gordon, until he was elected district attorney for the 8th Circuit Court District (which includes Neshoba County) in 1971. He held that post for six years until, in 1977, he was elected and served as the 8th Circuit Court Judge.

Ten years later, Gordon resigned from the court and reentered private practice with his brother Rex and his nephew, Rex Jr. In 1990, he was reelected 8th Circuit Court Judge and has held the position since then. Gordon was sitting when Killen was indicted in 2005 and was the presiding judge when the murder trial began on June 13, 2005.

An event just before the trial began illustrates the mettle of the seventy-three-year-old judge, who looks as if he was sent straight from central casting.[16] A threat had allegedly been made on the judge's life by one of Killen's brothers, J.D. Killen. Gordon was informed of this and was offered the services of a bodyguard during the murder trial. He brushed off the idea, saying, "I'm not sure I want that. I've always been a two-fisted kind of guy. And if I take on a bodyguard, in a way I'm saying that I'm no longer capable of taking care of myself. I don't really like that thought."[17]

Ironically,[18] after Killen's trial concluded but before his August 12, 2005, bond hearing, J.D. Killen *again* allegedly tried to hire two men (who were plainclothes detectives) to kill the judge. According to documents filed by Attorney General Hood with the Mississippi Supreme Court, on July 26, 2005, J.D. approached the officers and told them: "'I'm pissed off and need some people taken care of because they had been running their mouth.'"

Another document filed by the attorney general quoted J.D. as stating to the officers: "[I have] a mule that needed to be shot, and [asked] the confidential informants [the detectives] if they would, for $3,000, be the ones to put the nails on him and make him stay." J.D. then showed the two undercover investigators the handgun he had and said: "The mule was old, and [I] know where the mule sits on his back porch." J.D. told them they could see the "mule" in the Neshoba County Courthouse on August

5—the day Gordon was scheduled to hear arguments about bail for Killen.

Hood noted, in his brief filed with the court, that J.D. "was adamant that he did not want anything to happen to the mule until after the hearing was completed." On July 28, 2005, Judge Gordon was informed of this latest threat on his life but, once again, refused police protection.[19]

Asked about the upcoming trial, Gordon, who had twenty-six years of experience on the Circuit Court bench, told a reporter:

> I accepted this case like any other. My responsibility is to provide a fair trial. The verdict of the jury will be the verdict of the jury. I don't know the facts of the case, but I do know the law and my duty—and that's to call it like it is. I can't allow the attention of the case to affect my rulings. And I won't.[20]

The judge did not read any books or articles about the 1964 triple murder; nor did he examine the 1967 federal trial transcript. He did, however, read news accounts of the upcoming trial. The only worry he had, as the trial was about to begin, was about Killen's health. "I was concerned that Killen could have some recurring disability that would delay the trial."[21]

To make the courtroom setting as comfortable as possible for Killen (who was in a wheelchair throughout the trial), Judge Gordon scheduled recesses so that Killen could rest in a room adjacent to the courtroom. He also had the county provide a nurse to minister to Killen in the event of any medical problem that might arise during the trial. She sat in the courtroom throughout the trial and came to his assistance on more than one occasion.

In court, Gordon works quickly and is all business. Unlike other judges, there are no cases languishing on his docket for years. And he has built a reputation as a very tough but fair judge. However, as black attorney Constance Slaughter-Harvey said: "He [Gordon] has a heart. He pretends to be tough, tough, tough, but he's very fair and he has a heart."[22] While she has seen other kinds of judges since she began practicing law in Mississippi in 1973, "I have never seen Judge Gordon discriminate."[23]

During a recess called because a witness was delayed in getting to the court, the judge came over to a few of us who were chatting about the trial. We were standing just behind the wood railing separating the on-lookers from the officers of the court. Gordon, who came from his chambers, was in shirtsleeves when he casually inserted himself into the conversation.

He apologized to a reporter who had written a story describing his stern, no-nonsense, manner from the bench. He told her that it was a good story but that he really *did* have a sense of humor and enjoyed telling stories and jokes—off the bench, of course. Then he said, to all of us: "I'll laugh at your jokes if you'll laugh at mine." During his sentencing statement, Gordon complimented the journalists from the bench, calling them professionals in every sense of the word.

(A month later, however, at the famous Neshoba County Fair, he told the crowd that the reporters came to Philadelphia, Mississippi, "expecting the judge to be in overalls, [and] expecting lawyers to wear Levi blue jeans and shorts."[24])

Mitch Moran, Killen's defense counsel, "jokingly" told a reporter before the trial began that Judge Gordon is like the old Texas judge Roy Bean: "He'll arrest you, try you, convict you, and hang you in the same day."[25]

Judge Gordon and his wife, Polly, have four grown children and two grandchildren. He has a favorite vacation spot in the Ozarks, in Arkansas. After the Killen trial and sentencing ended, Gordon, quickly pulling off his tie, told me in his chambers that's where he and his wife were going for a few days. "Just to wind down from the trial," he said. He planned on riding his four-wheeler over the twenty-eight acres he owns there.[26]

He is also an avid horseman. "I like to carry my horses up there and ride the trails. I like riding my four-wheeler. And we enjoy visiting with our neighbors, who have lived there all our lives. . . . But you know, I only get up there about three times a year. Seems like I'm busier than I've ever been."[27] As he told me before we parted, he is planning on running in 2006 for reelection. If he does run and if he is reelected, I have no doubt that he will continue to visit his Ozarks hide-away only three times a year.

The Twelve Jurors and Five Alternates

On Wednesday, June 15, 2005, the first day of testimony at the Killen trial, the 8th Circuit Court Clerk's Office released the names of the seventeen jurors and alternates who would hear the case—sequestered. To assure maximum attention from the seventeen Neshoba County residents, Judge Gordon chose not to announce who would serve as jurors and who were the five alternates until after summation by counsel and before his charge to the twelve jurors.

On Monday and Tuesday, June 13 and 14, the judge and all counsel participated in the voir dire—jury selection—process. More than 400 Neshoba County residents received a summons to appear in court on those days although only around 180 showed up to be interviewed by counsel and the judge during the two days.

A few were dismissed because they could not read or write. In the case of a dozen potential jurors, they were dismissed because they were over sixty-five years of age. When the judge asked the group questions about their health or hardships they might face, three dozen stood up to say they would suffer financial or other hardships if they were picked to serve. Most of those citizens were also dismissed by Gordon.

Some were excused because they expressed fear for themselves if they served; or "felt sorry" for Killen because of his age and/or his dreadful logging accident; or because they were, as was the case with at least three potential jurors, kin to Killen. A handful of other potential jurors were dismissed because they were close friends of the defendant.

Others said that they had "unshakable opinions" about the case. One person answered the jury questionnaire question regarding his feelings about the prosecution of Killen, with the following comment: "Bullshit! Been too long a time." He was dismissed from the juror pool.

Duncan addressed the juror pool at one point on day two to urge them "not to be influenced by Killen's age" and the fact that he is a Baptist preacher. "I mean," he said to the large group sitting in the courtroom, "we're all sinners, aren't we? Some of us are just worse than others." Then he said something that went to the heart of the prosecution's case: "Tell me you'll treat them [the three dead civil rights men] like they were from here and were our neighbors."

By Wednesday morning, the two sides agreed on the final seventeen members of the juror panel. The panel of seventeen was an interesting cross-section of Neshoba County residents, reflecting the many economic and social changes in the county since the 1964 murders took place.

There were four teachers and one librarian. Two others were nurses and another two worked in an automobile manufacturing plant. One juror was an office manager, one was an engineer who moved to the county five years ago from California. Rounding out the cohort were a casino games auditor, a chicken farmer, a social worker, a manufacturing plant worker, a chicken plant worker, and, finally, a homemaker.[28] The seventeen-person cohort that heard the evidence consisted of nine white women, four white men, two black men, and two black women.

The Prosecutors: Mark Duncan and Jim Hood

Mark Duncan, forty-six years old, was elected district attorney in November 2003 and formally took over the position in January 2004. (He served out his predecessor's [Ken Turner III's] final three months when Turner resigned in November 2003.) Duncan had served four terms (sixteen years) as assistant district attorney, all under Turner.

"I have a vague memory of something going on [in 1964], but did not understand what it was," recollected Duncan recently. As a six-year-old in 1964, Duncan doesn't remember the killings.

As I grew older I learned of the murders through news reports, books, etc. It was something that was talked about, but more in whispers than in open conversation. I learned that most people here didn't like what happened. They hated what these killers had done to the reputation of their home, but were powerless to do anything about it. . . . No one here condoned the murders; they just got tired of the bad publicity.[29]

Duncan's father and mother owned and ran a General Motors car dealership in Philadelphia. "I have a brother and a sister. My parents raised us to be honest and respectful of others. My father told me that a man may not have anything else in the world, but if he was honest, he would always have his word. . . . My mother taught us to always treat others like we would want to be treated."[30]

One of the few times during the trial that Duncan became livid with rage was after Oscar Kenneth Killen, Edgar's younger brother, testified for the defense. On cross-examination, Duncan asked Oscar if he knew that Edgar was a member of the Klan. Oscar said he did not. "No sir, I didn't ever know it. I've heard more talking to that your daddy and granddaddy was in the Klan than I have him, to tell the truth."[31] At the next recess, Duncan angrily denied Oscar's accusations. He told reporters that "he had never seen or heard any evidence that his father or grandfather were Klan members."[32]

Duncan is a Philadelphia, Mississippi, native, and attended Philadelphia High School, where he played defensive end for the football team. However, his first and only passion in sports is golf. He told journalist Sid Salter (who, incidentally, played high school football alongside Duncan) that as a kid "I played 50–60 holes a day." For Duncan, golf prepared him for his job as a prosecutor. "You sometimes get bad bounces on the course, and you have to accept it and move on. Sometimes you get a bad case and you have to use your experience and ingenuity to make the best case you can."

He, too, attended Ole Miss where he earned a bachelor's degree in banking and finance in 1981. He attended Ole Miss law school, graduating two and one-half years later. He began his private law practice in Philadelphia in 1983. He was then appointed, part-time, as the city's public defender. And in 1988, Ken Turner III hired Duncan as his assistant district attorney.

Duncan and his wife, Joni (who were university sweethearts), have a teenaged son. "[My wife and I] do everything together," he told Salter. "I am miserable when we are apart. I get told quite often that my wife could have done a lot better than me, and they are right, but I am happy that she is easy to please."[33] His life, as reporter Jerry Mitchell observed, "is much like many of those in this city of about 7,300 residents. It revolves around his family, church, and going to Wal-Mart."[34]

It turns out that Duncan is a gourmet cook—"he has a catfish specialty to die for," said one of his friends.[35] It is a skill that took time to develop, he told a local reporter. "I couldn't cook in college but as I got older I started going places and eating in different restaurants and eating things that I like but couldn't get in restaurants around here. So I learned to cook things that I like to eat."[36] One of Duncan's favorite dishes to prepare is fried fish, "served elegantly over a plate of meuniere sauce and topped with pecan butter."[37]

Duncan as prosecutor is not a grandstander, argue many Neshoba County residents. "He's just doing his job," said seventy-one-year-old Philadelphia resident Leon Baxstrum. He is, by all accounts, an aggressive prosecutor. Fenton DeWeese, a local lawyer and member of the Philadelphia Coalition, said that "when Duncan's at bat, he's very aggressive. He is very serious at what he does."[38]

Duncan's view of his job in the Killen trial reflects his focused, nononsense attitude: "I am just a prosecutor. My job in this case was to hold a man accountable for his role in these killings. That is the only reason the case was pursued. It was not done for any social cause. That is not the role or purpose of bringing any prosecution."[39]

A year before the Killen trial began, the newly sworn-in attorney general Jim Hood told a reporter that he was solidly committed to solving the 1964 Neshoba County murders "if at all possible."

When I lay my head on my pillow at night I want to know that I've done the right thing. [He conducted his own interviews with] several witnesses because [he didn't] want some investigator to tell me about that person. I prefer to eyeball my witnesses. . . . A lot of it's just for my own personal knowledge and the satisfaction of knowing the facts.[40]

Forty-three-year-old Jim Hood was elected Mississippi attorney general in November 2003 and took office in January 2004. Jim is one of three siblings; he has an older sister and a younger brother. Hood grew up in Houlka, Mississippi, and, when his home was fire-bombed, moved to close-by Houston, Mississippi, where he attended public schools.

He describes himself as a "rough-edge country guy." His father was a county prosecutor—a fact Hood believes explains why their home in Houlka was torched.[41] Jim initially wanted to become a medical doctor, following in the footsteps of his grandfather. However, he changed his mind and went to law school after attending Ole Miss. He, too, received his law degree from Ole Miss in 1988, five years after Duncan.

Hood had planned on a career as an oil and gas attorney, which can be a very lucrative profession. During the 1987 election season, Hood worked on Mike Moore's campaign for attorney general; Moore was so impressed with Hood that he brought him on as an intern and, after Hood received his law degree, Moore hired him in 1988 as a special assistant attorney general in charge of the Drug Asset Forfeiture Unit.

Hood, in 1995, and 1999, successfully ran—and was reelected—for the office of district attorney, 3rd Circuit Court District. In the eight years before he became attorney general in January 2004, Hood tried more than 100 criminal cases.

Hood *knew* that he was going to bring the 1964 triple murder case to a grand jury as soon as he took his oath of office. "Murder has no statute of limitations and those affected never forget one of their family members who've been murdered. I want to know 20 years from now when the dust settles that I've done all I could do [to bring closure to the families of the three civil rights workers who were murdered in 1964]."[42]

His philosophy as prosecutor developed, in part, as a result of Hood's own family tragedies, especially the murder of his cousin (see Chapter Four). According to Hood, "The victim [and his family] has a right. That, really, is why I'm in this case in Philadelphia."[43]

Hood and his wife, Debbie, live in Jackson and have three young children.

The Defense Counsel: Mitch Moran and James McIntyre

Mitch Moran, forty-three, has been practicing law in Carthage, Mississippi, for less than a decade. He grew up in San Diego, California, where his father worked for NASA. The family then moved to Houston, Texas. Mitch received his undergraduate degree from Northwestern University, then returned to the South, to Louisiana, where he took up farming as a livelihood.

Moran is an avid hunter. He attended Mississippi College in Jackson, where he received his law degree in 1996. He chose Mississippi College simply because it was the closest school to his much-used deer camp.[44]

After graduation, he worked for Phillip Martin, the chief of the Mississippi Band of Choctaw Indians, while he started up his private practice. His legal practice has Moran handling mostly criminal defense work. Most of his clients are, as Moran said, "little guys." Ironically, they are mostly minority clients, "many of them arrested on drug charges," he told a reporter in 2005.[45]

He became involved in the Killen case shortly after Killen's indictment and arrest for the murder of the three civil rights workers. Moran said that seeing Killen in jail moved him to take the case:

When I saw an 80-year-old man without his false teeth, laying on the concrete floor of the jail cell, I knew it wasn't right. . . . [The justice system should take dangerous criminals off the streets]. This case is not going to serve any of that. Whether Killen did it or not, we need to put it in God's hands because that is going to happen soon enough. . . . In this case, Killen is a minority. He's been singled out.[46]

Moran believes that Killen and the others were not prosecuted by the state of Mississippi in the 1960s because of the presence of segregationist racial politics in the state. "So now, 40 years later, politics again: 'Hey, we can prosecute him at our advantage and get votes, make a name for ourselves, popularity, whatever.' Our justice system and the [Mississippi] political arena are too close together."[47]

District Attorney Duncan, told of Moran's observations, said to reporter Jerry Mitchell:

Anybody thinks I'm prosecuting this case for politics doesn't know me very well. When you're in the prosecuting business, you can't make decisions on whether to prosecute based on politics. You make your decisions based on the evidence, the law, and nothing else. *All Mitch Moran is doing is playing to the jury when he makes statements like that* [my emphasis].

As already noted, one of Moran's defense strategies prior to trial was to allow Killen to be interviewed at least four times between January and June 2005. "At least," said Moran, "it humanized him. That's the basic reason [for the television interviews]." Hood and Duncan knew, however, that the reason for the Killen conversations was because the defense needed to portray Killen—to potential jurors watching or reading these interviews—as a pathetic old man, and not a cold-blooded killer of "outside agitators."

Moran has some interesting observations about the human condition in America. He believes that

When it comes to racial matters, everybody's prejudiced. If you're not, then there's something wrong with you. I am a white Anglo-Saxon, half German-Irish. Proud of it. Don't want to be anything else. We have a Miss Black America. We don't have a Miss White America. We've got the NAACP, but we don't have anything for the white people. What's the big deal?

In Moran's view, "Killen didn't plan crap. He took orders. He drove people around. Ran his mouth and possibly had knowledge it was going to happen."[48]

Moran himself was at one time (2003–2004) about to meet up with District Attorney Duncan in another extremely ironic way. The defense counsel

was arrested in 2003 for attempting to buy methamphetamine, just shortly after defending a client in court that had been charged with possession of meth. . . . His case falls under the jurisdiction of the District Attorney for District 8 in Mississippi, Mark Duncan, [who] is trying the state's case against Killen along with Mississippi Attorney General Jim Hood. *There is a chance that the man Moran has been arguing against throughout this case, could be the same man that tries him later on the meth charge* [my emphasis].[49]

How very ironic this scenario would have been—however, the charges were dropped recently. As Moran's wife, Wendy, told me, when someone is a powerful defense attorney, that person ruffles the feathers of law enforcement in his defense of his clients, and, occasionally, the local authorities "will go after you."[50]

The Morans live in Carthage, Mississippi, and have three young children.

James McIntyre, seventy-two, is Killen's other defense attorney. A conversation with McIntyre quickly uncovers the reality that he "is clearly a[n old-time] believer."[51] McIntyre says that he's "just an old Mississippi lawyer, that's what I am, just trying to earn a living."[52] He regularly repeated that line in public, to the Killen trial jurors, when interviewed on radio and television, and to any reporter he can find or that finds him. And he is very easy to find.

Although he is a whiz at using the media, McIntyre does not like them at all nor does he believe anything they say or write. In his conversation with me, he noted that reporters, especially people like Jerry Mitchell, slant everything. "They're masters at words, and," he said in a serious tone of voice, "they're better using words than lawyers."[53]

McIntyre "has a florid red face, squashed down with years so that he resembles a blow-dried bullfrog. His speech is a raspy Mississippi drawl, and he is armored in a fiercely pressed lawyer's power suit. He doesn't show the tiniest drip of sweat in the unrelenting heat."[54] McIntyre was born in Alto, Texas, in 1933 and went to law school in Mississippi. His father was an engineer. During the Eisenhower administration (1953–1961), McIntyre, serving in the U.S. Navy, was assigned to the President's Honor Guard for one year (1954–1955). After military service, he became a science teacher.

He gave that up for law. Both he and Moran received their law degrees from Mississippi College of Law in Jackson (formerly known as Milsaps College of Law). During the administration of Mississippi Governor Ross Barnett (1960–1964), McIntyre was one of the governor's major speech writers. He has practiced law in Jackson for more than four decades. He is a widower with three grown children and six grandchildren.

In the 1967 federal conspiracy trial against the eighteen Klansmen indicted in federal court for conspiracy to take the constitutional rights and liberties secured by the U.S. Constitution away from Michael Schwerner, James Chaney, and Andrew Goodman, McIntyre was Sheriff Lawrence Rainey's defense counsel. Rainey was acquitted by the all-white jury in 1967. "I won that case. I damn sure did win it," he proudly boasted to Sugg.

He joined the defense team a few months after the indictment. McIntyre told me that about a month after Moran took the case, "he called me up and asked me to help him prepare for trial. He's the lead counsel in the Killen case."[55]

He agrees with Moran's assessment that the trial is purely political and totally without any redeeming legal value. "This is a sad, sad, very sad day for the state of Mississippi. Mississippi should go forward, not backward. But Mississippi has seen fit to come in with charges against an old man." On the phone with me and during the trial itself, McIntyre said that Killen would not get a fair trial because he was not being tried by his peers. "They're all dead," he exclaimed.[56]

And, again and again, during the trial and outside facing the television cameras, McIntyre railed against the "selective enforcement" of the criminal laws in Killen's case while ignoring the terrible crimes committed daily in Jackson. "Why open up all of this old crap?"

I've been robbed with a gun held to my head. I've had four burglaries in one month. I'd like the state of Mississippi to tell me how this case is going to reduce any of the real crime that happens every day. Why doesn't the state protect us from real crime, rather than *persecute* an old man. Make no mistake, this is not a prosecution. It is a persecution [my emphasis].[57]

The Trial Environment

My seat at the trial was in the first row, off center and almost directly behind the defense counsel table and the defendant, Edgar Ray Killen.[58] From that spot, I was able to appreciate the dynamics that took place inside the courtroom.

I was always about 10 feet from Killen. It was an unforgettable experience for me. I had written about Killen's role in the murders of the three young civil rights workers. I had read the 1967 federal trial testimony and the 1964 confessions obtained by the FBI from no less than three of the eighteen Klansmen who participated in the June 21, 1964, triple murder. I'd read the 2000–2001 Price interviews with Moore and others, conversations that could not be introduced in the trial because Price died in 2001. To many, the Preacher was a cruel, vengeful murderer. And there he was, sitting in a wheelchair, a few feet from me.

Killen had a penchant during the trial to spin in his wheelchair and view the audience, smiling at his wife and family, but grimly staring at others, including me. He and I regularly had staring contests where we would peer into each other's eyes. I had never been this close to evil; to an alleged cold-blooded, anti-Semitic racist who had no reluctance to kill in order to maintain a "white Christian civilization." Frankly, these staring battles were a very scary time for me, but Killen's eyes always moved away first. Killen has cold eyes, magnified by the spectacles he wears. His wardrobe never changed: open-collared shirt, a jacket, chino pants, and loafers.

Inside the courtroom stood an array of Mississippi Highway Patrol officers, each one attired in grey and blue, seemingly custom-tailored, uniforms and wearing stiff grey "Smokey the Bear" hats. Their uniforms highlighted their Mike Tyson builds. Most of these superbly attired and physically fit officers were assigned to the governor's office but were on temporary duty assignment to the Neshoba County Courthouse for the trial.

In addition to the highway patrol officers, there were also more ordinary FBI agents and Mississippi Bureau of Investigation (MBI) officers, Neshoba County Sheriff's Deputies (most of them, unlike the svelte, muscled highway patrol officers, had bellies hanging over their belts), and, finally, local Philadelphia police officers, working security.

Security was just as impressive outside the courthouse; barricades surrounded the building and law enforcement officers were stationed all around the court. Judge Gordon told the jurors that the court would provide food, care, and protection—"we will have security for you." He spoke the truth; there was ample security for everybody who attended the trial.

On Monday, the first day of voir dire proceedings, chubby, young-looking, bearded J. J. Harper, from Cordele, Georgia, the Imperial Wizard of the American White Knights of the Ku Klux Klan, greeted Killen when the defendant entered the courthouse in a wheelchair. Harper and other Klansmen, much to the chagrin of defense counsel, were there "to support our Christian brother."

The courtroom is on the second floor, up a long flight of stairs. To get there everyone must go through a metal detection device. No cameras were allowed in the courtroom, other than those of Mississippi Educational Television and an Associated Press photographer.

In accord with Judge Gordon's no-nonsense public persona, the courtroom itself is bereft of any fancy trappings. There are no murals adorning the walls, nor any portraits of famous Mississippi jurists and generals. It is a completely wood paneled, rectangular room. The only color comes from the two flags—the American flag and the Mississippi flag—found directly behind the judge's bench. On the wall, in between the flags, is the Mississippi State crest. These items provide the only color in the courtroom. Over one of the side exits, there is a large, antique-looking clock.

It is a fair-sized courtroom, with room for about 170 visitors. News reporters were seated by lot every morning at 7:30 a.m., for there are less than three dozen seats reserved for more than sixty reporters. The necessary space limitations made for strange neighbors. For example, Georgia Imperial Wizard Harper was seated next to Ben Chaney, the younger brother of one of the three murdered young men! In another arrangement reminiscent of *The Twilight Zone*, seated in front of Wizard Harper and his Klan friends were Schwerner's widow, Rita Schwerner Bender, and her husband and son, while Bender, in turn, was seated directly behind Killen's brother, sister, wife, and stepson.

Unlike forty years ago, the jury pool of almost two hundred persons included about fifty black residents of Neshoba County, which is roughly the percentage of blacks living there. There were also a few Choctaw Indians in the jury pool. Regarding the jurors, Judge Gordon did something very uncommon even before the opening arguments were heard this afternoon. He sat the twelve jurors and the five alternates (thirteen whites and four blacks) without informing the group and the rest of the world who the actual jurors were and who were the alternates.[59]

During the regular recesses that the judge called throughout the short trial to accommodate Killen, the courtroom quickly became a "gathering place" where different clusters of onlookers met and talked about the latest testimony and other subjects. There were no less than five separate clusters of people that instantly formed up: Killen's family and friends; Rita's group; the prosecutor's cluster, the Philadelphia Coalition cohort, and the news reporters crowd (those who chose not to interview someone in another cluster).

Killen's group was generally eight or nine people. It was made up of Killen's brothers, sister, wife, stepson, and other close, former Klansmen friends of the defendant. Standing and sitting almost directly under the large antique clock, they talked quietly and occasionally smirked at the bevy of news reporters working on their stories nearby.

Some of the seventy or so reporters covering the trial were attractive females in their late twenties and early thirties. A few of them drew ogles from the Killen cluster and others, especially the bright, very attractive, and very talented reporter for the *New York Times*, Shaila Dewan.

They were especially attracted to her after they heard a rumor that on her way to Philadelphia from Jackson, she was traveling quite fast. Although there was a highway patrol car with blue flashing lights trying to pull her over, she continued driving until she reached the courthouse. Only then was the officer able to "introduce" himself to the young—and very surprised—attractive reporter. Intent on getting to the Neshoba County Courthouse, Dewan evidently never heard the siren nor saw the flashing blue lights, but she never received a speeding ticket.

Whether the story was true or not, Dewan became the center of attention for a brief period of time. Her colleagues as well as some of the mature men in the courtroom, including some of the Neshoba County deputies, appreciated the story's cheeriness while all were intensely focused on the murder trial. Her alleged escapade instantly became Philadelphia's newest "urban legend."

Another group bunched around Rita Schwerner Bender, a sixty-two-year-old lawyer from Seattle. She was there initially as the first witness for the prosecution and then, for the rest of the trial, as an observer. During recesses, she was the center of animated conversation; it seemed that she met old civil rights companions during every recess. Men in their sixties visited with her during these recesses; they had been youthful civil rights colleagues of her and her husband in 1964.

They recalled Mickey's last hours spent with them before his fateful ride to visit the burned-out Mt. Zion United Methodist Church. Hugs and kisses were the norm in this small group, as well as remembrances of the evils they experienced in Mississippi forty years ago. Roscoe Jones, now fifty-eight, was one of the members of Rita's circle of friends. He was, in 1964, an NAACP Youth Council worker in Meridian, when he met and worked with the Schwerners. "I didn't realize how much [this trial and seeing Rita] made me realize that I am a warrior and that I need to be back," he said to a reporter during one of the recesses. "I didn't realize that I hadn't put this behind me."[60]

Some of us clustered around the two prosecutors, Jim Hood and Mark Duncan, and chatted about recent goings-on in the courtroom. On one occasion, J.D. Killen passed by this cohort and cussed us out, telling Duncan that he wasn't "goin' to get reelected next time." Duncan just smiled at the comment.

Members of the Philadelphia Coalition attending the trial—including Stanley Dearman, Fenton DeWeese, Jewell McDonald, Leroy Clemons, and the group's advisor, Susan Glisson—formed themselves into a discussion group at the first recess. Like the other courtroom groups, the coalition members gathered to talk about the last witness, the next witness, what Jerry Mitchell said in the *Clarion-Ledger* that morning, and so on.

The final semiorganized cluster consisted of the horde of reporters. However, during these recesses, they were generally helping each other out in the preparation of their news stories about the day's trial events. "What was the name of the guy who said the Klan did many good things?" asked one reporter. Immediately, others gave the reporter the name and the correct spelling. For the reporters, these recesses gave them time to fill in the blanks in their stories. They were too busy working to aimlessly chat. Their aimless chatter began when they went to Peggy's Restaurant for lunch every day.

While these clusters were chatting away, law enforcement slowly walked around the courtroom, making sure that there was peace in the place. Some of the sheriffs enjoyed their stops at the reporters' group and chatted with a number of the young female journalists.

The Jury Selection Process in the Killen Trial

The selection of the twelve jurors and five alternates from among the hundreds of residents of Neshoba County was a critically important element of the trial. This process, termed *voir dire*, in the Killen trial took about two and one-half days. Once the jury is selected, sworn in, and impaneled, the actual trial begins.

Voir dire involves the questioning of potential witnesses—by the trial judge, the prosecutors, and defense counsel—in order to select a panel of jurors who are "capable and willing"[61] to fairly and impartially examine the evidence in the case, in light of the applicable law, in order to determine whether or not the prosecutors have met the burden of proving beyond a reasonable doubt the guilt of the defendant. It takes place in open court and in the judge's chambers. In attendance for this selection process are the lawyers, the judge, jury consultants for the lawyers, and the defendant. While the process in the courtroom is public, the voir dire held in the judge's chambers is not—until the trial transcript becomes available.[62]

Before Judge Gordon proceeded with questioning of jurors, in chambers—with lawyers for both sides and the defendant present—he met individually with jurors who claimed either hardship problems or who held opinions about the case that merited exclusion from jury service. "We are going to hear your problems in chambers," he told those sitting in the courtroom, "so as to not cause [jurors] any embarrassment."[63]

The first phase of the in-chambers proceedings dealt with claims of hardship problems by prospective jurors. Primarily, these were economic hardships (e.g., an out-of-state business, a farmer with forty-two cows and haying to be done), mental health problems (child with brain injury syndrome, "mind not good," nervous breakdown), family responsibilities (nursing a four-month-old baby, caregiver to aged parent), and health disorders (bladder problem, steel plate on spine, sleeping disease). For the most part, Judge Gordon excused these persons.[64]

The second phase of the in-chambers proceedings dealt with claims made by some prospective jurors that they had opinions about the case or were friends with the defendant himself or were related to Killen or one of the three dead civil rights workers, or were clients of the defense counsel.

Some asked to be excused because they knew Killen to be "a real outstanding member of our community." One potential juror said that "Killen violated one of the Ten Commandments" and he couldn't examine the facts impartially. A Choctaw nurse told the group that "I can't listen to the evidence because I have love for the victims and their families." Another potential juror angrily said that the trial was a "waste of time and taxpayer dollars" and that he could not "hear the evidence impartially." After hearing from this group of individuals, the second phase ended and the participants reentered the courtroom for dismissal of jurors because they had opinions that strongly suggested they could not act impartially as jurors in this case.

The next phase of voir dire involved the questioning in court of jurors' answers to questions on a jury questionnaire[65] that was received by them when they were summoned for jury duty. After each prospective juror answered the questions, the questionnaires were returned to the court. Copies were made and distributed to defense and prosecution lawyers for their examination—using jury experts to assist them. During this phase of voir dire, the lawyers for both sides asked some jurors about the meaning of some of their answers.

The questionnaire was a seven-page document. It consisted of (1) questions about occupation, residency in the county, marital status, family information, education, occupation, church affiliation, possible kinship to Killen or members of his family, and (2) open-ended questions such as "What is your opinion about [the murder charges] being brought against Edgar Ray Killen at this time?" and "What is your opinion about why these charges are being brought against Edgar Ray Killen at this time?"

There followed (3) a list of names of people to whom the juror may be related "by blood or marriage, no matter how remote." Included on the list were the names of all the Klansmen involved in the 1964 murders, names of Killen's kin and his friends, and (4) a list of organizations such as the Anti Defamation League, the American Civil Liberties Union, American Nazi Party, FBI, John Birch Society, Internal Revenue Service, KKK, NAACP, National Rifle Association, SCLC, SNCC, and the WCC. Jurors were asked to indicate if they had ever been a member of one or more of the listed groups. The last question, an open-ended one, was: "Do you have any personal experiences or feelings that may affect your services as a juror in this case, or you feel should be brought to the court's attention?"[66] The final actions taken on Monday were motions by counsel for both sides to excuse potential jurors for cause, i.e., because their answers demonstrated a possible lack of impartiality.

The various phases of Monday's voir dire process were repeated on Tuesday for the second group of potential jurors. By Wednesday morning, there was a pool of potential jurors from which the court would select the seventeen who would serve as jurors and alternates. Before that could happen, however, there was a final voir dire opportunity by both sides to ask potential jurors questions about their answers, especially the open-ended ones.[67]

Mark Duncan addressed the jury pool in open court and presented a number of questions addressing a variety of issues for all of them to ponder. Duncan asked jurors to raise their hand if they had any concerns with the following aspects of the case, so that he could get their names:

- The attorney general's office participating in the criminal case
- Killen's age
- That Killen is in a wheelchair
- That it has taken more than forty years to have a criminal trial
- That there is no statute of limitations on a charge of murder
- That Killen is a preacher
- That the trial would be televised
- Killen's interviews televised during the spring of 2005
- Their ability to treat Schwerner, Goodman, and Chaney "as if they were from here and [were] our neighbors and friends"
- Did they have knowledge of any of the defense witnesses?[68]

A few hands went up after Duncan discussed these issues and he took their names down for consideration by the prosecution team. The defense counsel waived their voir dire.

After this phase, the "jury wheel" was spun by the court clerk and seventeen persons were asked to take a seat in the jury box. This, however, was not the end. At this point in voir dire, the lawyers, the defendant, and Judge Gordon went into his chambers in order to determine the changes in the jury makeup.

In chambers, the lawyers gave Gordon the names of jurors they wished to dismiss for cause. Only one juror was identified by the prosecution; the defense did not move to strike anyone for cause. After the one juror was dismissed, both sides were then given the opportunity to employ peremptory challenges, i.e., to dismiss jurors without giving any reason. In the Killen case, each side had twelve peremptory challenges that could be used to select the jury of twelve. In addition, each side had two peremptory challenges that could be used to select the five alternates. In this case, both sides used all their peremptory challenges and, within the hour, they had agreed on the final panel of seventeen. The final segment of the voir dire process was the swearing in of the jury by Judge Gordon: "Do you and each of you solemnly swear that you will well and truly try the issue between the State of Mississippi and Edgar Ray Killen and a true verdict give, according to the evidence and the law, so help you God?"[69]

On Wednesday, June 15, 2005, the arguments in the case began after the lunch recess.

In the Killen voir dire process, both sides used jury consultants to assist them in the more than two days of voir dire proceedings in court as well as in the months before the trial began when jury questionnaires had to be examined. The prosecutors' primary consultant was Andrew Sheldon, a sixty-three-year-old expert from Atlanta, Georgia. Sheldon is a lawyer who went back to university and received a Ph.D. in clinical psychology.

Prior to the *Killen* trial, as a pro bono consultant, he assisted state and federal prosecutors in Mississippi in murder trials involving 1960s-era Ku Klux Klan murders, including the De La Beckwith, Bowers, and Avants trials. Sheldon was also the person who put together the juror questionnaire used in the case.

The defense attorneys' consultant—their *only* jury "expert"—was their client, the Preacher, Edgar Ray Killen. Who else but the Preacher knew all about the residents of Neshoba County? When asked whether the defense hired someone like Sheldon, Mitch Moran answered: "There's no need to hire a professional. We got Edgar Ray. He says he's a jury consultant. He says he's done other cases."[70]

(One "reality" is suggested in Moran's response to the journalist: Everybody, friend or foe, agrees that Killen is a talker par excellence; moreover, they would also see eye-to-eye that Killen often told tall stories.)

149

Killen took an active role in the screening of all the potential jurors, taking notes, reading the questionnaires, and talking with Moran and McIntyre. For the first two days of the trial, Killen attentively sat through endless hours of questioning of prospective jurors in the courtroom and in Judge Gordon's chambers—alongside the counsel for both sides. When he emerged at the end of each of the two days, Killen carried "a pad of notes about the views of the panelists and even wheeled his chair to the court clerk's desk [in the courtroom, next to the judge's bench] to verify which of those summoned had been excused for bias."

After the final panel was announced by the clerk on Wednesday morning, Killen seemed very pleased. "After Moran showed him the final list, he smiled and flashed an 'OK' sign to his wife and stepson in the audience."[71]

Before the trial began, Judge Gordon spoke to the jurors:

> Ignore everything but the evidence presented in this case. Be very responsive to the court, to the attorneys, and give Mr. Killen and the State a fair trial. Just let the chips fall where they may. If you are of the opinion that the evidence is there, then return a verdict of guilty. If the evidence is not there, then return a verdict of not guilty and just let the chips fall. You are not obligated to anyone. What we are doing and what we have done will be recorded in the history of Neshoba County.

When the case is over, he concluded, "we should be proud of what we have done."[72]

6

The Murder Trial of Edgar Ray Killen, June 13–21, 2005: Testimony and Post-Trial Events

It's not the perfect verdict, I suppose. But you have to understand
that it was not a perfect case.
Neshoba County District Attorney Mark Duncan[1]

Edgar Ray Killen is a political prisoner.
Richard Barrett, Nationalist Movement[2]

After nearly forty-one years, the trial that nobody thought would ever take place took place. The Neshoba County Courthouse square was barricaded; it was also surrounded by police and a number of huge television trucks from CNN, Court TV, Mississippi Public Television (which televised the trial from beginning to end), and other Jackson television stations.

Reporters from major—and minor—domestic newspapers were present, but so were reporters from Sweden, Denmark, England, and other European nations. At least three documentary film production companies were present, two from the United States and one from Scotland.

And, at one time or another, the families of the three victims were in the courtroom, to testify as witnesses for the prosecution and to observe the trial from minute to minute.

The trial itself took all of eight days, from selection of the jury through the jury verdict. The first two and one-half days were spent selecting the panel of jurors who would hear the case. More than half of the 400 Neshoba County residents who received a summons to appear did not show up for a number of reasons, some procedural, others substantive. Fear was a substantive reason given by some. Dr. Andrew Sheldon, a jury consultant for the prosecutors, recalled that one potential juror who was excused said that he had recurring nightmares "that my house is goin' to be firebombed."[3]

On Monday, Day 1, June 13, about 120 people responded to the jury call; a third of them were black residents. They silently entered the courtroom and waited to be called to answer questions. At the end of the first day, only about 30 potential jurors were asked to return on the following day.

On Tuesday, Day 2, June 14, another 57 potential jurors took seats in the courtroom, awaiting their turn to be quizzed by counsel. On the morning of Day 3, the panel of jurors was finally agreed upon by both sides.

On the afternoon of Day 3, June 15, brief—fifteen minutes for each side—opening arguments were presented. However, the judge, evidently not accustomed to televised proceedings in his court, failed to turn the audio switch to the correct setting. As a consequence, both the State's and the defense's opening remarks were neither broadcast nor taped. After the arguments were presented, Judge Gordon recessed the trial until 8:20 a.m. the following morning. This was done, he said, so that jurors could go home before being sequestered for the balance of the trial.

The case for the prosecution was presented to the jurors on Days 4 through the morning of Day 6, June 16–June 18. However, before the witnesses began their testimony, Judge Gordon made a most important, though expected, ruling. The defense counsel argued that documents and testimony from the 1967 federal trial, including three confessions by Klan members identifying Killen as the mastermind behind the three murders, not be admitted into evidence at this trial. This morning Judge Gordon ruled that prosecutors would be allowed to use transcripts from the 1967 trial.

As noted below, more than half of the two and one-half days of prosecution witness testimony was spent by "actors" for the prosecution reading portions of the 1967 federal trial transcripts.

On Saturday afternoon of Day 6, June 18, the defense began its arguments on behalf of Killen. Moran's presentation, joined by McIntyre, was much shorter, about a day *in toto,* and then the defense rested its case.

By Monday afternoon of Day 7, June 20, the last of the defense witnesses testified, and both sides presented emotional closing arguments. These arguments ended about 3 p.m. in the afternoon. Judge Gordon then announced who the twelve jurors were and dismissed the alternates. After the five persons left the courthouse, Gordon gathered the twelve jurors in a semicircle in front of the bench and proceeded to instruct them as to the appropriate laws and about their responsibilities as jurors. At 5:50 p.m. that afternoon, Judge Gordon dismissed the jurors for the day.

On Day 8, Tuesday, June 21, 2005, exactly forty-one years to the day Michael Schwerner, James Chaney, and Andrew Goodman were executed, the jury found Edgar Ray Killen guilty of three counts of manslaughter. Sentencing took place two days later, on Thursday, June 23, 2005.

The Trial of Edgar Ray Killen, June 15–21, 2005

Strategies and Opening Statements

For the prosecutors, more than half of their two-day case against Killen consisted of the reading of parts of the 1967 trial transcript[4] in which now-deceased witnesses implicated Killen as the ringleader/planner of the murderous events of the night of June 21, 1964. Jerry Mitchell wrote that prosecutors' success in this week's trial . . . could hinge on their ability to make the dead come to life. About half the witnesses expected to testify this week are dead. Attorneys and others will read their testimony from the 1967 federal conspiracy trial into the record. "It's going to be an important part of the trial," said D.A. Mark Duncan.[5]

Although the prosecution subpoenaed five of the living Klansmen, none were called by the prosecution because the five had already called the prosecutors' bluff. Both young prosecutors knew that the Klansmen would remain silent but they hoped against hope that a guilty conscience would appear. None popped up and the prosecutors had to present the worst possible type of evidence—readings from an old transcript. Generally, testimony that is read bores its listeners. What was missing from the prosecution's reading of testimony was the *drama* associated with successful prosecutions of murder cases.[6]

Mitch Moran, the lead defense attorney, indicated that the reading of the 1967 transcript was "the whole heart of this case." The defense strategy, in part, was to challenge the introduction of the 1967 trial transcript because the 1942 Mississippi Criminal Code did not allow the introduction of such evidence and that the section was still on the books when the crime took place. (The state's evidence section in the Criminal Code was amended in 1972 to permit the reading of transcripts into the record so long as cross-examination took place at the time of the live testimony.)

While Killen would have loved to testify,[7] Moran and McIntyre's strategy was to keep the Preacher quiet by not having him take the stand in his own defense. For the two defense counsel, the State's case against Killen—consisting in large part of read testimony from the 1967 trial and emotional but irrelevant testimony from the widow of one of the dead men (Rita Schwerner Bender) and the mothers of the other two (eighty-nine-year-old Dr. Carolyn Goodman and eighty-three-year-old Mrs. Fannie Lee Chaney)—was very weak.

The opening arguments by opposing counsel were short—fifteen minutes each—based on the judge's instructions to them in his chambers. The opening statement in any criminal trial "draws a sketch of the evidence that the State intends to prove in this case," said Attorney General Hood to the jurors.[8] After the prosecution's opening arguments, it is the defense's turn, in its opening statement, to tell the jurors how it plans to show that the State has not met the burden of showing guilt beyond a reasonable doubt.

Hood's opening statement indicated that the State was going to present facts, based on witness testimony, and that some of the witnesses will be "speaking from the grave." At one point, Hood pointed his finger at the seated Killen and told the jurors that the Preacher told the Klansmen in 1964 that "God sanctions" the killings of the three civil rights workers. Even though Killen did not pull the trigger, said Hood, according to Mississippi criminal law, Killen's role as organizer made him "just as guilty as those who pulled the triggers."

He painted Killen as the mastermind behind the June 21, 1964, killings. Killen was a Kleagle—an organizer and recruiter for the Klan in Mississippi—and, Hood said, helped organize the Meridian Klavern. Killen was so attentive to the details of the murder plot that he told the men he rounded up to purchase rubber gloves and wear them when the three men were murdered.

> The State intends to prove that not only did Killen plan this murder, he organized the Klan there [Meridian] to bring them here [Philadelphia] to commit murder, and then he tells people afterwards about how their bodies were disposed of. The State believes that after we put on our evidence in this case, you will find this defendant guilty of three counts of murder. Thank you.[9]

It was now Mitch Moran's turn to speak to the jurors. His task, he began, was to point out "what the evidence is going to show you, what we plan to show you, a common sense approach to the situation. . . . We want you to look only at the evidence that mentions Edgar Ray."[10]

He surprised the courtroom and the prosecutors when he told the jurors that Killen was a member of the Klan and that Mr. Killen did recruit other Klansmen to "kick butt, kick [the three young men's] butts out of Neshoba County. He was a part of it, as far as being a member of the Klan. Does that make him guilty of murder? No," said the lead defense counsel to the jury. "He was just a bystander in an organization a lot of other people were in. [But] the Klan is not on trial in this case," he asserted.[11]

It also surprised and angered Killen, who had for four decades denied ever being a member of the Mississippi Klan's Neshoba County Klavern—but who, at the same time, thoroughly enjoyed the notoriety of being identified as the mastermind behind the killings.

Further angering Killen, Moran labeled the Preacher as a "messenger boy," a "gofer," or a "runner" for the real leaders of the Neshoba Klan—the Sheriff's Office men, Rainey and Price.

> I've been in the South long enough to know that a sheriff of a county basically runs the county. The evidence is going to show that somebody like Edgar Ray Killen did not tell Sheriff Rainey what to do. That's just not what happened. Edgar Ray Killen didn't tell Cecil Price [the deputy sheriff] what to do. He didn't tell the Highway Patrolman what to do. Edgar Ray was just a bystander.[12]

In a final surprise move, Moran also conceded that Killen "had knowledge of the murders. But he's not on trial for having knowledge that this crime was going to be committed. He is on trial for being the main perpetrator."[13] Alluding to the confession (1964) and, later on, the testimony of one of the 1967 informants, Horace Doyle Barnett, the lead defense counsel seemed to give the prosecutors an unexpected concession. Moran told the court that the defense accepted Barnett's assertion that Killen told him: "we have a place to bury them, and a man to run the dozer to cover them up." However, he reiterated to the jurors, "knowledge of aspects of a crime is not criminal action."[14]

The opening arguments ended in the early afternoon of the third day. Judge Gordon recessed the trial until 8:30 a.m. the following day, Thursday, June 16, 2005, at which time the prosecution would present its case against Edgar Ray Killen.

The Prosecution's Case

The case for the prosecution took less than two days to present to the jurors. However, the first day of testimony, Thursday, June 16, was a chaotic one that ended in the late morning when Judge Gordon recessed the court. There were fourteen witnesses for the prosecution. Six were dead witnesses "speaking from the grave"; eight were living witnesses.

In order of appearance, the fourteen witnesses for the State were

Thursday, June 16: Rita Schwerner Bender
Friday, June 17: Nell Miller, wife of Carleton Miller
    Carleton Wallace Miller, Klansman, Meridian Police Sergeant
    (transcript)
    Ernest Kirkland, friend of Schwerner and Chaney (transcript)
    Earl Poe, Philadelphia policeman (transcript)
    Minnie Lee Herring, wife of jailor (transcript)
    Dean Lytle, FBI agent
    Carolyn Goodman
    Jay Cochran Jr., FBI agent
    Delmar Dennis, Klansman, FBI Informant (transcript)
    Mike Winstead, felon
    James Jordan, Klansman (transcript)
    Mike Hatcher, Klansman
Saturday, June 18: Fannie Lee Chaney

Rita Schwerner Bender was the State's first witness and she testified for less than one hour. McIntyre cross-examined her for a few minutes.

But Killen was not in the courtroom to hear her testimony. Before the morning's proceedings began, he felt ill and waived his presence to hear the testimony. He was being treated by the nurse and by local paramedics (requested by the nurse) in the room set aside for him by Judge Gordon.

On arrival at the courthouse, Killen complained of a "smothering sensation" and was brought directly to his room and treated by the nurse for high blood pressure, which was above 200. The nurse called for an ambulance and Killen, sitting up on a stretcher, was taken to the local hospital.

This occurred out of sight or awareness of the judge, prosecutors, and defense counsel. And the prosecutor's first witness spoke about her life with Michael in east central Mississippi in the five months before he was murdered. There was, Rita Bender testified, constant harassment, late-night threatening phone calls, repeated moves from one rented house to another because the landlords were forced to evict them, and so on. She talked about hearing that the car her husband was using that fateful day was found, burned and shattered, in a swamp. "That's when it hit me for the first time," she said to the jury, "they were dead. There was no realistic possibility they were alive."[15]

Defense counsel McIntyre briefly cross-examined Bender. Did she have "personal knowledge of the events?" Her answer: "I have a lot of personal knowledge of the events."

McIntyre then rephrased the question: "Do you have *personal* knowledge of the actual murders?" He then asked her: "Do you have any personal knowledge of Edgar Ray Killen?" Bender replied that she had "no personal knowledge" to both questions.[16] McIntyre then asked her: "Then why did the state of Mississippi call you to testify?" Without any answer to these questions, he sat down and she left the witness stand.[17]

The second prosecution witness was Nell Miller, the widow of a Meridian police sergeant who testified against Killen in the 1967 federal trial. However, before she began her testimony, at 9:45 a.m., Judge Gordon interrupted the prosecutor to recess the court and call counsel to his chambers.

The nurse had informed Judge Gordon of Killen's condition and that the paramedics were ready to remove Killen to the local hospital. One of the paramedics, Kevin Smith, met with the small group in the judge's chambers and informed them that Killen's blood pressure was over 210 and that he had a rapid heart beat that necessitated transporting him to the hospital. About an hour later, while still in chambers, the judge had a conference call with the doctor treating Killen. Dr. Patrick Eakes said that Killen was being treated for high blood pressure and that the defendant had to stay in the hospital overnight.

Gordon asked Moran and McIntyre if Killen would agree to waive his presence while the prosecution presented its witnesses. After speaking to Killen at the hospital, they gave Gordon his answer: No. Killen wanted to be present for the testimony against him. McIntyre said to the judge: "He (Killen) said he didn't want to be cantankerous. He said tell the judge 'I don't want to be cantankerous.' He said 'I'd like to get it over with,' but he said 'I just feel like I need to be there.'"[18] With that information, the judge then reconvened the court and recessed the trial until Friday morning at 8:30 a.m.

Killen remained in the hospital overnight and was released early the following morning. He arrived at the courthouse in time for the 8:30 a.m. reconvening of the jurors and lawyers. The second day of the prosecution's case began promptly. It was a full day—the only full day of the trial. The prosecutors presented twelve witnesses—six dead and six living—to the jurors.

Viewing the witness list, and the order they were scheduled to testify, illuminates the prosecution's strategy. The first witness, Rita Bender, told the jurors about the hostile environment she and her husband found when they arrived in Mississippi.

The second witness was Nell Miller, the widow of a Meridian police sergeant, Carleton Wallace Miller (who died in 1972). She told the court that Killen visited their home on at least three occasions after the three young men were murdered. McIntyre, again, asked Mrs. Miller whether she had any personal knowledge of Killen's involvement in the murders, and she answered in the negative.[19]

The third witness, from the grave, was Nell Miller's husband. Miller was a lifelong friend of Killen's and a member of the Lauderdale County Klan organization in 1964. In the 1967 federal trial, he testified about a back-room conversation he had with Killen a few days after the three civil rights workers were murdered. Killen, he testified, shared the details of the murder plot, and how he had "gotten together" the Klansmen who participated in the killings. He also testified that "Mr. Killen told us [Meridian Klansmen] to leave Goatee alone, that another unit was going to take care of him, that his elimination had been approved by the Imperial Wizard [Sam Bowers]."[20]

Having laid out the environment and the preplanning with the first three witnesses, the fourth witness, Ernest Kirkland, from the grave, placed the three civil rights workers at the burned-out Mt. Zion United Methodist Church on Sunday afternoon, June 21, 1964, about 1 p.m. He was one of the members of the church and a friend of Schwerner and Chaney. He was the last person, other than the murderers and the jailors, to see them alive.[21]

The fifth witness, also speaking from the grave, was Earl Poe, a Philadelphia Highway Patrolman who spoke with Deputy Sheriff Cecil Price after Price, later that afternoon, pulled the trio over for speeding and escorted them to the Philadelphia city jail.[22]

Poe's facts were followed by testimony from the jailor's wife, another dead witness, Minnie Lee Herring. Her testimony established the trio's actions while in the city jail from 3 p.m. until about 10 p.m. when they were finally released after paying a $20 speeding fine.[23]

The seventh witness was the FBI agent, Dean Lytle, who was present when the trio's burned station wagon was removed from the Bogue Chitto swamp the day after they were murdered. Photos of the charred car were introduced by the prosecutor and identified by Lytle.[24]

After the lunch recess, the court heard testimony from other prosecu-

160

tion witnesses. The eighth to testify was Andrew Goodman's mother, ninety-year-old Dr. Carolyn Goodman. She talked about her son's willingness to go to Mississippi and she read the last message she received from Andy, a postcard written after he arrived in Mississippi early on the day of his death:

> Mom and Dad: I have arrived safely in Meridian, Mississippi. This is a wonderful town, and the weather is fine. I wish you were here. The people in this city are wonderful, and our reception was very good. All my love, Andy.[25]

The ninth witness to testify was Jay Cochran Jr., a retired FBI laboratory examiner who examined the dead men's car in June and who was present, in August, when the three bodies were dug up on the Old Jolly farm. On cross, Moran asked Cochran if there was any evidence found by him linking Killen to the crime. Cochran answered in the negative.[26]

The tenth witness was Delmar Dennis, a Baptist minister, a member of the Klan, and an FBI informant. From the grave Dennis testified that Killen told him before the murders that "Goatee" was targeted for elimination. In 1964, he told FBI investigators what had occurred and signed a confession. However, Dennis was asked to continue to remain in the Klan and provide the FBI with additional information. At the 1967 trial, he said that Killen swore him into the Meridian Klavern in March 1964. At that time, Killen told Dennis and others that "there would be things that the Klan would need to do and among these would be the burning crosses, people would need to be beaten and occasionally there would have to be an elimination."

"What did he mean by elimination?" asked the prosecutor, John Doar, in 1967.

Dennis's answer: "Killen meant killing a person. He explained that any project that was carried out by the Klan had to be approved by the Klan's [state leader, Sam Bowers]. . . . Killen said the elimination order for

Schwerner had already been approved by the state officers of the Klan and had been made part of their program."[27]

The eleventh witness was Mike Winstead, currently a prisoner in a Mississippi prison. He was serving a fifteen-year term for sexual battery (rape). He testified that, after the murders, he overheard a conversation between Killen and Winstead's grandfather. Although only eleven or twelve years old at the time, Winstead specifically remembered his grand-father asking Killen if he was involved in the murders and Killen's re-sponding that he was very involved in the planning of the killings.[28] On cross, Moran challenged Winstead's credibility, noting again and again that the witness could not remember any other facts about that time.[29]

The twelfth witness on Friday was James Jordan, a member of the Meridian Klan. He, too, spoke from the pages of the 1967 federal trial transcript. He was one of the Klansmen who met with Killen in the late af-ternoon of June 21 in Meridian. Killen told that group that they had to do a job "that needed to be done—to have the civil rights workers' rear ends tore up." He spoke about Killen's successful efforts to round up the seven-teen Klansmen and about the meeting Killen had in Meridian "just before 6 p.m." where he laid out portions of the plot and gave the men their as-signments: "Alton Roberts, you get gloves, and shovels. Make sure we have enough guns, we have a dozer operator," and so on.[30] He also told the jurors that Killen met them in Philadelphia to show them the jail and to explain what they were to do after the three men were released from the jail. Then Killen left for the funeral home to establish his alibi because, he told Jordan and the others, he would be one of the first men to be ques-tioned by the FBI.

The thirteenth witness, Mike Hatcher, a Klansman and a member of the Meridian police department from 1961 to 1982, was the last witness of the day. He told the jurors of the June 22 conversation he had with Killen. According to his testimony, Killen had a pistol he wanted Hatcher to dis-pose of "and then he proceeded to tell me that we got rid of them civil rights workers."

We got rid of those Civil Rights workers, and you won't have no more trouble out of Goatee, and he began to tell me [the whole story], . . . shooting them and killing them and buried them in the middle of a pond dam out here off highway 21 where a pond was being built. They were buried in a shallow grave, and that the bulldozer operator, who I believe he told me was a Tucker, got there the next morning to cover them up . . . under that pond dam. He told me that the car was supposed to have been covered up, too, but they [had] trouble, and didn't get to [burying it]. . . . He told me that he was at the funeral home, signed the book, made sure he talked with people in front and rear of him, and that was his alibi, and I told him, well, good.[31]

On cross, Moran asked whether Killen told Hatcher that "[Killen] planned it; did he? He did not tell you he planned that?"

Hatcher: No, sir.

Moran: And, in fact, would not every member of the Klan or a lot of members of the Klan have the same knowledge that [Killen] had when he told you that?

Hatcher: I can't answer that.

Moran: Have you ever seen Edgar Killen give Sheriff Rainey orders?

Hatcher: No, sir.

Moran: Do you have any personal knowledge of any evidence or anything that would show you that Edgar Killen killed the Civil Rights workers?

Hatcher: My personal knowledge would only be from what people told me.[32]

Judge Gordon scheduled the trial to continue on Saturday, June 18, and the prosecutors put on their fourteenth and final witness, eighty-two-year-old Fannie Lee Chaney. She talked about the last time she saw her son. He was picking up books to take to the CORE office where the civil rights workers had installed a children's library. "J.E. never came back. He never came back." She also spoke from the stand about the threats to her own life after James went missing and how these frightening calls and drive-by's of her house led her to move her family to New York.[33]

This time, defense counsel McIntyre did not have any questions for the State's last witness.

The prosecution then rested its case. It was now the defense's turn to respond to the State's case against the Preacher. McIntyre immediately called for Judge Gordon to issue a directed verdict of not guilty because of lack of evidence. The judge rejected the motion and the defense presented only five rebuttal witnesses.

The Defense Counterattack

The first defense witnesses Saturday morning were Killen's family members, his sister Dorothy Dearing and his brother, Oscar Kenneth Killen. Both testified that Killen was with them and other family members for a "father's day" party—with over fifty family members present—until about 4 or 5 p.m.[34]

Oscar testified that he saw his brother "about 7, 8 p.m." in a Philadelphia funeral home.[35] The Preacher was there to officiate at the wakes of two deceased persons. (Ironically, one of the dead whose family was ministered to by Killen that evening was the four-year-old niece of Stanley Dearman's wife. Dearman and his wife were in attendance.)

It was during District Attorney Mark Duncan's cross-examination of Oscar that the Preacher's brother told the court:

> Oscar Killen: I still don't know if [Edgar Ray Killen] was [a Klansman], but I've heard talk that your daddy and granddaddy was in the Klan, more than I have [Edgar]. Sure have. That's honest. I swore on the bible, gentlemen, that's the way I've heard it all these years.[36]

> Judge Gordon: I orally instruct the jury to disregard the emotional statement of Mr. [Oscar] Killen. Don't hold that [outburst] against the defendant in this case.[37]

Afterwards, Duncan told a reporter that "I had to restrain myself" when Oscar, smiling as he said them, threw out those "fighting words."[38]

The third witness for the defense was a retired Baptist minister, the Reverend James Kermit Sharp. He was, he said, "friend, neighbor, and ministers together" with the defendant.[39] His testimony was, at heart, a testimonial to Killen's "very good character" and Christian values and to the fact that Killen could never be a part of a brutal, premeditated murder of another human being. Killen was, said the character witness, "a very good man."[40]

On cross, Hood asked the preacher about the Klan's religious views.

Hood: They believe the Bible says you shouldn't intermingle races—do you know where those scriptures are?

Sharp: Not off hand.

Hood: Do you believe those who organized this crime should pay for what they did?

Sharp: I think all sin will answer in payment of some kind.

Hood: So is it fair to say that those who committed this crime should be held responsible by the State of Mississippi, shouldn't they?

Sharp: I suppose so.[41]

The Reverend was the last witness of the day for the defense.[42] The trial was adjourned in the early afternoon by Judge Gordon until Monday morning, June 20, 2005.

The following day, Sunday, June 19, was Father's Day and there were, as in the past, two memorial services celebrating the lives of the three dead civil rights men. The "Memorial Service Commemorating 41 Years" was held at the Mt. Zion United Methodist Church. Its theme: The Ultimate Sacrifice. It began at 2 p.m. with the invocation by Mississippi Rabbi Debra Kasoff. After songs, including the NAACP's signature hymn, "Lift Every Voice and Sing," members of the Philadelphia Coalition spoke, in very emotional tones, about the past, present, and future of justice in Mississippi. Then Fenton DeWeese, another coalition member, introduced the keynote speaker, State Senator Gloria Williamson.

The tears began after the keynoter's address. Rita Bender, Carolyn Goodman, and Ben Chaney spoke poignantly about, respectively, their dead husband, son, and brother. After another heart-rending civil rights hymn, "We Shall Overcome," was sung by the large group, wreaths were laid at the foot of the very small memorial plaque on the church's land. The memorial plaque's words summed up the history of a violent era in Mississippi's recent past:

> On June 21, 1964, voting rights activists James Chaney, Andrew Goodman, and Michael Schwerner, who had come here to investigate the burning of Mount Zion church, were murdered. Victims of a Klan conspiracy, their deaths provoked national outrage and led to the first successful prosecution of a civil rights case in Mississippi.

On Monday morning, June 20, the trial's last day of testimony and closing arguments, the defense presented their last witnesses. There was a surprise witness for the defense: fifty-two-year-old Dave Winstead, a long-time friend and neighbor of the Preacher[43] and the older brother (by three years) of Mike Winstead, the felon who had testified for the prosecution on Friday. Dave disagreed with his brother's earlier testimony. "I saw his testimony on TV. He's lying."[44]

> Moran: Have you ever seen Edgar Killen at your grandfather's house on a Sunday?
> Winstead: No.
> Moran: Never?
> Winstead: Never.
> Moran: Would you believe your brother under oath?
> Winstead: No.

Winstead was followed on the witness stand by a former four-term mayor of Philadelphia, Harlan Parks Majure. He was another character witness for Killen. He also testified that he saw Killen at the funeral home the evening of June 21, 1964.

He stunned everybody in the courtroom when, on cross by Duncan, he said that the Ku Klux Klan did a "lot of good things," and that it was a "peaceful organization."

> Duncan: [If he was in the Klan] would that change your opinion [about his good character]?
> Majure: No, sir, because I know some things about the Ku Klux Klan that a lot of people really don't know.
> Duncan: Do you know they are a violent organization?
> Majure: Not necessarily so. They did a lot of good things.
> Duncan: Would you call them a peaceful organization?
> Majure: As far as I know, it's a peaceful organization.[45]

The final tactic of the defense was to call Mike Hatcher back to the witness stand. That led to another recess because Hatcher was in Meridian and it would take over an hour to bring him, with a police escort, into the courtroom.

Hatcher had already testified for the prosecution that Killen, a day after the 1964 killings, told Hatcher that "we took care of the civil rights workers."

> Moran: Now, Mr. Hatcher, can you read your answer [given in the 1967 trial].
> Hatcher: Yes, sir, I will be glad to read the answer. I would also like to make an explanation to that answer.
> Moran: OK.
> Hatcher [reading from 1967 trial transcript]: *He [Killen] told me that the three had been taken care of, and the bodies were buried.*[46]

Judge Gordon then permitted Hatcher to explain the discrepancy between his 1967 testimony and the testimony he gave on Friday, June 17, 2005:

Hatcher: In 1967, from the early part when the Klan started in '64, you've got to realize at that time the conditions, law enforcement people, secret members, sympathizers, and the people that had been talking and had been told they were going to be killed, and me, being a young man and what I knew, *I only gave as much information as I did at that time at the Court, and the reason for it was that what I'm saying, because I didn't want to be killed back then,* and I wouldn't say that I was scared, but I feared Jesus Christ, and I feared what might happen to me back then, and I answered the questions that they asked [my emphasis].[47]

Moran: In 1967, you lied?

Hatcher: I did not lie. I only gave the amount of information to a certain extent, and as I said, the conditions back then and all is the reason for that.

Moran: Is it not also true that in the 1967 trial, that you stated that Edgar Killen told you he had nothing to do with it?'

Hatcher: Yes, yes, sir. I could have, . . . and again, I go back to the reason why I did that.[48]

On cross, Attorney General Hood showed Hatcher a May 4, 1967, statement given to the FBI by Hatcher. In it, he told the FBI that Killen told him that "we got rid of the Civil Rights workers."

A bit later, facing redirect from Moran, Hatcher told the Court that

If somebody come down and told you what Mr. Killen told me, at the time, there was nothing I could do about it unless I wanted to leave where I was born and raised, get my name changed and all that. I was aware of the FBI's plan [for witness relocation], and I never said anything, because of the threats then and the people that I knew was in the Klan and what could happen.[49]

Moran: Was the testimony you gave Friday, is that correct, or was the testimony in 1967 correct?

Hatcher: Partially 1967 correct, and honest to God's truth, Friday correct.

Moran: Did you lie in 1967?
Hatcher: I guess you could say I lied.
Moran: OK. You lied under oath; is that correct?
Hatcher: Like I said, I guess you could say I lied.[50]

At the conclusion of Hatcher's redirect testimony, the defense rested its case. The jurors had heard all the evidence presented by both sides; it was time for them to be "instructed in the law and to receive the closing arguments of the attorneys." After the jury instructions were given, Judge Gordon recessed the court. The closing arguments were to be given with everybody's stomach full.

The Closing Arguments

On Monday afternoon, June 20, the closing arguments began. Each side had one hour. The lectern was placed so that the speaker faced the seventeen jurors head-to-head. The prosecution spoke first.

Hood said: "Evil flourishes when good people sit idly by and do nothing."[51] This criminal trial should have occurred decades ago, he said, "but law enforcement did not do their duty." Because of that failure to do the right thing, the case "fell in our laps." Was it too late, as asked, "to look back at the skeletons of our past? No it isn't. The defendant has counted on time. He has counted on time passing, that memories will fade, but those memories preserved in these transcripts when those people spoke from the grave, are the truth then, and they are the truth now."[52]

This trial, Hood continued, in part is about honoring the memories of the three murdered civil rights workers. "They came down here doing God's work. They were helping their fellow man. They worked on a library over in Meridian. They set up a community center. They were here in peace. They weren't troublemakers. They were doing the same things that we are doing in Iraq right now."[53]

Killen was not an accessory to murder; he was charged with murder because of his leadership role in planning the deaths of the three young men. He was the "mastermind of all of [the plan]"; he was "the main man,"[54] said Hood, who was at this time holding up large photographs of the three men's dead bodies as they were uncovered by the FBI in August 1964.

Then he pleaded with the jurors: "Don't let God deal with Killen; that's shirking your duty. He's a murderer," said Hood. The prosecutor repeated the accusation: "He is a murderer and we have shown you the central role he played as the Klan main man." Your duty, he told them, "is to make sure that you make a decision and follow the jury instructions, without sympathy and without concern or fear or anything."

> Our duty is to give a fair trial for the defendant and for the victims, those victims that saw the venom that night out there on that dark road when they were shot in a road ditch and just left lying there in a road ditch, without an opportunity to ask God to forgive them, without a fair trial like we have given this defendant. They just took them out and shot them and threw them in a grave.[55]

Hood then proceeded, again, to "talk about Killen and your duty to him." The evidence clearly showed his hand in the planning of the executions of the three civil rights workers. "He did it all, and then, like a coward, he went and hid in the funeral home." He concluded with a reference to the tenseness when, on Saturday, Oscar Killen's fighting words jolted Hood.

> You saw the venom in his brother when he talked on the witness stand. You saw that venom. That venom is sitting right there seething behind those glasses. That coward wants to hide behind this thing and put pressure on you. He wants you to be weak and not do your duty to find him guilty of this crime. This is the man right here that has that venom, and there he sits, wanting your sympathy. What he doesn't want you to know is that he left these young boys in a grave, no funeral, no casket, dumped in there like a dog.[56]

Pointing his finger at Killen, Hood then added, loudly, words that visibly pricked the defendant's feelings: "Killen is a *coward.*" Killen reacted instantly to this wound, saying above a whisper: "You son-of-a-bitch."[57]

At this point, the prosecutors reserved the balance of their time and the defense began its closing arguments to the jury. The old country lawyer, James McIntyre, spoke first. "A terrible thing happened 41 years ago. It's awful. It's grotesque. I have nothing but compassion for the victims, the families, and the old ladies that have testified."[58]

However, in a criminal trial, jurors must "listen to the evidence and follow the law." The State has to meet the "beyond a reasonable doubt" burden of proof in order for the jury to convict a defendant. "The State has not met that burden. There is a great deal of reasonable doubt," McIntyre maintained.[59] He said that Mike Hatcher and all the other witnesses for the prosecution lied in 1967; "they were paid FBI informants," claimed McIntyre.

If they all lied, then why this trial at this time—forty-one years after the murders were committed? He answered his rhetorical question: The State wanted to put a show on television.[60] This trial has absolutely nothing to do with justice. "I'm an old country lawyer, trying to make a living," he said, without much modesty, "and I've done the best I could to bring justice and fair play before this jury. Is there justice and fair play in evidence in this trial? Nah. I suggest it is not,"[61] McIntyre said. Closing, he implored the jurors: "Go forward, not backward. You must acquit Edgar Ray Killen."

After a brief recess, Mitch Moran took to the lectern to conclude the defense's closing arguments. "Let the chips fall as they may. There is no *credible evidence* beyond a reasonable doubt that Killen was anything but a gofer, a messenger, for the Klan higher-ups. The State has not shown a shred of proof beyond a reasonable doubt that Killen was the godfather."[62]

The final words were uttered by the local prosecutor, Philadelphia-born-and-raised Mark Duncan. He reminded the jurors of the promise they made during the voir dire proceedings to treat the three dead men as if they had been born and raised in Philadelphia, Mississippi. Two of them, he said, "came down to Mississippi because they wanted to help others, and it cost them their lives."[63]

In a final emotional message to the jury, Duncan spoke to the jurors as fellow residents of Neshoba County.

> Is a Neshoba County jury going to tell the rest of the world that we are not going to let Edgar Ray Killen get away with murder any more? Not one day more! For 41 years tomorrow, it's been Edgar Ray Killen and his friends who have written the history of Neshoba County.[64]

He then talked about the impact that the movie *The Gladiator*, starring Russell Crowe, had had on him. "What you do in life," said Crowe's character in the movie to his fellow gladiators, "echoes through eternity." Duncan asked the jury to be as heroic in real life as the general was in the film. "What you do today when you go into that jury room is going to echo throughout the history of Neshoba County from now on. You can either change the history that Edgar Ray Killen and the Klan wrote for us, or you can confirm it."[65]

The closing arguments ended at about 3:30 p.m. Judge Gordon then pared the jury down to the twelve members by excusing the alternates. Immediately afterwards, the jury retired to deliberate and determine what their judgment would be in the case of *Mississippi vs. Killen*. Two hours later, Judge Gordon, after being told by the jury forewoman that they were divided 6–6, called a recess until the following day, Tuesday, June 21, 2005.

The Jury Verdict

At 11:18 a.m., on Tuesday, June 21, less than three hours after the jury had resumed their deliberations, we were all ushered back into the courtroom. The jurors had arrived at a unanimous verdict. In minutes, the room was packed with tense, emotionally drained onlookers.

Gordon warned the audience not to demonstrate in any manner. "We are in a court of justice," he said to the silent, nervous throng. "However imperfect the jury system, it has worked," he remarked, and, "it will work again today." With that, the clerk ushered the jurors into the courtroom. Killen was white; an oxygen tank was providing him with pure air. He looked straight ahead—his eyes on the judge, a man from his tiny hometown.

The twelve formed another semicircle facing the judge. The fore-woman gave the sheet of paper containing the jury's judgment to the judge. He looked at it—carefully, slowly, deliberately. Killen, along with almost 200 pairs of other eyes, was staring at the paper, trying to read the jurors' verdict.[66]

The day was, eerily, the forty-first anniversary of the slaying of Schwerner, Chaney, and Goodman. The judge gave the verdict to Patti Duncan Lee, the clerk of the 8th Circuit Court. Lee read it aloud:

> Count 1. We, the jury, find the defendant, Edgar Ray Killen, as to Count One, guilty of manslaughter.
> Count 2. We, the jury, find the defendant, Edgar Ray Killen, as to Count Two, guilty of manslaughter.
> Count 3. We, the jury, find the defendant, Edgar Ray Killen, as to Count Three, guilty of manslaughter.

As some jurors said to the media afterward, finding Killen guilty of planning the premeditated murders "beyond a reasonable doubt" was not a realistic path for many of them to take because of the poor quality of the evidence. At the end of the first two hours of deliberations on Monday, June 20, they were divided 6–6—not "deadlocked" or "hung," as reported in the press. Six jurors said that while they believed Killen was guilty of murder, the prosecutors had not made the case for guilt "beyond a reasonable doubt." The other six said he was guilty of murder—the prosecutors had made the case for murder to their satisfaction.

Warren Paprocki, the fifty-five-year-old engineer who had moved to Neshoba County five years earlier, wrote about the verdict for the *Los*

Angeles Times.[67] All the jurors, he wrote, were familiar with the 1964 event; none of the jurors "fit the stereotype of Mississippi that seems so prevalent, even today." Of the jury's decision, Warren wrote, "We found Killen guilty of manslaughter because that's what the evidence supported. . . . The jury was initially split between those who felt he was guilty and wanted to convict him of murder and those who felt he was guilty and were frustrated because the state did not present sufficient evidence to convict him under the jury instructions."

Paprocki insisted that there was no "jury nullification" (that is, when a jury reaches a conclusion not based on the facts and law presented to them). "We focused on what was presented in the courtroom." The problem was the lack of evidence accompanied by the jury's instructions. According to those instructions, given to them by Judge Gordon, conviction of Killen on murder charges had to be based on proof beyond a reasonable doubt that Killen either "pulled the trigger or that others had been acting under his specific direction to kill the three men." Six of the jurors, insisted Paprocki, did not see any evidence that "Killen gave them [the Klansmen] any instructions to perform a specific act."

For the jurors to convict Killen without that specific evidence would mean, said the engineer, that "we would be acting in the same spirit as the Ku Klux Klan. We would have been setting the law aside and subverting [the rule of law] to suit our own purposes. Killen received a fair verdict, based on the evidence [and the rule of law]."

Another juror, Troy Savell, the history teacher, said that the prosecution "never came close" to proving that Killen was guilty of murder. Savell was one of the six jurors who voted "not guilty" in the initial tally of jurors on Monday afternoon.[68] "Some of us," had great difficulty with the reading of the 1967 trial transcript, he told Jerry Mitchell. Some of the jurors simply dismissed it out of hand.[69]

A second vote indicated that the jurors were now split 7–5 in favor of convicting Killen for the 1964 murder of the three young men.

Then Paprocki recounted that he spoke up, arguing that there must be a unanimous guilty verdict of some kind. "It would be a hell of a deal" if Killen walked out of court *again* because *another* jury was deadlocked.

A third vote was taken after his comments and the jury voted 11–1 in favor of manslaughter. After a bit more discussion, the fourth, and final, vote was taken: 12–0, guilty of manslaughter. As Savell said afterwards, although the State's case was weak, "there was no doubt Killen went to Meridian and recruited those men."[70]

Paprocki told Shaila Dewan immediately after the jurors were dismissed that "I heard a number of very emotional statements from some of the white jurors. They had tears in their eyes, saying that if they could just have better evidence in the case that they would have convicted him of murder in a minute. Our consensus was that the state did not produce a strong enough case."[71]

Mark Duncan, for one, did not blame the jury. As he told us afterwards: "I think it was asking a lot of a jury to convict a man on testimony of people who they couldn't see. All they had were words on paper. So I can't criticize the jury at all."[72]

Others were not at all charitable about the verdict. Rita Bender was not as forgiving of the jurors as were the two prosecutors.[73] Standing outside the Courthouse after the verdict, she said:

> The fact that some members of this jury could have sat through that testimony, indeed could have lived here all these years and could not bring themselves to acknowledge that these were murders, that they were committed with malice, indicates that there are still people unfortunately among you who choose to look aside, who choose not to see the truth.[74]

But Shirley Vaughan, the jury forewoman, said, sadly: "With the little amount of evidence that we had, we did the very best that we could."[75]

Chapter Six

Sentencing the Preacher

The courtroom was heavily guarded on sentencing day. Dozens of law enforcement agents were in the oak-paneled room, with a phalanx of highway patrol officers standing in front of the railing separating the onlookers from the lawyers, facing the more than 150 reporters, family, and other attendees. Killen was sitting in his wheelchair, wearing a bright yellow Neshoba County Jail jumpsuit.

Judge Gordon looked at Killen and then began to speak.

Those of you who have never been Judge do not understand the problems that a sentencing Judge has at this stage of the trial. . . . In all the years I have sentenced persons, I've never really learned how to do it. . . . I've just have done what I thought was the best thing to do in keeping with the law, my oath, my responsibility to my oath, to the people, and to the Defendant that's before me.[76]

Gordon then asked: "Is sixty years (the maximum sentence) an *excessive sentence* for this convicted killer? Should age and health be factors in determining the length of the sentence? I have to pass on a sentence to a person who is 80 years old. A person who has suffered a serious injury. [And] there are those of you in this courtroom that would say a sentence of 10 years would be a life sentence."[77]

Then Gordon solemnly said: "Edgar Ray Killen, come around. Bring Mr. Killen around in front of the Bench." Killen's wheelchair was pushed so that the defendant faced the judge. Then he answered the questions he had posed.

I take no pleasure at all in pronouncing sentence. The three gentlemen who were killed, each life has value, and each life is equally as valuable as the other life, and I have taken that into consideration. That there are three lives involved in this case, and the three lives should absolutely be respected and treated equally.

176

Therefore, Edgar Ray Killen, in Count One, it is the sentence of this Court that you serve twenty years in the custody of the Mississippi Department of Corrections (MDOC). In Count Two, it's the sentence of this Court that you serve twenty years in the custody of the MDOC, with this sentence to run consecutive to the sentence pronounced upon you in Count One. In Count Three, it's the sentence of this Court that you serve twenty years in the custody of the MDOC, with this sentence to run consecutive to the sentence pronounced upon you in Counts One and Two.

Mr. Killen, you are submitted to the custody of the Sheriff of Neshoba County.[78]

In the courtroom we all sat in stunned astonishment. No one had expected the maximum, a sentence of 60 years, in the case. Rita Schwerner Bender, for the first time since the trial began, broke into an enormous smile and hugged her husband.

Judge Gordon then asked the defendant if he had anything to say. "None, your honor," the Preacher responded. Gordon then ordered the sheriff to take Killen back to the jail.

A minor incident in Killen's first hours in the Neshoba County Jail suggested the mind-set of the eighty-year-old convicted felon. He was asked routine questions by the black jailers, queries asked of all prisoners when they first arrive at the jail.

One question was whether Killen had suicidal thoughts: "Do you have any thoughts about killing yourself?" Killen replied: "I ain't thinking about killing myself. I'll kill you before I kill myself."[79]

The Manslaughter Verdict Explained

People who followed the short trial in the media had many questions.[80] For example: "How can the prosecutors jump shift from a murder charge to a manslaughter charge?" In Mississippi, Judge Gordon pointed out in open court, all murder trials include a lesser offense, manslaughter, if requested by prosecutors. Mississippi statute 97-3-19 (1)(3) states: "An indictment for murder or capital murder shall serve as notice to the defendant that the indictment may include any and all lesser included offenses thereof, including, but not limited to, manslaughter." Additional Mississippi statute, Miss. Code Ann. Sec. 97-3-27 (1994), defines manslaughter as follows: "The killing of a human being without malice, by the act, procurement, or culpable negligence of another, while such other is engaged in the perpetration of any felony, except rape, burglary, arson, or robbery, or while such other is attempting to commit any felony besides such as are above enumerated and excepted, shall be manslaughter." In the *Killen* case, because of the paucity of new evidence generated by the prosecutors before the trial, the State asked that the lesser offense of manslaughter become part of the jury's consideration. Judge Gordon agreed.

The State had very little new evidence to present in 2005. From the very beginning of their reexamination of the cold case, both prosecutors were concerned about that dilemma.[81] The prosecutors' case boiled down to testimony read from the 1967 federal trial and live testimony from the three victims' family members, from two retired FBI agents who were involved in the 1964 search for the trio, from a convicted rapist whose statements were weak and probably not credible, and from a retired Meridian policeman who had to confess, under cross-examination, that he lied in the 1967 trial. No live prosecution witness could identify Killen as the planner of the executions. Still, testimony from 1967 showed that Killen had told Meridian Klansmen that he needed them because three civil rights workers needed "their rear ends tore up"—thus raising the pivotal question for jurors of whether Killen planned for them to be killed. If he did, it was murder. If not, it was manslaughter. However, as the defense noted—again and again—to the jurors, there was no way that they could have cross-examined these dead FBI informants. They impeached the credibility of the 1967 informants, calling them liars and Judases. The defense also presented live witnesses who placed Killen at a funeral home the night of the murders (not that he had to be present to be convicted of murder; yet, this alibi planted seeds of doubt). In its summation, the defense repeatedly argued that the 1967 FBI informants, whose testimony was read into the 2005 trial, were liars who took money from the federal government in return for their lies. Moran and McIntyre claimed that the State did not come close to meeting the burden of showing "guilt beyond a reasonable doubt."

Duncan told the jury in his summation that "we" (Hood and Duncan) believe strongly that the evidence presented showed that Killen deliberately planned the executions of the three men, but if there was a question whether they had shown "guilt beyond a reasonable doubt" of murder, then the jury should consider the lesser charge of manslaughter. Given the general weakness of the State's case, manslaughter quickly became a very viable option for the prosecutors and, as it turned out, for the jurors as well.

While there was not guilt beyond a reasonable doubt that Killen plotted the murders, there was guilt beyond a reasonable doubt that Killen's actions inexorably led to their murders, and therefore he was guilty of manslaughter. There was no "jumpstarting" by the prosecutors—under Mississippi's criminal code, the jurors could consider manslaughter as a "lesser offense" and very likely chose the verdict that best matched the evidence as presented.

Reactions to the Sentence

Immediately after the sentencing hearing ended, Rita Bender stood at the front of the courthouse. "Visibly moved," she said to the press: "It didn't hit me until I saw them take [Killen in his yellow jumpsuit] away."[82]

Ben Chaney said to the onlookers on the courthouse lawn: "I want to thank God that today we saw Preacher Killen in a prison uniform taken from the courthouse to the jailhouse." James Chaney's daughter, Angela Lewis, who was only ten days old when her father was murdered by Klansmen, said: "There was a knot in my stomach until [Judge Gordon] actually gave the sentence. The only thing I could do was sit and hope and pray it would be the maximum on all three convictions."[83]

179

The Philadelphia Coalition members held a press conference immediately after the sentencing hearing ended. The group issued a statement
that commented about the trial and about what needed to happen in Mississippi in the future. "An ancient proverb teaches that a journey of a
thousand miles begins with one step. Neshoba County has taken that first
step."

After thanking the two prosecutors and the citizens of Neshoba
County, saying, "Today justice was served," the statement went on: "But
we have only begun our work here. . . . We must now seek the truth. We
call on the state of Mississippi, all of its citizens in every county, to begin
an honest investigation into our history. While it will be painful, we must
understand the legacy of racism that continues to divide us, and to prevent all of us from participating fully in the promise of democracy." The
group then issued a challenge and a promise:

> We challenge our fellow citizens to join us in an honest appraisal of
> the past. Knowledge brings truth and the truth brings freedom. . . .
> We have a purpose for the future: to seek the truth, to insure justice
> for all, and to nurture reconciliation. And so we promise in our own
> community to see this journey through to the finish line. But we can-
> not do it alone. . . . Join us in that struggle.

Mississippi politicians applauded the verdict and the sentence. "To-
day's verdict is a testimony to the community of Philadelphia and
Neshoba County," said Chip Pickering, a Republican member of the U.S.
House of Representatives. Continuing, he noted that

> [The Philadelphia Coalition] is a local, community organization that
> has promoted healing and sought justice, and today's verdict goes a
> long way toward both of those goals. The images and perceptions of
> the past do not reflect today's Mississippi, where we have the largest
> number of elected black officials in the country, where we celebrate

common cultures and history, where civil rights and justice prevail, and where reconciliation is a greater priority in our communities than in many other areas of the country.

The sole Democratic Representative from Mississippi in the U.S. House of Representatives, Benny Thompson, echoed Pickering's remarks. "Justice has finally arrived in Mississippi," he said. However, Mississippi "must now redouble its efforts to make sure that all its citizens are embraced and assured an equal opportunity to participate in every aspect of society. The world will be watching Mississippi and shame on the state if it does not seize this opportunity to improve the quality of life for all of its people."

Both U.S. senators from Mississippi, Republicans Trent Lott and Thad Cochran, spoke about the verdict. Cochran said he was "impressed" with both the verdict and the "determination and skill" of Mississippi Attorney General Jim Hood. "He should be congratulated for the diligence and success of his efforts." Lott said that the verdict in the Killen trial "shows that we can indeed pursue justice, and Mississippi has taken the lead in doing that." The trial is "a testament to the integrity of our state and to the professionalism of Mississippi's judicial system, and particularly to the Mississippians who served on the jury."

Republican Governor Haley Barbour also commented on the verdict. In his statement to the *Clarion-Ledger* Editorial Board, he said that now "there's closure" for residents of Philadelphia and Neshoba County as well as closure for the families of "the young men murdered in a heinous way" forty-one years ago. The goal of the prosecutors in the case, he said, was to seek justice. The two prosecutors believed they had the evidence needed to convict Killen "and they were right," concluded the governor.

Editorials and op-ed columnists in Mississippi and across the nation commented positively on the trial's conclusion and on the positive change in the behavior of Mississippi's residents.

Jackson Clarion-Ledger, June 22, 2005, *Neshoba:* 41 Years late but justice is done. Forty one years is a long time to wait for justice, but justice has finally been done with the murder conviction of Edgar Ray Killen.

The great danger in the Killen conviction would be that Mississippi stopped searching for justice in the Neshoba murders. One conviction does not atone for what was in fact a mob lynching of James Chaney, Andrew Goodman and Michael Schwerner. One conviction does not wipe the slate clean. As long as Klan members who participated in the scheme to kill the three civil rights workers live, the search for justice must continue. The rest of the guilty should face justice as well. Attorney General Jim Hood said he offered immunity from prosecution to some of those surviving Klansmen in exchange for testimony against Killen. The survivors declined the offer and refused to testify. So the next order of business would seem the convening of another grand jury to consider charges against Killen's co-conspirators. Justice in the Neshoba killings is a destination that has not yet been reached.

But the people of Neshoba County and the judicial system there should rightly be commended for taking a huge first step toward taking responsibility for making "justice for all" a phrase that resonates in their environs again. While 41 years late, guilt has finally been assigned by a Neshoba County jury and a harsh sentence handed down in punishment by a Neshoba County judge in the 1964 case.

Finally, Mississippi is learning, not burning.

The Daily Mississippian,[84] June 29, 2005, *And Justice for All:* We should use this trial and case as a glimpse into the current plight of the black community in this state and elsewhere. Blacks today still face many of the economic, political and social injustices they faced in the 1960's at the height of the civil rights movement. De Jure, legally defined, designated segregation has been broken, but de facto segregation still exists. . . . The trial must be a catalyst for the entire state to conduct a painful and close examination of its past and its future. . . . The trial was a first step. Now begins the more difficult task of changing the state for the better, something else that has not happened much over the past 40 years.

Mississippi Sun Herald, June 29, 2005, *Weight of the World No Longer on Shoulders:* Things are changing in Philadelphia, Neshoba County, and Mississippi. [It] is memorable, noteworthy, and ironic that a Klansman provided one of the clearest examples of that change.

Washington Post, Neely Tucker column, June 26, 2005: They got Edgar Ray Killen. Not the black people he so detests. Not the reporters from New York and Washington and London, whom he loves to taunt and threatens to shoot. Not the card-carrying ACLU commies. No, it was Edgar Ray Killen's neighbors—conservative white folk who vote Republican in overwhelming numbers—who dropped the hammer on him in the Philadelphia, Mississippi courthouse. And lifted a historical weight from themselves.

Boston Globe, June 30, 2005: Of course intolerance still exists, and there are still bigots among us. But surely the most striking transformation in American life is . . . the uprooting of a virulent racial hatred that much of this country once took for granted. In 1964, Mississippians like Killen made it a priority to hunt down civil rights workers. In 2005, Mississippi makes it a priority to hunt down men like Killen.

Joplin (MO) Globe, June 22, 2005: Still, symbols matter. If they didn't, Ronald Reagan would never have opened his 1980 campaign for the presidency in Philadelphia, Miss., which had a nationwide reputation for only one thing—the murders of Chaney, Goodman and Schwerner. In going there to declare "I believe in states' rights,"

Reagan sent a not-so-subtle message to a certain segment of the white South—those who continued to resent the civil rights move-ment—that he sympathized with them. Now, perhaps, Philadelphia can be used as a symbol of a hopeful future, not a reminder of a hate-ful past. At the time of the murders, Killen and his ilk believed that white men in Mississippi could kill black men with impunity. It turns out they were wrong.

Los Angeles Times, June 24, 2005, *No Peace, No Justice:* The Missis-sippi trial of former Ku Klux Klan leader Edgar Ray Killen in the 1964 slayings of three civil rights workers amounted to a U.S. ver-sion of the truth and justice commissions more commonly associated with nations such as South Africa or El Salvador. It reminded us that this country too is still finding its way out of a shameful past.

The Motions Hearing, June 27, 2005, and the Start of the Killen Appeals Process

On Monday, June 27, 2005, there was a motions hearing in Judge Gor-don's courtroom. Convicted killer Edgar Ray "Preacher" Killen was in court. He wore his yellow Neshoba County Jail jumpsuit. The courtroom was nearly empty; only a few reporters and television cameramen were present. For forty minutes, McIntyre and Moran presented motions that urged the judge to order a new trial for Killen.[85]

They presented a motion for a new trial for Killen because the indict-ment handed down in January 2005 did not mention manslaughter. A grand jury indictment, they argued, cannot be changed by the court. A judge has no power to change, or modify, or amend the indictment, refer-ring the court to Article III, clause 8, of the Mississippi Constitution and to *Haley vs. Mississippi,* a 1988 state court decision directly on point.

District Attorney Duncan responded to the motion. He pointed out, as did the judge earlier during the trial, that Mississippi law is clear that manslaughter is always included as a lesser included offense when there is a murder charge.

Moran then moved for a retrial because the statute of limitations had run out of time. Manslaughter was done in the act of kidnapping the three workers and there is a two-year statute on that crime. "Irregardless [*sic*], we had no notice about kidnapping when we cross-examined witnesses during the trial," Moran told the Judge. Afterward, McIntyre told us, as he stood in front of the courthouse: "We came here prepared for murder, then, in the middle of the stream, they changed horses. I know everybody wants Killen shot in the head at sunrise, but he's entitled to a fair trial before they shoot him."

Additionally, the defense contended that there should be a new trial because their requests for continuances were denied by the court; because Killen's Sixth Amendment right to a "speedy" trial was violated; because there was a "selective prosecution" by the State; because there was "no newly discovered evidence" presented by the prosecutors; because the "Constitution-makers didn't intend for a man to be prosecuted for a crime he allegedly committed 41 years ago"; and because there were serious questions surrounding the use of the 1967 transcript. Finally, the defense argued that the prosecutors had "some illegal contact with jurors during the trial itself."

The judge denied all these motions for a retrial. "As Mr. Duncan has pointed out, I've ruled on almost every issue that you have developed this morning or that you have presented to the Court this morning."[86] There is nothing in your motions that is valid, he said to defense counsel. "Therefore, your motion for a new trial is overruled."[87]With that, the judge adjourned the motions hearing. The question of bail for Killen was not raised; bail bond motions can only be discussed after the defense has filed a notice of appeal with the clerk's office.

Killen was immediately taken to prison after the motions hearing ended. He was held in isolation at the Central Mississippi Correctional

Institute, in Rankin County, Mississippi, until the state's classification process was completed. Newly convicted prisoners are evaluated according to the severity of their crime. "Manslaughter is pretty high [on the scale], especially three counts," said Chris Epps, the Mississippi Department of Corrections (MDOC) commissioner.[88]

Epps told me that, because of the crimes Killen committed, he will be labeled either a medium or a maximum security prisoner and will remain in the Rankin County prison or be shipped to Parchman State Prison (a maximum security facility north of Jackson, Mississippi) to serve his time. In either location, he continued, and regardless of his final classification, Killen will be in isolation in a cell for twenty-three hours a day, Monday through Friday. Weekends and holidays, he will remain in his cell for twenty-four hours a day. The Parchman facility has a fifty-six-bed prison hospital in case the Preacher needs additional medical treatment.[89]

The Killen case was now a part of the Mississippi appeal process. As heard in the defense motions before Judge Gordon, the primary arguments would revolve around allegations that the State violated a number of Killen's due process rights protected by the U.S. and Mississippi Constitutions.[90]

Asked about who will pay the costs of this process after the motions hearing ended Monday, June 27, 2005, defense attorney James McIntyre told reporters that at least "five respected citizens" promised to cover all the costs associated with Killen's appeal.

Appeals to the Mississippi Supreme Court may take another year or so before Mississippi jurists reach final judgments. And then there is the possibility of an appeal to the U.S. Supreme Court, a process that may take another year before the Court decides whether to hear Killen's appeal.[91] If Killen was released on bail pending the outcome of these appeals, it is possible that he may die while still a free man. The next step for the defense attorneys, then, was to see if Killen could be released from prison on a bail bond while awaiting the outcome of the appellate process.

Defense Motion for Bail Bond for Killen
and Judge Gordon's Two Responses,
August and September 2005

On August 12, 2005, less than thirty days after the defense filed its notice of appeal to the Mississippi Supreme Court in the Neshoba County circuit court clerk's office, a bail bond hearing was held in Judge Gordon's courtroom. A sentencing judge in Mississippi has a great deal of flexibility in determining whether a convicted felon can be released on bail pending the outcome of an appeal to the Mississippi Supreme Court. Mississippi law, however, does not allow appeal bonds to be granted by a judge if the defendant has been "convicted of felony child abuse or any offense in which a sentence of death or life imprisonment is imposed." However, using "the greatest caution, and only when the peculiar circumstances of the case render it proper," the judge of the district in which conviction was had" may grant an appeal bond.[92] "A person convicted of any felony other than those enumerated in subsection (1) of this section shall be entitled to be released from imprisonment on bail pending an appeal to the Supreme Court." However the trial judge can deny bail to a convicted felon "upon making a determination that the release of such person would constitute a special danger to any other person or to the community."[93] The two questions Judge Gordon had to ponder and answer, on the basis of evidence presented by counsel, were whether Killen was a flight risk and whether he would pose a "special danger to others or to the community" if he was released on bond.[94]

The August 2005 Killen Appeal Bond Hearing
The day for the hearing was Friday, August 12. Killen, dressed in his yellow jail jumpsuit, was all smiles as he entered the courthouse. About fifty family members and friends entered the courtroom to support and, for some, to testify on Killen's behalf. A handful of Philadelphia Coalition

members sat on the other side of the room, joined by Jerry Mitchell and a few other reporters.

The two defense attorneys put on at least seven witnesses, including three Baptist preachers, to testify that Killen was neither a flight risk (he was, after all, still in a wheelchair and in great pain) nor a dangerous threat to the community.

Marcus Harrington, of Union, Mississippi, testified that Killen was a "peaceful man." And Gerald Crenshaw, sixty-three years old, said that Killen, who baptized him when he was sixteen years old, "has been a dear friend all my life."

Edgar Ray Killen took the stand in a dramatic manner. He took the oath showing great pain in his right arm. (Quite noticeably he used his left hand to raise and then hold up his right arm.) He complained about a lack of medical care since he had been incarcerated at the Central Mississippi prison in Rankin County.

> They checked me through the lines like a cattle auction. I'm very unhappy with the treatment I've received. I can barely sleep. The court won't like it, but I bribed a black convict, and he got me a pillow out of the trash can. . . . I still don't understand how I could lie in severe pain for 24 hours and no one even brings me an aspirin. I'm not a drug addict.[95]

(On cross examination by D.A. Duncan, Killen said: "I can't write anymore with my right hand and I have to feed myself with my left.")

Mark Duncan was in court to present the case against granting the bail bond. However, Attorney General Jim Hood was absent from this important hearing. Duncan did not put on a strong case for denying the bail bond. He presented the two Neshoba County jailers, Willie Baxter and Kenny Spencer, who questioned Killen about suicide six weeks earlier. Their claim that Killen threatened to kill them before he would commit suicide was ridiculed by Moran and McIntyre on cross.

Moran asked Baxter: "Did you think he was going to come out of his wheelchair and kill you?" Baxter said that he took Killen's comments seriously and saw them as threatening. McIntyre asked Spencer on cross: "You thought Mr. Killen would rise from his wheelchair and attack you? He's 80 years old!" Spencer did not answer.[96]

McIntyre then called, as a rebuttal witness, the Neshoba County sheriff, Larry Myers. The sheriff told the court that his deputies had absolutely no problem with Killen while he was in the custody of the sheriff's office.

Duncan also introduced into the proceedings a letter from Rita Schwerner Bender.

> Mr. Killen has made public statements applauding the murders of my then-husband Mickey Schwerner, James Chaney, and Andrew Goodman. By those statements, he has repeatedly let the community know that he continues to believe in the use of violence to suppress any person with whom he disagrees. If [he] is released on bail, he will continue to spread his venom and hatred. . . . He will continue to intimidate and threaten, and to encourage others to act in brutish disregard of the rights of the citizenry. He will indeed constitute a special danger to the community.

The district attorney also presented the 1974 transcription of a taped conversation between Killen and the wife of a private investigator who had been tailing Killen and his married lady friend. This taped evidence was used to convict Killen in 1975. The recorded threat was presented by Duncan in August 2005 to show that Killen was a danger to the community in 1975 and will continue to be a menace to members of the community if released on a bail bond in 2005.

After hearing arguments from the prosecutor and the defense team, Judge Gordon granted Edgar Ray Killen a $600,000 bail bond. "It is not a matter of what I feel," Judge Gordon said, "it's a matter of law."[97] The prosecution, continued Gordon, did not meet the burden of showing that Killen was a flight risk or that he was, in his weakened medical condition, a serious threat to the community. By Friday evening, the family and friends of the Preacher secured property pledges that satisfied the $600,000 requirement. A very happy Killen, wearing a white broad-rimmed cowboy hat, was freed from the Rankin County prison.

Jim Prince, the editor of the *Neshoba Democrat* and the cochair of the Philadelphia Coalition, was distraught over the judge's action. "What's so disheartening about seeing Mr. Killen released is that I felt a majority of the people of Neshoba County had spoken and said he ought to be behind bars. For him to be released is just an atrocity, and it sends the wrong message to hate-mongers and these white supremacists in the Klan."[98]

Ironically, at about this time, Richard Barrett, the head of the racist Nationalist Movement, requested permission from the Neshoba County sheriff to hold a "Killen Appreciation Day" on September 18 on the lawn of the Neshoba County Courthouse. "It's an old-fashioned Mississippi homecoming. It's held for sports figures and beauty queens. Why not political prisoners?"[99] Barrett said that the granting of the bail bond was "a victory. He'll never see the inside of a jail cell." Then he said:

> There are still many people who think, and perhaps rightly so, that sometimes vigilante justice is needed when ordinary government doesn't do its job—in this case keeping Schwerner, Goodman, and Chaney [*sic*] out of Mississippi. [Killen] should be honored for not backing down, for not groveling. They'll want to shake his hand for just having a good old Southern redneck backbone that's kept Mississippi strong ever since there's been a Mississippi.[100]

Jewell McDonald, another member of the Philadelphia Coalition, was visibly shaken by this turn of events. She told Mitchell: "We're searching for terrorist cells all over the world, and we've got one right here in Philadelphia. He is just as dangerous."[101]

After Gordon's decision and Killen's release, Attorney General Hood, on August 17, 2005, took the matter to the Mississippi Supreme Court, asking the state's highest appellate court to hold an emergency session and to hear oral arguments on whether the bail bond judgment should be reversed. He claimed that Judge Gordon "abused his discretion" when he granted the bail bond to Killen. Hood presented a number of documents to show that Killen posed a serious threat to citizens of Philadelphia and Neshoba County. He asked the justices for thirty days to "fully brief these matters" and to supplement the petition with additional materials.

One of the documents presented to the Supreme Court was under seal; however, defense attorney McIntyre (correctly, as events proved) told the press that the sealed document contained information that Edgar Ray Killen's brother, J.D. Killen, threatened the life of Judge Gordon before the trial began in mid-June 2005.

On September 8, 2005, the Mississippi Supreme Court denied Hood's request for an emergency session to hear the state's appeal of Judge Gordon's decision.

The September 2005 Hearing before Judge Gordon

Days after the Mississippi Supreme Court order, however, things changed drastically for Edgar Ray Killen. On Friday, September 2, 2005, a Winston County deputy sheriff telephoned Jerry Mitchell to tell the reporter that he had seen Killen walking unaided as he filled his vehicle with gas. "He was walking with no problem. I was very surprised," said Connie Hampton, who saw him at the Conoco station in Philadelphia.[102] Five other Neshoba County deputy sheriffs also told Mitchell and Duncan that they had seen Killen driving around the county.

The next day Mitchell's story ran on page one of the *Jackson Clarion-Ledger*. The prosecutors immediately asked for another hearing before Judge Gordon to determine whether or not Killen should be rejailed. Mark Duncan, for the prosecutors, asked the judge to reconsider the granting of a bail bond because Killen "apparently misrepresented his physical condition to the court."[103]

On September 12, 2005, after hearing testimony that Killen was walking around Philadelphia, Judge Gordon said: "That's incredible to me. I feel fraud has been committed on this court." Confessing in court that he had released Killen "on the basis of sympathy," the judge determined that there was no way Killen could show such rapid medical improvement—unless there was a medical miracle or there was intentional lying and fraud committed by the defendant in August.

Furthermore, Judge Gordon, taking judicial notice of Killen's willingness to attend the September 18 "Killen Appreciation Day," said that Killen's decision to attend the celebration "seems to me . . . grounds to deny bond. This trial involved the death of three persons who died in a cruel, heinous and atrocious manner. They were murdered."

In his written order returning the Preacher to prison, Gordon wrote: "Without the testimony of the defendant's poor physical condition the court finds that the defendant has failed to show by clear and convincing evidence that he is not a danger to the community."

At the conclusion of the hearing, Killen was taken back to the Rankin County prison where the eighty-year-old will remain in his isolation cell for the rest of his sixty-year sentence.

Killen's well-known fondness for stretching the truth pops up one final time after his return to a prison cell. It appears in a letter he wrote on September 30, 2005, to a convicted felon, Travis Golie, an inmate in the prison in Fort Madison, Iowa. (Golie was serving time for robbery and had written Killen months earlier, praising the Klansman for refusing "to give up the fight.") In his letter, Killen explains to Golie why his bond has been forfeited:

> Since I wrote you I went home [and] made an appeal bond. [Afterwards, Attorney General Hood] investigated the judge [Gordon, and] found where several years ago [Gordon] was involved with a county

sheriff's drugs so [Hood] warned [Gordon]: "We expose you or you forfeit [Killen's] bond." So I lost my bond. . . . So I am right where your other letter came too [sic].[104]

In a way, this barely understandable letter reflects the tragedy of Mississippi in the century of Jim Crow. Edgar Ray Killen was one of thousands, extending into the highest ranks of Mississippi government, of hateful men who terrorized the state's citizens into frightened silence in the face of the racial brutalities that occurred daily.

Meanwhile, the Preacher's defense lawyers have submitted their briefs to the Mississippi Supreme Court. Based on earlier decisions of the Mississippi Supreme Court, analysts see little chance of his lawyers successfully overturning his conviction. For one thing, Judge Gordon's ruling on the admissibility of the 1967 trial transcripts was on solid state precedential ground, said Ole Miss Law School professor Michael Waterstone.[105] The same conclusion would hold regarding the forty-one year delay in bringing felony murder charges against a defendant. There is no statute of limitations on such a charge and, although the State's prosecutors were inactive, that fact does not turn into a reason for reversal of the conviction. As the Mississippi Supreme Court concluded, in the De La Beckwith case, "Miscreants brought before the bar of justice in this state must, sooner or later, face the cold realization that justice, slow and plodding though she may be, is certain in the state of Mississippi."

After Killen was returned to the Rankin County prison, Richard Barrett announced that "Killen Appreciation Day," to have been held September 18, 2005, was cancelled. The "political prisoner" was unable to attend.

Closure, of Sorts

Mark Beason is a sportswriter for the *Northeast Mississippi Daily Journal.* He grew up in Neshoba County, born in 1974, ten years after the murders of the three young civil rights workers. His essay, "Common Bond Age, Friendship, Not Color," appeared in the *Neshoba Democrat* on June 29, 2005. He spoke about the question of closure.

> As far as closure, I hope there is some for the family members of the slain civil rights workers. They're the ones who truly deserve it. For those of us whose lives will always be a part of the community, there won't ever be any. I'm happy they convicted Edgar Ray Killen and I'm happy he won't ever be a free man. But the verdict does make me mad in a way. It makes me mad because it took 41 years to get something done. . . . It makes me mad that my hometown will always be known for "Mississippi Burning" and not the Philadelphia I grew up with.[106]

When the conviction of Killen came down, Clyde Haberman, a *New York Times* columnist, met with Dr. Carolyn Goodman, Andrew's mother. She is a woman who has, for half of her ninety years, lived with the death of her twenty-year-old son. For Haberman, *closure* "suggests that there is a single moment or event [that] will somehow end the abiding pain of having lost a loved one."[107] And he asked Mrs. Goodman about that concept.

"It isn't the greatest word," she said, but "there is really not a better word to describe her feelings" now that Killen has been found guilty of the murders of Goodman, Chaney, and Schwerner.

"That's justice enough for me," she said to Haberman. "It's good that he will be off the streets." She recalled something her late husband, Robert Goodman, said to her almost forty years ago. Sooner or later, we'll "have justice." He was right, she added. "And now she has it. Perhaps," concluded Haberman, "that qualifies as closure, after all."

7

Beyond 2005:
Truth, Reconciliation, and
Change in Mississippi

> I hope this case is just a beginning and not an end. I hope this
> conviction helps to shed light on what has happened.
> *Rita Schwerner Bender*[1]
>
> Long term, Mississippi earned its reputation, and it's going to take a
> long time to correct it.
> *Reverend Dolphus Weary*[2]

The trial of Edgar Ray Killen is the story of change in Mississippi over
the past four decades. The Killen criminal trial is also the prism through
which we can understand and appreciate the nature of change in Mississippi. Having lived in Mississippi between 1976 and 1982 and having
visited the state many times since then, most recently to attend the
Killen trial, I believe I have a sense of the people, their values, and the
nature of change in Mississippi. And I believe that, in the words of a very
popular protest song of the 1960s civil rights era, "the times they are a-
changin'."

The Killen trial must be seen as the very beginning of a profound
"sea change" in Mississippi. When the whole truth is spoken and
recorded in history books—a very slow process, to be sure—people will

see a fundamental transformation of the institutions and the people of Mississippi. The Killen trial is but a single step on the long path to truth and understanding and reconciliation in Mississippi.

The Need for Justice and Truth

While there were no *living* witnesses for the prosecution to testify about Killen's role in the murders of the three civil rights workers in 1964, the prosecutors were able to paint a portrait of a prior era in Mississippi when there flourished a culture of impunity, one that condoned—at the highest levels of state government—brutal actions by the Klan and other extremist organizations.

By painting this portrait, Duncan and Hood achieved both an immediate and a long-term goal. The immediate purpose was to achieve justice: to convict Edgar Ray Killen for his major role in the murders of Schwerner, Chaney, and Goodman. As noted, the prosecutors had to overcome two catastrophic events in the effort to achieve this goal: the death of Cecil Price in 2001 and the suicide of Bob Stringer in 2004.

They also had to face the prospect that jurors might be turned off by the reading of parts of the 1967 federal criminal conspiracy transcript. (And their fears were partially realized, as some jurors said to reporters—after the trial ended—that the reading of the transcript was not helpful.)

Furthermore, two of their living witnesses—Mike Hatcher, the former Klansman, and Mike Winstead, the convicted felon who appeared in court in chains and wearing his prison jumpsuit—turned out to be less than helpful to the prosecution.

However, a picture of the reality of life for blacks and a few others in Jim Crow, racist Mississippi did emerge. It emerged through the reading of transcripts, the testimony of retired FBI agents, the heartrending testimony of Rita Schwerner Bender, Carolyn Goodman, and Fannie Lee Chaney.

196

Even the testimony of Hatcher and Winstead helped flesh out a portrait of 1950s–1960s Mississippi. Although Hatcher's testimony was belittled by the defense in an effort to discredit him, his testimony about, in his words, "fearing for my life because of the conditions in the state of Mississippi at that time,"[3] buttressed the prosecution's effort to tell the truth about Mississippi's culture of impunity in 1964.

Laying out the truth led to Killen's conviction for the planning of three homicides in June 1964. For all their posturing, the defense lawyers were unable to make dents in the truth-telling process. Although Rita Bender's testimony—and the testimony of the FBI agents, and Carolyn Goodman, and Fannie Lee Chaney—was tossed off by McIntyre and Moran as irrelevant and off the legal question of murder, those many words helped complete the portrait of the state in one of the cruelest periods of its history.

Killen's conviction for manslaughter and Judge Gordon's sentencing of Killen to sixty years in prison meant that the immediate goal of the prosecutors was met. As a former colleague of mine, Les McLemore, said after the trial ended: "Justice has clearly been done."[4]

The long-term goal of the prosecution was also achieved by Duncan and Hood. Ben Chaney spoke to the long-term goal when he said, after the sentencing phase ended: "First justice, then truth is established within."[5]

The prosecutors' broader goal was to place truth in the record, in the transcript, in the news stories on television, on the radio, in the press, on the DVD of the trial prepared by Mississippi Public Television, to lay out the unvarnished truth about an unholy era in Mississippi's history. Lay it out so that public school teachers can draw upon these truths to educate their students about the reality of life in segregated, racist Mississippi. Lay it out so that young parents and other adults in the state come to grips with and understand the truth about race relations in a very different Mississippi from what it was not too long ago.

In this effort to bring racial truths to the surface in Mississippi, Susan Glisson and the William Winter Institute for Racial Reconciliation have played and will continue to play a major role. Susan's work with the multiracial coalition in Philadelphia, Mississippi, should become the statewide model for racial and economic problem solving and reconciliation, said Les McLemore, a professor of political science at Jackson State University.[6]

> The coalition is important in and of itself. Just the fact that they [with Glisson's help] did it. It is more important to have the coalition continue to have an ongoing dialogue that is sustainable and that can, hopefully, become a model for other communities all across our state and for our state as a whole. . . . The challenge is to make this sustainable so that we can identify issues, concerns, and challenges we can address in this same way.[7]

In addition to working closely with the Philadelphia Coalition, the William Winter Institute for Racial Reconciliation (WWIRR) has been working with other communities all across the state to achieve the same goal. That objective is to bring different classes and races together so that these newly organized groups can begin to discover the truth about its past, and to address some significant issues that need to be resolved.

Through this process Glisson believes that reconciliation can take place. The following information, taken from the WWIRR Web site, illustrates the kinds of activities that have taken place just in the past five years.

Batesville, Mississippi[8]
The work in Batesville has been heavily centered on teaching Concord youth how to . . . collect the histories of their membership and the surrounding community.

Brookhaven, Mississippi
Working with the local community group Serving All People, WWIRR co-sponsored a community health and education fair in

Brookhaven in the summer of 2003, seeking to bring together community residents to improve knowledge about health concerns.

Clarksdale, Mississippi

. . . Through training and leadership development, [a youth oral history] project . . . teaches young people to document the history of their communities and, in turn, to support their engagement in local issues to bring new energy to solving local problems.

Documentary Films

In May 2005, the Institute completed production of a 34-minute documentary film on the 1961 Freedom Rides. The film showcases the crucial role of young people, black and white, in helping to dismantle segregation. The film is available to high schools for free and has a companion web site with oral histories, interactive forums for young people, and lesson plans for teachers.[9]

Drew, Mississippi

In spring 2001, WWIRR, in partnership with Delta State University, secured a Mississippi Department of Archives and History Grant for the Holly Grove Community Development Corporation for the restoration of the Drew, Miss., Rosenwald School for use as a community center.

Holly Springs, Mississippi

In partnership with Ole Miss's Department of English, WWIRR co-sponsors the Marshall County Correctional Facility Writing Project. . . . The class encourages all types of writing from its participants. Almost all of the participants in the workshop have not only found that their general writing skills improve, but that creative writing is in and of itself a therapeutic activity.

Jackson, Mississippi

In spring 2002, WWIRR secured a grant from the First Amendment Center for Lanier High School in Jackson, Mississippi. The First

Amendment School Project is transforming Lanier, an all-black, inner-city high school, into a laboratory of democracy. Through the practice of First Amendment principles, as in the creation of a school newspaper and a school constitution, students will learn the importance of engaged and informed citizenship through the application of the freedoms protected in the First Amendment. In turn, the transformation of the school will serve as a catalyst for community renewal and reconciliation.

McComb, Mississippi

In 2004, the Institute began serving the city of McComb as it sought to reexamine the experience of 1964's Freedom Summer. Forming a new biracial community group, the Institute helped begin an oral history project and began working with the McComb City school district to explore curriculum development on civil rights history.

Newton, Mississippi

In spring 2003, the Institute partnered with a biracial planning committee working to honor the legacy of Medgar Evers, a native of Newton County. In conjunction with the Medgar Evers Institute, the project commemorated the legacy of Evers during the 40th anniversary of his assassination.

Oxford, Mississippi

In fall 1999, WWIRR began working in the local community to help identify issues of concern and to help build local alliances to address those concerns. The result is OLAMOS, the Oxford-Lafayette Amos Network, a faith-based coalition for systemic change in the local community. Partnering the national IAF, Industrial Areas Foundation, OLAMOS trains local leaders to identify and solve problems in the Oxford area.

Resource Guide for Communities

In Spring 2005, the Institute made available to local town and city leaders across Mississippi a 78 page guidebook for community organizing. The guide includes case studies of Institute work as well as a compendium of organizations and initiatives across the country that seek to improve race relations through the arts, education, community revitalization, and economic development. Its title is: "We Are the People We've Been Waiting For: Equipping Communities for Change."[10]

Rome, Mississippi
In spring 2000, WWIRR helped the Rome Community Development Corporation to implement a grant for construction of sewer system. By helping to build the infrastructure of the community, WWIRR has helped create a foundation for other community projects that include rebuilding a former drug haven into a youth community center, a youth arts program and an oral history project of the community's history. This spring, the Institute helped to initiate a children's library and collected more than 600 books for ages K–12. The summer 2003 reading program, "See the World through Books," awarded individual and group prizes for books read. In the summer of 2004, the Institute trained the youth in Rome to conduct oral histories of their community. The young people then visited the campus for a 2-day retreat of classes, web site development, and recreation. In June 2005, several young people from Rome, along with their parents, attended the civil rights education summit in Philadelphia, MS. They presented a workshop on Sunflower County civil rights history.

Sunflower County Freedom School
Begun in 2000, this innovative program is an independent nonprofit organization dedicated to educational excellence and leadership development in Sunflower County, Mississippi. Founded by Teach for America alumni, it uses the history and spirit of the 1960s freedom struggle to motivate young people to become capable and compassionate leaders in their communities. The project has participated in other WWIRR projects and UM hosts its summer programs with involvement from SEED students and support from WWIRR staff.

Another undertaking of WWIRR was the "This Little Light" Oral History Project. The program trained secondary school students in three towns across Mississippi—Rome, Batesville, and Greenwood—to operate tape recorders and video cameras. The purpose was to have these students interview blacks and whites in order to create oral histories of their towns that document the bad times in the state.[11]

Clearly, the WWIRR and other organizations Glisson helped to create across Mississippi must continue their work in order for significant change to take place in Mississippi. It is encouraging for Mississippi's future to see these positive, proactive efforts by Mississippi's residents. There are other initiatives currently being planned by the WWIRR—in conjunction with Mississippi residents in towns and cities—to bring truth and reconciliation to Mississippi in the twenty-first century.

While it is a major challenge, it may not be an insurmountable one. Like all such Herculean projects, progress is measured one day at a time, one step at a time, one town at a time. Glisson's ultimate goal is to see race forums "in every county in Mississippi, creating a safe environment for difficult discussions."[12]

Truth and Reconciliation in Mississippi

The terrible truth about Mississippi's Jim Crow/KKK era, brought out before and especially during the trial of the Preacher, is a necessary precondition for reconciliation between the races in Mississippi. For too many decades, most good people in Mississippi, the *bystanders,* were too frightened to even talk openly about the terrible events that were taking place—or had taken place—in their homeland. Even in 2005, during Killen's trial, there were some residents of the city and county who were genuinely fearful about the possibility of being chosen to sit on the jury—or even speaking to a news reporter.

Until the 1990s the *perpetrators* of these crimes against humanity were walking the streets of Union and Philadelphia, in Neshoba County, without any concern about the possibility of indictment and prosecution for their criminal acts. However, once the grand jury handed down the indictment against Killen, the fear and the humiliation of many of the bystanders began to subside.

After truth becomes manifest, becomes visible, then reconciliation can happen. Reconciliation is a healing process; however, it takes time to work—if it is ever going to work. Charles R. Wilson, the director of the Center for the Study of Southern Culture at the University of Mississippi, said, after the trial ended:

> Those images from the 1960s have haunted us and complicated reconciliation between blacks and whites—and even northerners and southerners. [The Killen verdict] was a real landmark. There have been a lot of civil rights murders and cases, but this one was particularly dramatic because it involved northerners and southerners, Jewish Americans as well as black Americans. This verdict will help the healing process, without question.[13]

The Reverend Charles Griffin, the fifty-five-year-old black pastor of the Mount Ary Baptist Church in Philadelphia, agrees with Bishop Desmond Tutu's admonition that there must be, in addition to truth, "*a physical transformation*, a changing of the quality of life of the most deprived," in order for reconciliation of the races to occur. Griffin believes that "although race relations are greatly improved, some general areas need to be addressed," especially "economic improvements for African Americans and political empowerment."[14]

The catastrophic Class 5 Hurricane Katrina that battered Alabama, Mississippi, and Louisiana in September 2005 reawakened Americans to the plight of the poor and minorities in America. Coinciding with the devastating force of nature, the U.S. Census Bureau published its income and poverty data for 2004. While income was stable, "the nation's official poverty rate rose from 12.5 percent in 2003 to 12.7 percent in 2004 [compared to 24.6 percent in 1989].[15] There were 37.0 million people in poverty in 2004, up from 35.9 million in 2003."[16]

> Black households had the lowest median income in 2004 ($30,134) among race groups. Asian households had the highest median income ($57,518). The median income for non-Hispanic white households was $48,877. Median income for Hispanic households was $34,241. . . . The South continued to have the lowest median household income of all four regions. . . . The poverty rate declined for Asians (9.8% in 2004, down from 11.8% in 2003), remained unchanged for Hispanics (21.9%) and blacks (24.7%) and rose for non-Hispanic whites (8.6% in 2004, up from 8.2% in 2003). . . . For all children under 18, both the 2004 poverty rate (17.8%) and the number in poverty (13.0 million) were unchanged from 2003.[17]

As Jonathan Alter wrote in *Newsweek,* "it takes a catastrophe like Katrina to strip away the old evasions, hypocrisies, and not-so-benign neglect."[18] The states hit hardest by Katrina, Mississippi and Louisiana,[19] are among the five poorest states in the nation. These very fundamental economic and social issues and fissures are the kinds of issues that must be addressed in order for truth and reconciliation to work in Mississippi.

In short, the task of the WWIRR, and other similar organizations in Mississippi,[20] is a huge one: The initiation of conversations with people who come from different classes and many races will eventually overcome what was once referred to in the administration of President Richard M. Nixon (1969–1974) as government's "benign neglect" of the poor and of minorities. Statistically, the poverty levels continue to decrease since the 1960s civil rights era; however, as Hurricane Katrina pointed out to the world, there still remains a large number—in the millions—of poverty-stricken people living in America in 2005.

Change in Mississippi

The convictions of Killen, De La Beckwith, and other aging, unregenerate Klansmen, called "the poster boys of that time and place" by one columnist, are "welcomed [for] they have a broad symbolic significance. They show that the struggle for justice, while long and arduous, can bear fruit in the most barren soil."

> *But while symbols are important, they should not be mistaken for substance.* . . . While the crimes that occurred during segregation were rarely systematic . . . they were *systemic.*
>
> They were born from a system of segregation that worked to preserve white privilege in the face of a concerted progressive onslaught—a system in which the white community had to collude in order for it to function. *While the scale and nature of these privileges may have changed, the privileges themselves still exist* [my emphasis].[21]

This is extremely grim criticism of Mississippi and of the events taking place in the state, and some argue it is not valid. "There *is* a great deal of change in Mississippi in the areas of education, political participation, leadership, and economic activity [since the three civil rights workers were murdered in 1964]," says Dr. Arthur G. Cosby, director of the Social Science Research Center at Mississippi State University.[22] And U.S. Census Bureau data bears his assessment out.[23]

Other writers, born and raised in Mississippi or in the South, while agreeing that serious social problems still exist in Mississippi, nevertheless disagree with Younge's pessimistic view of the systemic continuation of white privilege in the South. They see, instead, not a "rebooted," racist Mississippi but a substantively transformed Mississippi. While true, complete racial fairness is a lodestar, perhaps not attainable anywhere, there is, as a noted columnist wrote, "movement. What was Mississippi Burning is, surprisingly often, Mississippi yearning."[24]

Karl Fleming was one of the first reporters to arrive in Philadelphia, Mississippi, in June 1964 to cover the then-breaking story of the disappearance of Schwerner, Chaney, and Goodman. Forty-one years later, Fleming, a native Southerner, covered the Killen trial for the *Los Angeles Times* and saw a fundamentally altered Mississippi.[25]

Walking around the courthouse square in Philadelphia, he spoke with local cops—black and white officers, male and female, as well as other denizens of the small town—including Anne Pullin and her clients at Peggy's Restaurant. They were all pleasant, and gracious, and very forthcoming. He observed:

> It could have been a mere performance, an example of surface-deep Southern hospitality masking the same old feelings—but it wasn't. The truth is that the change in the South in the years since Goodman, Chaney, and Schwerner were killed has been profound. . . . A native Southerner myself, I find that the South today is so transformed that it's hard for most people to understand what it was once like.[26]

William Raspberry, the highly respected black Mississippi-born syndicated journalist, shares Fleming's sentiments. "Visiting Mississippi leaves me both *hopeful and despairing*. Mississippi is a state of confusion—the symbol of racism and backwardness and arguably the state that is trying hardest to repair the damage caused by racism [my emphasis]."

For Raspberry, the five trials and convictions of Mississippi Klansmen that have taken place since 1990 in state courts are symbolic. However, he believes that they are "powerful symbol[s] of a desire to atone not just for the crime of murder but for the prevailing attitude that, for many Mississippians, made lynching acceptable."[27]

Certainly the new, emergent attitude, reflected in the events that led to the June 2005 trial of Edgar Ray Killen, is a clear indicator that change has occurred in the state.

In 1964, a young Bob Moses, the codirector of the 1964 COFO Mississippi Summer Project and Field Secretary for the Student Nonviolent Coordinating Committee (SNCC), at the time an offshoot of Martin Luther King Jr.'s Southern Christian Leadership Conference (SCLC), said that Mississippi was the "middle of the iceberg" of racism. Through the speaking of formerly unspeakable truths, in part through the criminal trials and convictions of elderly Klansmen such as De La Beckwith and Killen, the iceberg has finally been breeched and with the breech, the truths of that era have emerged. With this reality, there is at last the beginning of racial reconciliation.

And then, after a true portrait of real Mississippi is painted, and after racial reconciliation begins to take shape in the state, there must inevitably—but probably very slowly—come the end of economic and social discriminations based on race and national heritage.

As Rita Schwerner Bender said, Killen's conviction was "a beginning, not an end" of a process that will ultimately lead to a drastically improved environment in the Magnolia State. A recent and very encouraging example of this "beginning" occurred on March 20, 2006. Governor Haley Barbour signed legislation creating the Civil Rights Education Commission. Mississippi Senate Bill 2718 created the commission to work directly with the State Department of Education to establish a civil rights history curriculum for all grades in Mississippi's public shcools. Susan Glisson observed that "the Philadelphia Coalition was the catalyst for this legislation. One of the first things the coalition agreed upon as a goal was education of civil rights history."[28] Things do change, sometimes for the better.

Notes

Introduction

1. Quoted in Richard Rubin, "The Ghosts of Emmett Till," *New York Times Sunday Magazine*, July 31, 2005, pp. 30–35.

2. Quoted in Stanley Dearman, "His Whole Life Led to Decision to Be in Mississippi in 1964," *Neshoba Democrat*, April 26, 1989, p. 1.

3. On the lawn of Edgar Ray Killen's property in Union, Mississippi, is a plaque. On it is the Ten Commandments, including, of course, the sixth commandment.

4. See, generally, Howard Ball, *Murder in Mississippi: United States v. Price and the Struggle for Civil Rights* (Lawrence: University Press of Kansas, 2004).

5. Indictment, State of Mississippi, Neshoba County, Mississippi, January 6, 2005.

6. Jerry Mitchell, "Grand Jury Indicts Killen in '64 Killings," *Jackson Clarion-Ledger*, January 7, 2005, p. A1.

7. Ibid.

8. Langston Hughes, *Scottsboro Limited: Four Poems and a Play in Verse* (New York: Golden Stair Press, 1932), p. 1. Hughes wrote this small book to raise money for the Scottsboro Defense Fund. In 1931, a group of young black hoboes was arrested and charged with the rapes of two white women who were also riding the rails in Alabama. Within days, the men were charged, convicted, and sentenced to death. There were a number of appeals to the U.S. Supreme Court on their behalf. They were innocent of all charges; both women were prostitutes, and one of the women recanted her trial testimony. Nevertheless, it took decades for all the men to be released from jail.

9. For example, the public schools were peacefully integrated in Neshoba County in 1971.

10. While I was standing in the courtroom during a recess, talking with the Neshoba County District Attorney, one of Killen's brothers, J. D. Killen, told Duncan what will happen to him when he runs for reelection next time. "We'll gonna [*sic*] make sure you lose," he said, grimly.

Chapter One. Change in Mississippi:
Mississippi vs. Edgar Ray Killen in Perspective

1. Quoted in Neely Tucker, "Mississippi Turning," *Washington Post,* June 16, 2005, p. C01.

2. Jerry Mitchell, "Bill to Honor Victims of 1964 Slayings Not Called Up for Vote," *Jackson Clarion-Ledger,* January 26, 2005, p. A1.

3. Michael Schwerner, James Chaney, and Andrew Goodman were the three young men who were killed on the night of June 21, 1964, by eighteen Klansmen outside Philadelphia, Mississippi. See, generally, Howard Ball, *Murder in Mississippi: United States v. Price and the Struggle for Civil Rights* (Lawrence: University Press of Kansas, 2004).

4. The group was charged with conspiracy to deprive the three civil rights workers of their constitutionally protected rights and liberties, Section 241 of the U.S. Code. See, generally, Ball, *Murder in Mississippi.*

5. Quoted in Gary Younge, "Racism Rebooted," *Nation,* July 11, 2005, p. 12.

6. Quoted in Arnold Lindsay, "Relations Calm in Neshoba," *Jackson Clarion-Ledger,* June 12, 2005, p. A1.

7. Esther Iverem, "On the Road: Mississippi, Past and Present," Voices of Civil Rights: Bus Tour, at http://www.voicesofcivilrights.org/bustour/journal_entry16.html.

8. Manuel Roig-Franzia, "Ex-Klan Leader Convicted in '64 Case," *Washington Post,* June 22, 2005, p. A01.

9. See James Silver, *Mississippi: The Closed Society* (New York: Harcourt, Brace and World, 1963).

10. The WCC was created initially in Mississippi, just a few months after the watershed 1954 U.S. Supreme Court decision ending separate public schools for black children and white children, *Brown v Board of Education of Topeka, Kansas.* Within six months, WCC chapters popped up across the South.

11. See, generally, Neil McMillan, *The Citizens' Council: Organizing Resistance to the Second Reconstruction* (Urbana: University of Illinois Press, 1971).

12. Quoted in Shaila Dewan, "In a Small Town, a Trial Mirrors Familiar Divisions," *New York Times*, June 21, 2005, p. A1.

13. Roig-Franzia, "Ex-Klan Leader Convicted."

14. Quoted in Shaila Dewan, "In a Small Town."

15. See, generally, Yasuhiro Katagiri, *The Mississippi State Sovereignty Commission: Civil Rights and States' Rights* (Jackson: University Press of Mississippi, 2001).

16. Beth Bonora, a jury consultant for the prosecution team, quoted in Dewan, "In a Small Town."

17. Quoted in Roig-Franzia, "Ex-Klan Leader Convicted."

18. See, generally, Raul Hilberg, *Perpetrators, Victims, Bystanders: The Jewish Catastrophe, 1933–1945* (New York: HarperCollins, 1992).

19. Roig-Franzia, "Ex-Klan Leader Convicted."

20. See, for example, Younge, "Racism Rebooted," p. 10.

21. "Remarks by Secretary of State Dick Molpus, Ecumenical Memorial Service, Mount Zion Church, June 21, 1989," http://www.neshobajustice.com/molpus1989.htm.

22. Interview, Dick Molpus, taped, June 29, 2005, Jackson, Mississippi.

23. Quoted in Jerry Mitchell, "Almost Half in Neshoba Survey Favored Trial in '64 Killings," *Jackson Clarion-Ledger*, July 5, 2005, p. A1.

24. See for example, Dearman's interview with Dr. Carolyn Goodman, "His Whole Life Led to Decision to Be in Mississippi in 1964," *Neshoba Democrat*, April 26, 1989, p. 1.

25. Quoted in Mark Minton, "Mississippi: In Search of Justice," *Arkansas Democrat-Gazette*, January 30, 2005, p. D1.

26. Ibid.

27. Quoted in Younge, "Racism Rebooted," p. 11.

28. Quoted in Ball, *Murder in Mississippi*, p. 144.

29. Stanley Dearman, editor of the *Neshoba Democrat*, for decades condemned in editorials the inaction of the legal community, especially the county prosecutors, for refusing to bring murder charges against the Klansmen who participated in the killings of Schwerner, Chaney, and Goodman. Florence Mars is another brave citizen of Philadelphia who spoke out against the Klan and wrote a book about the 1964 murders: *Witness in Philadelphia* (Baton Rouge: Louisiana State University Press, 1977). Still another person who supported equal rights and befriended Michael Schwerner was Buford Posey, a white resident of Philadelphia who was forced to leave the state immediately after the deaths of the three civil rights workers in late June 1964. On the night of their murders, Posey received a phone call from a man he believes was "Preacher" Killen, who told him, "We took

care of three of your friends tonight. You're next!" After the threat, Posey left town. See Ball, *Murder in Mississippi*, p. 62.

30. Editorial, "Was Justice Really Served?" June 22, 2005, http://www .workers.org/2005/editorials/civil-rights-0630/index.html.

31. Quoted in Younge, "Racism Rebooted," pp. 12–13.

32. Some of the results of reopening racial murder cases in the 1990s by state prosecutors follow: (1) Klansmen Bobby Frank Cherry and Thomas E. Blanton Jr. were indicted in May 2000 by an Alabama grand jury for the bombing murders of four Birmingham, Alabama, black girls in the September 1963 bombing of the Sixteenth Street Baptist Church; both men were convicted of murder in separate trials, Cherry in 2001 and Blanton in 2002; (2) Byron De La Beckwith was convicted in 1994 for the June 1963 murder of Mississippi NAACP Field Secretary Medgar Evers; (3) In his fifth trial, in August 1998, Mississippi Ku Klux Klan Imperial Wizard Sam Bowers was convicted for ordering the 1966 murder of a local black civil rights leader, Vernon Dahmer Sr.; (4) three Klansmen from Humphrey County, Mississippi, were brought to trial in November 1999 and convicted of manslaughter in the 1970 murder of Rodney Pool, a one-armed sharecropper; and (5) Mississippi Klansman Ernest Avants was convicted in March 2003 for the killing of a black sharecropper, Ben Chester White, in 1966.

33. Jerry Mitchell, "Killen's Arrest Challenges Nation's Views of Mississippi," *Jackson Clarion-Ledger*, January 11, 2005, p. A1. In May 2005, the body of fourteen-year-old Emmett Till, murdered in Money, Mississippi, in 1955 for allegedly whistling at a white woman, was exhumed by the FBI. If the examination turns up information about Till's death, there may be further legal action by federal or state authorities. See note 32 for the four other Mississippi trials that took place beginning in the 1990s. Meanwhile, in July 2005, Henry Lee Loggins, now eighty-two years old but in 1955 a young black who was taken with Till by the whites who murdered Till, indicated through his son that he would be willing to talk to prosecutors about the murder if he received immunity from prosecution. Immunity, said his son, Mayor Johnny Thomas of Glendora, Mississippi, "would give him freedom to speak about the situation." At the 1955 trial of two white men, Roy Bryant and J. W. Milan, one witness said there were four white men and three blacks in a truck with Till. Both Bryant and Milan were acquitted of the murder in September 1955. One month later the two men confessed their guilt to a reporter for *Look* magazine. See Jerry Mitchell, "Immunity Sought in Till Case," *Jackson Clarion-Ledger*, July 29, 2005, p. A1.

34. See Sheila Byrd, "Mississippi Opens Inquiry into 1964 Deaths," *Burlington Free Press*, July 23, 2005, p. 2A.

35. See "Media Alert: Mississippi Learning," *Jackson Free Press*, July 20, 2005, www.jacksonfreepress.com.

36. Byrd, "Mississippi Opens Inquiry," p. 2A.

37. Poll results published in Mitchell, "Almost Half in Neshoba Survey."

38. In his novel *Intruder in the Dust*, William Faulkner wrote, of the past: "The past is not dead. It's not even past."

39. Quoted in Younge, "Racism Rebooted," p. 14.

40. Majure gave an example of the Klan's "good deeds": When a husband was known to beat his wife, the Klan would pay him a visit to suggest that he act like a good Christian in his relationship with her. See Circuit Court of Neshoba County, Mississippi, *State of Mississippi vs. Edgar Ray Killen*, No. 05-CR-0006-NS-G, 2005 (Killen trial transcript).

41. See the latest *Intelligence Report* data on Ku Klux Klan and other hate groups, published annually by the Southern Poverty Law Center, Montgomery, Alabama, http://www.splcenter.org/intel/intelreport/intrep.jsp.

42. Tucker, "Mississippi Turning."

43. According to data collected by the U.S. Department of Justice, between the 1880s and the 1960s, more than 4,700 lynchings took place. Mississippi alone had almost 600 public executions. See also James Allen, Hilton Als, John Lewis, and Leon F. Litwack, *Without Sanctuary: Lynching Photography in America* (Santa Fe, NM: Twin Palms, 2000).

44. The Ku Klux Klan was born in Tennessee in the months immediately following the conclusion of the Civil War. It resurfaced again in the 1920s and, once more, in the early to mid-1960s.

45. http://www.olemiss.edu/winterinstitute/.

46. This excellent June 22–24, 2005, program for teachers, The Chaney, Goodman, and Schwerner Living Memorial Civil Rights Education Summit, was held in the Philadelphia middle school. It unintentionally but fortunately coincided with the Killen trial in Philadelphia. The almost fifty teachers were able to attend the last day of the trial. See the coalition's civil rights tour brochure "Roots of Struggle, Rewards of Freedom: African-American Heritage Driving Tour" at http://www.neshobajustice.com/RootsofStruggle.pdf.

47. Susan M. Glisson, "On Truth and Freedom," *Wellspring* 2, 1 (May 2005): 5.

48. See, generally, Howard Ball, *Prosecuting War Crimes and Genocide: The Twentieth-Century Experience* (Lawrence: University of Kansas Press, 1999), for a discussion of the TRC experiences in international reconciliation efforts after conflict has ended. The South African Truth and Reconciliation Commission (TRC) was set up in 1995 by the Government of National Unity to help deal with what happened under apartheid. The conflict during this period resulted in violence and human rights abuses from all sides. No section of society escaped these abuses. The TRC is based on the document "No. 34 of 1995: Promotion of Na-

tional Unity and Reconciliation Act, 1995" (available at http://www.doj.gov.za/trc/ index.html). The TRC effects its mandate through three committees: the Amnesty Committee, Reparation and Rehabilitation (R&R) Committee, and Human Rights Violations (HRV) Committee. The Commission is currently in suspension while the work of the Amnesty Committee is completed. The remaining work of the R&R and HRV Committees has been designated to the former Chairs of those Committees, and now forms part of the Amnesty Committee.

49. Telephone interview, Susan Glisson, September 6, 2005.

50. "Michael Schwerner's widow was in a Civil Procedures class I taught at Rutgers University," wrote U.S. Supreme Court Associate Justice Ruth Bader Ginsburg. "She was a woman of diminutive size, but large courage." Letter, Justice Ruth Bader Ginsburg to Howard Ball, February 1, 2005.

51. Statement of the Philadelphia Coalition, January 21, 2005. See http://www.neshobajustice.com/.

52. Donna Ladd, "Mississippi Learning," *Jackson Free Press*, July 20, 2005, p. 2. Compare her words with those spoken by Bishop Desmond Tutu, the Chair of the South African Truth and Reconciliation Commission: "Our people have been committed to the reconciliation where we use restorative rather than retributive justice, which is a kind of justice, that says—we are looking to the healing of relationships, we are seeking to open wounds, yes, but to open them so that we can cleanse them and they don't fester; we cleanse them and then pour oil on them, and then we can move into the glorious future that God is opening up for us." See "Archbishop Desmond Tutu, October 6, 1999" (A NewsHour with Jim Lehrer Transcript), http://www.pbs.org/newshour/bb/africa/july-dec99/tutu_10-6 .html.

53. South African Bishop Desmond Tutu, a Nobel Peace Prize recipient and the chair of the South African TRC, said that reconciliation would not work unless there was a change in the ways in which economic goods are delivered to the people: "Our commission's report underscored the importance of a physical transformation, of changing the quality of life of the most deprived, and we have said that unless the gap between the rich and the poor, which is very wide, is narrowed, *then you could just as well kiss reconciliation goodbye*, and, therefore, we are urging those who have—for their own sakes—to be eager to participate and drive on the process of transformation in South Africa [my emphasis]." See ibid.

54. *Jackson Clarion-Ledger*, July 17, 2005, p. 1.

55. William Raspberry, "Racial Fairness Still a Dream, but There's Movement in Mississippi," *Jackson Clarion-Ledger*, June 22, 2005, p. A16.

56. "Archbishop Desmond Tutu, October 6, 1999."

Chapter Two.
The 1964 Murders and the Long Silence, 1964–1989

1. Quoted in Howard Ball, *Murder in Mississippi: United States v. Price and the Struggle for Civil Rights* (Lawrence: University of Kansas Press, 2004), p. 81.

2. Ibid., p. 119.

3. "Excerpts from Barbour Speech," online at http://www.neshoba democrat.com/main.asp?Search=1&ArticleID=8267&SectionID=20&SubSection ID=330&S=1.

4. See, generally, Sally Belfrage, *Freedom Summer* (New York: Viking, 1965).

5. Quoted in Jerry Mitchell, "Mississippi's Best Hope," *Jackson Clarion-Ledger*, June 12, 2005, p. A1.

6. Quoted in John Sugg, "Mississippi Emotion," *Truthout/Report*, June 20, 2005, http://www.truthout.org/docs_2005/062005N.shtml.

7. An observation by David Sims, a civil rights worker who lived in Meridian and from whose house the three men left to visit the burned-out church in Neshoba County. Quoted in ibid.

8. Quoted in Mitchell, "Mississippi's Best Hope."

9. COFO, the Council of Federated Organizations, was created in February 1962 to function as an umbrella organization to unify local and national civil rights groups such as the NAACP, CORE, and SNCC. Bob Moses, of SNCC, was the director of COFO.

10. Nine years earlier, in the 1955 murder trial of two white men charged with the murder of fourteen-year-old Emmett Till, both defense attorneys, in their closing arguments to the jury, said the same thing. Joseph Kellum told the twelve white men that they were "absolutely the custodians of American civilization." John W. Whitten, Jr., the other defense counsel, in his closing said: "There are people in the United States who want to destroy the way of life of Southern people. . . . I'm sure that every last Anglo-Saxon one of you men in this jury has the courage to set these men free." Both quoted in Richard Rubin, "The Ghosts of Emmett Till," *New York Times Sunday Magazine*, July 31, 2005, pp. 33, 34.

11. In the mid-twentieth century, the *Jackson Clarion-Ledger* was an ally of the White Citizens' Council, the State Sovereignty Commission, the segregationist state government, and the Klan. Indeed, it was designated by a national press association as the "worst paper in America" at the time.

12. Jim Prince, "Historical Context of 1964 Civil Rights Murders," *Neshoba Democrat*, April 28, 2004, p. 1.

13. Philadelphia Coalition, *Neshoba County: African-American Heritage*

Driving Tour, Philadelphia, Mississippi (Philadelphia, MS: Community Development Partnership, 2004), p. 20.

14. Who would do the shooting, who would use the backhoe to dig a burial site for the dead trio, whose property would be used to bury them, and who would give the guns used in the executions were some of the matters that Killen dealt with while Schwerner, Goodman, and Chaney were held in the jail. See Circuit Court of Neshoba County, Mississippi, *State of Mississippi vs. Edgar Ray Killen,* No. 05-CR-0006-NS-G, 2005, hereinafter cited as KTT (Killen trial transcript). See KTT, vol. 4, pp. 619–694 (transcript testimony of Carlton Wallace Miller and Ernest Kirkland); pp. 752–775 (Delmar Dennis transcript testimony); pp. 792–820 (James Jordan transcript testimony).

15. During closing arguments, the Mississippi Attorney General, Jim Hood, pointed to a seated and "seething" Killen and said: "It was a mob that murdered those young men, . . . and th[e] coward [who led the mob] is still sitting right here in this courtroom right there. . . . That venom is sitting right there seething behind those glasses. That coward wants to hide and put the pressure on you. . . . This is the man right here that has that venom. This is the man that needs to be held responsible, and there he sits, wanting your sympathy." At this instant, the Preacher murmured, "you son-of-a-bitch!" KTT, vol. 4, pp. 954–955; Howard Ball, "When Past Becomes Present," *Burlington Free Press,* June 20, 2005, p. 7.

16. Mitchell, "Mississippi's Best Hope."

17. Quotes from the trial transcript, *U.S. vs. Cecil Price, et. al,* 1967, KTT, Vol. 4, 674–675, 794–796. See, generally, Ball, *Murder in Mississippi.*

18. Quoted in Mitchell, "Mississippi's Best Hope."

19. Quoted in Ana Radelat, "Arrest Applauded Nationally," *Jackson Clarion-Ledger,* January 8, 2005, p. A1.

20. Quoted in Radelat, "Arrest Applauded." In the early 1970s Burns returned to Mississippi as the head of the NAACP in Mississippi.

21. Eastland made that observation when he spoke with President Lyndon Baines Johnson. See Ball, *Murder in Mississippi,* pp. 64–73, for additional "observations" by Mississippi state and national elected officials, all maintaining that it was a hoax. Even after the bodies were found, the Mississippi argument was that the three were murdered by COFO officials in order to create "martyrs" for the civil rights cause.

22. Quoted in Rubin, "The Ghosts of Emmett Till," p. 34.

23. Quoted in ibid., p. 32.

24. In 2005 the body of Emmett Till was exhumed by the FBI and law enforcement officials speculated that his murder would be reinvestigated, but Bryant and Milam have died; others have been named as possible coconspirators in Till's death. In March 2006 federal officials ended the review without taking any action.

25. Quoted in Mitchell, "Mississippi's Best Hope."

26. See Ball, *Murder in Mississippi,* for one speculative argument. See, generally, Jerry Mitchell, "Reward: Whether FBI Ever Paid Money Remains Matter of Speculation among Many," *Jackson Clarion-Ledger,* January 8, 2001, p. A1.

27. Jerry Mitchell, "Mr. X 'Unsung Hero' in Slaying of 3 Men," *Jackson Clarion-Ledger,* June 13, 2005, p. A1.

28. Philip Dray, quoted in Mitchell, "Mr. X."

29. Ibid.

30. Quoted in Mitchell, "Reward."

31. Ibid.

32. The 1870 Enforcement Act was based on the power of Congress, in Section 5 of the Fourteenth Amendment (ratified in 1868), to pass legislation that would "enforce" the provisions of the Fourteenth Amendment.

33. 18 U.S.C. Section 241, the "conspiracy" statute, in part, states: "If two or more persons conspire to injure, oppress, threaten, or intimidate any person in any State . . . in the free exercise or enjoyment of any right or privilege secured to him by the Constitution or laws of the United States, . . . they shall be fined not more than $5,000 under this title or imprisoned not more than ten years, or both." In 1968, the Section was amended by Congress to provide for the possibility of life imprisonment if the conspiracy led to the deaths of persons. See Ball, *Murder in Mississippi,* pp. 115–118, passim.

34. Quoted in Ball, *Murder in Mississippi,* p. 80.

35. *Neshoba Democrat,* "Scorching Report Issued by Grand Jury," October 1, 1964, p. 1.

36. The grand jury report, in its entirety, was published in the *Neshoba Democrat,* October 1, 1964.

37. An incident at the December 1964 hearing before Commissioner Carter is a reflection of the time. Deputy Sheriff Cecil Price was late arriving at the federal courthouse in Meridian. The reason for the Klansman's tardiness, in his own words: "It took me an hour to get here this morning. I had to shake so many hands!"

38. In 1966, in the case of *United States vs. Cecil Price, et al.,* 385 U.S. 787 (1966), a unanimous U.S. Supreme Court, in an opinion written by Associate Justice Abe Fortas, invalidated Judge Cox's very narrow interpretation of Section 241, the "conspiracy" statute. For a general examination of the constitutional and statutory questions raised in the Price case, see, generally, Ball, *Murder in Mississippi,* pp. 101–110.

39. The "Allen" charge to a deadlocked jury is an instruction approved by the U.S. Supreme Court in the case of *Allen v. United States,* 164 U.S. 492 (1896), that "the jurors should examine the questions submitted with candor and with a proper regard and deference to the opinions of each other." Quoted in James A.

Ballentine, *Ballentine's Law Dictionary*, 3d ed. (Rochester, NY: Lawyers Cooperative Publishing Company, 1969), p. 61.

40. The seven found guilty were Sam Bowers, Cecil Price, Billy Wayne Posey, Wayne Roberts, Jimmy Arledge, Jimmy Snowden, and Horace Doyle Barnette.

41. One of the three men who walked out of the courthouse because the jury deadlocked was Edgar Ray Killen, the Neshoba County Kleagle who hatched the murder plot after Schwerner, Chaney, and Goodman were detained by Price and held in the Philadelphia jail. In his case, the jurors deadlocked 11–1 because a female juror could not convict a preacher man.

42. Quoted in Ball, *Murder in Mississippi*, p. 61. Barbara Arnwine, the executive director of the Lawyer's Committee for Civil Rights (LCCR), recalled that the LCCR sent lawyers to Philadelphia at the end of August 1964. "It was a horrible atmosphere, a lawless environment." Quoted in Redelat, "Arrest Applauded."

43. Associated Press, "Former Volunteer Finds Closure in Killen Conviction," *Jackson Clarion-Ledger*, July 10, 2005, p. A1.

44. Jim Prince, "Editorial: Why Stir Up the Past?" *Neshoba Democrat*, June 24, 2004, p. 1.

45. Rubin, "The Ghosts of Emmett Till," p. 36.

46. Quoted in Neely Tucker, "Mississippi Turning," *Washington Post*, June 16, 2005, p. C01.

Chapter Three. From Silence to Dialogue: Initial Efforts to Reopen the 1964 Murders Case, 1989–2001

1. Neely Tucker, "Mississippi Turning," *Washington Post*, June 16, 2005, p. C01.

2. Quoted in *CBS Evening News*, "Justice Late, but Justice Still," October 2, 2000. See http://www.cbsnews.com/stories/2000/10/02/eveningnews/main 237965.shtml.

3. Adam Nossiter, *Of Long Memory: Mississippi and the Murder of Emmett Till* (Cambridge, MA: Da Capo Press, 2002), p. 4.

4. Interview, Sid Salter, June 20, 2005, Philadelphia, Mississippi.

5. Mike Hatcher, testimony, Circuit Court of Neshoba County, Mississippi, *State of Mississippi vs. Edgar Ray Killen*, No. 05-CR-0006-NS-G, 2005, Vol. 4, p. 925.

6. Sid Salter, "Philadelphia Coalition Seeks Reconciliation in Neshoba Today," *Clarion-Ledger*, June 20, 2004, p. G1.

7. Stanley Dearman recollection; quoted in Associated Press, "Murder

Brought Charges to Mississippi Klan Leader, Minister Known as 'Preacher,'" *Connecticut Post,* June 27, 2005, p. A1.

8. Stanley Dearman, quoted in Mark Minton, "Mississippi: In Search of Justice," *Arkansas Democrat-Gazette,* January 30, 2005, p. A1.

9. A "jackleg" preacher is a preacher without a church, a traveling preacher.

10. From trial transcript, quoted in Jerry Mitchell, "Preacher Refused Plea Deal in '75," *Jackson Clarion-Ledger,* May 1, 2005, p. A1.

11. Jim Prince, "Mississippi Transitioning," *Neshoba Democrat,* June 24, 2004, p. 1.

12. In 1989, Mitchell published excerpts from the still-secret Mississippi State Sovereignty Commission (MSSC) files, documents that clearly show the symbiotic relationship between the commission, state government, the White Citizens' Councils, and the KKK. Rita Schwerner Bender, Michael Schwerner's widow, reads these and begins her long effort to get Mississippi law enforcement officials to bring murder charges against the Klansmen who committed the 1964 crime.

13. Stanley Dearman, interview with Dr. Carolyn Goodman, April 26, 1989, "His Whole Life Led to Decision to Be in Mississippi in 1964," reprinted in *Neshoba Democrat,* June 23, 2004, p. 1.

14. Quoted in Sid Salter, "Sunday Morning with Stanley Dearman," *Jackson Clarion-Ledger,* June 20, 2004, p. G1.

15. Ibid.

16. Dearman, "His Whole Life Led."

17. Quoted in Salter, "Sunday Morning."

18. The complete interview can be found at http://www.neshobademocrat .com/Main.asp?SectionID=20&SubSectionID=330&ArticleID=8246.

19. The "seventh inning stretch" is a hallowed tradition for baseball fans at any ballpark in America. Fans of the visiting team, in this case, the opponent of the Brooklyn Dodgers, would stand up and literally "stretch" in support of their team. Brooklyn Dodgers fans, however, stood up at the bottom of the seventh inning, the home seventh, and stretched for their Bums.

20. Dearman, "His Whole Life Led."

21. Salter, "Sunday Morning."

22. Dearman, "His Whole Life Led."

23. M. Susan Orr-Klopfer, *Where Rebels Roost: Mississippi Civil Rights Revisited* (2005, available at http://www.lulu.com/content/135246).

24. See, generally, Adam Nossiter's 1994 book, *Of Long Memory: Mississippi and the Murder of Medgar Evers* (Cambridge, MA: Da Capo Press, 2002, reprint), for an accurate account of the events that occurred after Mitchell's story was published in the *Jackson Clarion-Ledger.*

25. Minton, "Mississippi: In Search of Justice."

26. *CBS Evening News,* "Justice Late, but Justice Still."

27. Although Bowers did not mention Killen by name in the initial conversations with the state archivist, in 2004, he did tell state officials in the attorney general's office that Killen carried out the 1964 plot to kill Schwerner, Chaney, and Goodman. See, generally, "A Chronology: Turning Points in the Neshoba Slayings Case," *Jackson Clarion-Ledger,* June 22, 2005. Also see Bowers's March 30, 2004, interview with Jim Gilliland, Attorney General's Office, in Case File Number 2K.0076W, State of Mississippi, Office of the Attorney General, Public Integrity Division.

28. Segments of the interview found in Jerry Mitchell, "Interview Unfurls History," *Jackson Clarion-Ledger,* June 12, 2005, p. A1. Elsewhere in the interview, Bowers said that, in 1954, "I think I would have probably joined more enthusiastically in hanging a white [U.S.] Supreme Court Justice than I would be a nigger rapist, and I would do that even today." He labeled himself "a criminal and a lunatic."

29. Quoted in Howard Ball, *Murder in Mississippi: United States v. Price and the Struggle for Civil Rights* (Lawrence: University Press of Kansas, 2004), p. 144.

30. See, for example, her 2005 interview in Minton, "Mississippi: In Search of Justice."

31. His long-time deputy district attorney, Mark Duncan, was elected to the position in November 2003 and took office in January 2004.

32. Quoted in Minton, "Mississippi: In Search of Justice."

33. See Donna Ladd, "Unfinished Business: Mississippi's Struggles with Racist Past and Present," unpublished master's thesis, Columbia University School of Journalism, 2000.

34. Mississippi Oral History Program, University of Southern Mississippi, interview with Alton G. Bankston, November 17, 1999, p. 4. See http://www.lib .usm.edu/~spcol/coh/cohbankstona.html.

35. Quoted in "On the Road: Mississippi, Past and Present," Voices of Civil Rights: Bus Tour, at http://www.voicesofcivilrights.org/bustour/journal_entry 16.html.

36. Ana Radalet, "Former Governor Vying for Top DNC Post," *Jackson Clarion-Ledger,* December 8, 2004, p. A1.

37. Republican Kirk Fordice defeated Mabus in the 1992 election. Fordice was the first Republican governor of Mississippi since the nineteenth-century Reconstruction era.

38. Moore's successful strategy was to sue the tobacco industry to recover

all the state Medicaid funds expended to treat citizens who were unalterably addicted to tobacco and contracted a variety of illnesses due to their addiction.

39. See Moore interview on *Frontline*, "Inside the Tobacco Deal," February 1998, PBS, at http://www.pbs.org/wgbh/pages/frontline/shows/settlement/.

40. Ben Chaney, "Schwerner, Chaney, and Goodman: The Struggle for Justice," speech given in 1999 before the New York Bar Association. Reprinted in *Human Rights Magazine*, Spring 2000, published by the American Bar Association, Section of Individual Rights and Responsibilities. Speech available online at http://www.abanet.org/irr/hr/spring00humanrights/chaney.html.

41. Ibid.

42. Quoted in Ball, *Murder in Mississippi*, p. 146.

43. Quoted in Ladd, "Unfinished Business," p. 41.

44. Telephone interview, James Gilliland, August 24, 2005, Mississippi Attorney General's Office.

45. Editorial, *Neshoba Democrat*, May 3, 2000, at http://www.neshoba democrat.com/main.asp?Search=1&ArticleID=9396&SectionID=20&SubSection ID=330&S=1.

46. *CBS Evening News*, "An Old Wound Reopened," October 3, 2000. See http://www.cbsnews.com/stories/2000/10/03/evening news/main238302/shtml.

47. Telephone interview, James Gilliland, August 24, 2005. The other Klansmen interviewed in 2000 and/or in 2004 were Billy Wayne Posey, April 5, 2000 (and again in 2004 by Attorney General Hood); Sam Bowers, March 30, 2004; Jimmy Arledge, April 5, 2000; and Jimmy Snowden, April 6, 2000. Reports of the interviews are in the files of Case Number 2K.0076.W, State of Mississippi, Office of the Attorney General, Public Integrity Division.

48. Telephone interview, Jim Hood, August 17, 2005. At one point the attorney general said that Price would have made a great witness for the state and that it was a "darn shame that he died."

49. Ibid.

50. Ibid.

51. Horace Doyle Barnett's November 20, 1964, confession to the FBI, given in New Orleans, Louisiana, from FBI MIBURN file, dated November 24, 1964.

52. In an interview published in 1977, Price intimates changes in his attitudes about race and racism, evidently after watching the ABC-TV miniseries *Roots*. See Roy Reed, "Philadelphia, Miss.: Erasing Memories of Violence," *New York Times*, February 17, 1977, p. A1. In 2000, saying his views on integration had changed, Price remarked: "We've got to accept this is the way things are going to be and that's it." Quoted in Ball, *Murder in Mississippi*, p. 139.

53. Letter, Ken Turner III to J. Max Kilpatrick, November 17, 1999. From files of Mississippi attorney general, Jackson, Mississippi.

54. A "proffer" is an offer, in this case, by the Mississippi attorney general to Price, to provide immunity from any criminal action.

55. Report: "Interview—Cecil Ray Price," State of Mississippi, Office of the Attorney General, Public Integrity Division, March 5 and 27, 2000, 3 pp. The quotes that follow are taken from this interview.

56. Report, "Subject: Cecil Ray Price Polygraph," State of Mississippi, Office of the Attorney General, Public Integrity Division, August 17, 2000, Case Number: 2K.0076.W, p. 1.

57. Report: "Interview—Bob Stringer," State of Mississippi, Office of the Attorney General, Public Integrity Division, n/d, 2000, March 18, 2004, 2 pp. At the very end of the 2004 interview, typed in capital letters ten days later: BOB STRINGER COMMITTED SUICIDE ON MARCH 28, 2004.

58. *CBS Evening News*, "Justice Late, but Justice Still."

59. Quoted in Ball, *Murder in Mississippi*, p. 146.

60. Essentially Metz told Gilliland that on June 22, 1964, he met Killen in Philadelphia. The Preacher told Metz that he had received a phone call from an unidentified man who told Killen that the 'activity on Rock Cut Road' needed to be checked for any evidence possibly left behind after the murders. However, "according to Metz, Killen has never admitted involvement in the Philadelphia murders." Report: "Interview—George Metz," State of Mississippi, Office of the Attorney General, Public Integrity Division, Case File Number: 2K.0076.W, August 2, 2001.

61. Quoted in Minton, "Mississippi: In Search of Justice."

62. Nossiter, *Of Long Memory*, p. 3.

63. Brian MacQuarrie, "Mississippi Town Forges a Hopeful Future from Racist Past," *Boston Globe*, June 20, 2005, p. 1.

64. Ibid.

65. Ibid.

Chapter Four. Toward the Indictment of
Edgar Ray "Preacher" Killen, 2002–2005

1. Quoted in Michael E. Ross, "Freedom Summer's Agony Revisited," MSNBC, June 9, 2005, http://www.msnbc.msn.com/id/7209834/.

2. Quoted in Sheila Byrd, "Former Klansman Pleads Not Guilty," *Tallahassee Times*, January 8, 2005, p. 1.

3. Quoted in John F. Sugg, "Racial Healing in Mississippi," *Truthout/*

Report, June 29, 2005, http://www.truthout.org/docs_2005/printer_0629050
.shtml.

4. Quoted in Gary Younge, "Racism Rebooted," *Nation,* July 11, 2005,
p. 10.

5. Duncan assumed the position of district attorney in Neshoba County in
November 2003 because his boss, Ken Turner III, resigned during that month and
Duncan, who was the deputy district attorney, took over.

6. On June 14, 2005, during voir dire proceedings in the Killen trial,
Duncan confided to Jerry Mitchell: "I knew I would have to deal with [the case]
one way or another. I'm anxious to get done with this and go back to being a small-
town DA nobody ever heard of." Quoted in Jerry Mitchell, "High Profile Case Puts
Spotlight on Humble DA," *Jackson Clarion-Ledger,* June 15, 2005, p. A1.

7. Quoted in Mark Minton, "Mississippi: In Search of Justice," *Arkansas
Democrat-Gazette,* January 30, 2005, p. A1.

8. Sugg, "Racial Healing in Mississippi."

9. See, generally, Virginia Foster Durr, *Outside the Magic Circle*
(Tuscaloosa: University of Alabama Press, 1985, 1990), and John A. Salmond, *The
Conscience of a Lawyer: Clifford J. Durr and American Civil Liberties, 1899–1975*
(Tuscaloosa: University of Alabama Press, 1990).

10. See, generally, Howard Ball, *Hugo L. Black: Cold Steel Warrior* (New
York: Oxford University Press, 1995).

11. Her speech is located in the archives of the University of Alabama
School of Law, in Tuscaloosa, Alabama, under "1988–1989 100th Anniversary
Celebration of the Life of Justice Hugo L. Black."

12. Quoted in Sugg, "Racial Healing in Mississippi."

13. Ibid.

14. When the legislators found out about the black-white ratio and that
"Ole Miss" was not included because it did not have an accredited public administration program, many were livid, especially those who graduated from that university. However, that realization came after the legislation and the appropriations
for it had been signed into law by Winter. Consequently, whenever the legislative
newsletter had a story about these bright interns, it never published photos of
them.

15. During Governor Mabus's administration (1988–1992), Mabus, Molpus, and Moore, the three M's, were called the "Boys of Summer." Quoted in
Suggs, "Racial Healing in Mississippi."

16. Interview, Dick Molpus, taped, June 29, 2005, Jackson, Mississippi.

17. Suggs raised the question in his essay "Racial Healing."

18. Quoted in ibid.

19. Quoted in ibid.

20. Interview, Dick Molpus.

21. In 1997, then-President Bill Clinton inaugurated an unprecedented national conversation on race. "One America: The President's Initiative on Race" marked the first time a sitting president had called for such a dialogue without the catalyst of a major crisis. It suggested, on a federal level, the importance of dealing positively with race relations on a daily basis. Accepting the challenge to prod grassroots efforts, the University of Mississippi hosted the only deep-South public forum for One America. Preceded by dialogue groups representing ten constituency topics ranging from the arts to education to religion, the event highlighted elected delegates from each group. Sharing the insight and hopes of the more than 160 participants, the representatives crafted a frank yet civil discussion on one of our nation's most difficult subjects. The President's staff hailed the UM experience as the single most successful of the entire Initiative year. That recognition encouraged the University to formalize its dialogue process with the creation of an institute to promote racial reconciliation and civic renewal. Founded in 1999, the William Winter Institute for Racial Reconciliation builds more inclusive communities by promoting diversity and citizenship and by supporting projects that help communities solve local challenges. "The Institute for Racial Reconciliation fosters reconciliation and civic renewal wherever people suffer as a result of discrimination or alienation. The Institute identifies and disseminates information on effective models of cooperation. It supports leadership and community development through outreach projects in partnerships spanning local communities, policy-makers and education institutions. The Institute's non-partisan work is grounded in the equal participation of University representatives and local community members to discover and apply constructive responses to past and continuing inequities caused by exclusion." See their Web site at http://www.olemiss.edu/winterinstitute.

22. Glisson received B.A. degrees in Christianity and history from Mercer University, an M.A. in Southern studies from University of Mississippi, and a Ph.D. in American studies from the College of William and Mary. She has written *Neither Bedecked nor Bebosomed: Ella Baker, Lucy Mason and Women's Leadership and Organizing in the Struggle for Freedom* (forthcoming), and her teaching and research specializations are women's history, the civil rights movement, race relations, and religion.

23. See "Winter Heads Winter Institute for Racial Reconciliation," http://www.olemiss.edu/depts/south/register/fall03/sixteen.htm.

24. Interview with Susan Glisson, taped, June 24, 2005, Philadelphia, Mississippi. When I asked her who was responsible for getting things started in Neshoba County, she instantly answered: "Dick Molpus!"

25. Ibid.

26. "Sitting under a huge picture of Ronald and Nancy Reagan's visit to the Neshoba County Fair in 1981," Prince told one reporter that he initially was against reopening the 1964 triple murder case, "but gradually came to see that the town could not move on without some resolution. 'Philadelphia would benefit,' he said, 'because the trial would be the outcome of doing the right thing. There would be some vindication, some redemption, some soul-cleansing. It will be the atonement, really, for this old sin. We have only the legal system to go by. That's all we've got. . . . I tell people if they can't be behind the call for justice because it's the right thing to do—and that's first and foremost—then they need to do it 'cause it's good for business.'" Quoted in Younge, "Racism Rebooted," p. 11.

27. Quoted in Sid Salter, "Sunday Morning with Stanley Dearman," *Jackson Clarion-Ledger*, July 3, 2005, p. G1.

28. Billy Wayne Posey served six years in a federal penitentiary. After his release he returned to Meridian and, for a while, managed a convenience store located in Meridian's black community. He is now retired and still living in Meridian. He was one of the Klansmen interviewed by Hood and Duncan in the months before the grand jury met in January 2005. Like all the others, he refused to testify or to tell what he knew about the 1964 murders.

29. Interview, Deborah Posey, taped, June 22, 2005, Philadelphia, Mississippi.

30. Ibid.

31. Ibid.

32. Interview, Susan Glisson, June 29, 2005.

33. Interview, Fenton DeWeese, June 22, 2005, Philadelphia, Mississippi.

34. See http://www.neshobajustice.com.

35. Interview, Dick Molpus.

36. Quoted in Sugg, "Racial Healing in Mississippi."

37. Quoted in Salter, "Sunday Morning."

38. See http://neshobajustice.com/resolution.htm.

39. Editorial, "Justice Call 'Reshaping Neshoba Legacy,'" *Neshoba Democrat*, June 24, 2004, p. 1.

40. See his series, "Genetic Disaster: A Story of Fate, Faith, and Family," in the *Jackson Clarion-Ledger* archives, online at http://www.clarionledger.com/archives. Mitchell's series, ten essays about the medical monster that ravished his family, ran between 2001 and 2004, although he began his search for the monster in the 1980s. Jerry found out about the disease in 1974 when he was a fourteen-year-old kid nicknamed "Boo," watching his grandfather, "Daddy Sam," die a slow and painful death from the disease.

41. Family doctors began to refer to the muscular dystrophy in the family as hereditary inclusion body myopathy.

42. Mitchell, "Genetic Disaster," Part 9.

43. Mitchell, "Genetic Disaster," Part 1. Compare his thoughts with those of Jewell MacDonald (see Chapter Three), a black member of the Philadelphia Coalition.

44. The James Earl Chaney Foundation is a 501 (c) (3) not-for-profit Human Rights, Civil Rights and Social Justice Advocacy organization. Its mission: "Protecting the constitutional rights of all Americans. We are committed to the right of equal protection and treatment under law. We believe in a government that respects the rights of all Americans—equally and without bias in regard to race, creed, religion, ethnicity, and sexuality." See the organization's Web site at http://www. jecf.org.

45. http://www.jecf.org/Programs.htm.

46. Quoted on CNN, "Man Seeks Trial in Brother's 1964 Murder," at http://www.cnn.com/2004/LAW/02/24/mississippi.killing.ap/. Chaney's mother, who has lived in New York and New Jersey since she was forced to leave Meridian in 1964, testified in the 2005 murder trial of Edgar Ray Killen.

47. All quotes that follow are found in *Neshoba Democrat*, Archives, http://www.neshobademocrat.com.

48. Donna Ladd, "Dick Molpus Raises the Roof in Neshoba County," *Jackson Free Press*, June 20, 2004, at http://www.jacksonfreepress.com/comments.php?id=A3227_0_22_0_C.

49. "The voting Tuesday capped months of campaigning that put Mississippi in the national spotlight, pitting a well-known GOP operative critical of state spending against an incumbent who touted his efforts to improve education and job creation." Julie Goodman, "Republican Challenger Unseats Musgrove," *Jackson Clarion-Ledger*, November 5, 2003, p. A1.

50. Quoted in Jim Prince, "Neshoba Acknowledges '64 Murders," *Neshoba Democrat*, June 24, 2004, p. 1.

51. Editorial, "The Courage to Seek Justice," *Neshoba Democrat*, June 24, 2004, at http://www.neshobademocrat.com/main.asp?Search=1&ArticleID=8258&SectionID=20&SubSectionID=330&S=1.

52. Editorial, "Forty Years Later, Healing Begins," *Jackson Clarion-Ledger*, June 20, 2004, p. G4.

53. District Attorney Duncan was not at the meeting, for at the time he was prosecuting another murder case.

54. Telephone interview, Stanley Dearman, September 7, 2005.

55. Ibid.

56. Jerry Mitchell, "As Crime Victim, Hood Understands Wanting Justice," *Jackson Clarion-Ledger*, January 9, 2005, p. A1.

57. In Mississippi, it is legal to read testimony from an earlier trial if (1)

the witness had died and if (2) the witness was cross-examined by defense counsel in the earlier trial.

58. In part, Jordan's confession clearly indicated that Killen was the Klansman who met with Lauderdale and Neshoba County Klansmen in Meridian and worked out the plan for the tragic event that occurred on the night of June 21, 1964. For example, Jordan's confession states: "'Preacher' Killen asked if everyone had their guns, and everyone present said that they did. Killen advised the second [of two cars] that they should meet him on the west side of the courthouse in Philadelphia, Mississippi. . . . Killen got into the car and said that he would show the group where they could go so they could park and watch for the [civil rights] workers when they were released from jail." See FBI Archive documents, MIBURN File, for full confession.

59. Interview, Mark Duncan, taped, June 27, 2005, Philadelphia, Mississippi.

60. Quoted in Mitchell, "High-Profile Case."

61. While they spoke regularly about the case, the issue itself—whether or not the state should reopen the investigation into the murders of Schwerner, Chaney, and Goodman—was "rarely mentioned" during their respective 2003 campaigns. Interview, Mark Duncan.

62. Ibid.

63. Telephone interview, Jim Hood, taped, August 3, 2005.

64. Interview, Mark Duncan.

65. Ibid.

66. Report: "Interview of Jimmy Arledge," State of Mississippi, Office of the Attorney General, Public Integrity Division, Case File Number 2K.0076.W. An earlier interview took place on April 5, 2000.

67. Report: "Interview: Billy Wayne Posey," State of Mississippi, Office of the Attorney General, Public Integrity Division, Case File Number 2K.0076.W. Two earlier interviews took place on April 5, 2000, and on June 29, 2000. In the latter interview, Posey gave a statement to the investigators telling of his involvement in the June 21, 1964, murders. He "voluntarily provided the following information pursuant to a proffer letter." Posey subsequently refused to sign the proffer letter, in 2000 and, again, after his conversation with Hood in 2004.

68. Report: "Interview of Jimmy Snowden," State of Mississippi, Office of the Attorney General, Public Integrity Division. Case File Number 2K.0076.W. An earlier interview took place on April 6, 2000.

69. Report: "Interview—Sam Bowers," State of Mississippi, Office of the Attorney General, Public Integrity Division, Case File Number 2K.0076.W.

70. Telephone interview, Jim Hood, August 3, 2005.

71. Telephone interview, Jim Hood, taped, August 17, 2005.

72. Interview, Mark Duncan.

73. Ibid.

74. Telephone interview, Jim Hood, August 3, 2005.

75. Telephone interview, Jim Hood, August 3, 2005. See also Jerry Mitchell, "Crime Victim," p. A01.

76. Jerry Mitchell, "Neshoba Killings Probe Widens," *Jackson Clarion-Ledger*, December 19, 2004, p. A1.

77. All quoted in Mitchell, "Neshoba Killings Probe Widens."

78. In 2004, the grand jury consisted of whites, blacks, and members of the Choctaw Indian Tribe.

79. Quoted in Jerry Mitchell, "Grand Jury Considered 4 Suspects of 8 Living," *Jackson Clarion-Ledger*, June 12, 2005, p. A1.

80. A "no bill" decision by a grand jury means that there was little or no justification, or probable cause, for issuing an indictment against a person. According to *Ballentine's Law Dictionary*, a "no bill" is "an indorsement by a grand jury on an indictment, indicating "not found," or "not a true bill." James A. Ballentine, *Ballentine's Law Dictionary*, 3d ed. (Rochester, New York: Lawyers Cooperative Publishing Company, 1969), p. 852.

81. Quoted in Jerry Mitchell, "Killen Pleads Innocent in Civil Rights Killings," *Jackson Clarion-Ledger*, January 8, 2005, p. A1.

82. See her remarks in Manuel Roig-Franzia, "'Mississippi Burning' Case Reopened; 1 Man Arrested," *Washington Post*, January 7, 2005, p. A01. See also Jerry Mitchell, "Grand Jury Indicts Killen in '64 Killings," *Jackson Clarion-Ledger*, January 7, 2005, p. A1.

83. Bender's press statement found in Josh Getlin and Elizabeth Mehren, "Still a Long Ways from Justice," *Los Angeles Times*, January 8, 2005, p. 1.

84. Quoted in Robert D. McFadden, "First Murder Charge in '64 Civil Rights Killings of 3," *New York Times*, January 7, 2005, p. A1.

85. Quoted in Getlin and Mehren, "Still a Long Ways."

86. Jimmy Arledge was the other Klansman ordered to appear before the grand jurors.

87. Quoted in McFadden, "First Murder Charge." See also Roig-Franzia, "'Mississippi Burning' Case Reopened."

88. Quoted in Mitchell, "Grand Jury Indicts Killen." McIntyre, as already noted, is a seventy-two-year-old "good old boy" plugged into the white Jackson, Mississippi, city establishment. At the 1967 federal trial, he was Sheriff Lawrence Rainey's counsel. Rainey was acquitted.

89. Quoted in Jerry Mitchell, "Attorney: Odds against Killen," *Jackson Clarion-Ledger*, February 10, 2005, p. A1.

90. Jerry Mitchell, "Bowers May Be Called to Testify," *Jackson Clarion-Ledger*, February 20, 2005, p. A1.

91. See his organization's Web site at http://www.awkkkk.org.

92. Ibid.

93. Quoted in Jerry Mitchell, "Killen Bid to Dismiss Charges rejected," *Jackson Clarion-Ledger*, March 5, 2005, p. A1.

Chapter Five.
The Murder Trial of Edgar Ray Killen, June 13–21, 2005:
Participants, Environment, and Jury Selection

1. Quoted in Jerry Mitchell, "Killen Wanted to Shake Assassin's Hand," *Jackson Clarion-Ledger*, January 12, 2005, p. A1.

2. Quoted in Jerry Mitchell, "Seeing 80-Year-Old in Jail Cell Drew Defense Lawyer to Case," *Jackson Clarion-Ledger*, June 17, 2005, p. A1.

3. Quoted in Manuel Roig-Franzia, "Ex-Klan Leader Convicted in '64 Case," *Washington Post*, June 22, 2005, p. A1.

4. Quoted in Steven G. Watson, "AG Eyeing Potential Witnesses," *Neshoba Democrat*, June 24, 2004, p. 1.

5. Killen recounted this event in a 1999 interview he gave to the *Clarion-Ledger*'s Jerry Mitchell, whose story about the interview was published in 2005 ("Killen Wanted to Shake Assassin's Hand"). In the same interview, Mitchell asked Killen what should happen to the killers of the three civil rights workers. Killen's response: "I'm not going to say that they [the killers] were wrong."

6. Quoted in John F. Sugg, "Mississippi Lawyer: What's White Is Right," *Truthout/Report*, June 17, 2005, at http://www.truthout.org/docs_2005/061705C.shtml.

7. Ross Barnett was the fifty-third governor of Mississippi, from 1960 to 1964. During Governor Barnett's administration he vowed to maintain segregation in the state's public schools, even pledging to go to jail before he would allow integration. But in 1962, the U.S. Supreme Court directed Ole Miss, the University of Mississippi, to admit James H. Meredith, a black applicant. Meredith's enrollment at Ole Miss broke the color barrier in Mississippi, and his admission was the first step in the eventual elimination of all racial segregation in the state's public schools and universities. Barnett personally blocked Meredith from registering at the university even after the Supreme Court ruled. Finally, on September 30, 1962, a Sunday, Meredith was escorted onto the campus by federal marshals and Civil Rights Division lawyers led by Assistant Attorney General for Civil Rights

John Doar. Stationed on or near the campus to protect him were 123 deputy federal marshals, 316 U.S. Border Patrol officers, and 97 federal prison guards. Within an hour, the federal forces were attacked by a mob that would grow to number 2,000 and who fought them with guns, bricks, bottles, and Molotov cocktails. The marshals had been ordered not to shoot and so used teargas to try to stop the rioting. The violence continued until President John F. Kennedy sent 16,000 federal troops to the campus. When it was over, 2 people were dead, 28 marshals had been shot, 160 people were injured, and James Meredith became the first black student to attend the University of Mississippi.

8. U.S. Senator James O. Eastland (1904–1986), from Sunflower County in the Mississippi delta, was first elected to the Senate in 1941. From 1956 to 1978, he was the chairman of the powerful Senate Judiciary Committee. Eastland was a vigorous, vicious opponent of all civil rights legislation and a fervent supporter of Jim Crow, the White Citizens' Councils (WCC), the Klan, and the Mississippi State Sovereignty Commission. Eastland and his staff flaunted their racism, both in Washington and in Sunflower County, Mississippi. At a WCC rally in Birmingham, Alabama, in 1956, Eastland told the wildly cheering audience: "When in the course of human events it becomes necessary to abolish the Negro race, proper methods should be used. Among these are guns, bows and arrows, slingshots, and knives. . . . All whites are created equal with certain rights, among these are life, liberty, and the pursuit of dead niggers." See http://www.flakmag .com/books/senate7.html.

9. John Doar was assistant attorney for civil rights in the Department of Justice in 1967. He was the chief prosecutor for the federal government in the 1967 conspiracy trial of the 18 Klansmen, including Killen, who were charged with conspiracy to deprive the three civil rights workers of their constitutional rights. See, generally, Ball, *Murder in Mississippi : United States v. Price and the Struggle for Civil Rights* (Lawrence: University Press of Kansas, 2004).

10. Full interview found at www.nationalist.org/doc/ideology/killen.html. Part of the Lee sermon (titled "Payday Someday") follows: "Thus we learn that no man can evade God's laws with impunity. All of God's laws are their own executioners. They have strange penalties annexed. Stolen waters are sweet. But every ounce of sweetness makes a pound of nausea. Nature keeps honks pitilessly. Man's credit with her is good. But Nature collects. And there is no land to which you can flee and escape her bailiffs. Every day her bloodhounds track down the men and women who owe her. . . . 'Payday Someday!' God said it—and it was done! Yes, and from this we learn the power and certainty of God in carrying out His own retributive providence, that men might know that His justice slumbereth not. Even though the mill of God grinds slowly, it grinds to powder. Yes, the judgments of God often have leaden heels and travel slowly. But they always have iron hands

and crush completely." See Lee's Web site at http://www.baptistfire.com/articles/gospel/payday.shtml.

11. Quoted in Jeremy Hudson, "'64 Slaying Suspect Called Friendly," *Jackson Clarion-Ledger*, January 12, 2005, p. A1.

12. Interview, Marcus Gordon, taped, June 23, 2005, Philadelphia, Mississippi.

13. Ibid.

14. Ibid.

15. "I don't like to fly today," the judge told me in jest, "because I'm afraid those mechanics are about like I was—a very poor mechanic." Interview, Marcus Gordon, June 23, 2005.

16. During my interview with wiry Judge Gordon, who stands 6 feet 3 inches tall, with a distinguished mane of pure white, wavy hair, he asked me if I thought a movie would be made of this trial. Instantly I responded: "If they make the movie you'll play yourself!" Interview, Marcus Gordon, June 23, 2005, Philadelphia, Mississippi.

17. Quoted in Billy Watkins, "Judge for Killen Is Seen as Efficient, Organized, Respectful," *Jackson Clarion-Ledger*, June 13, 2005, p. A1. During my conversation with Judge Gordon, he told me that he "had no concerns about security, with the possible exception of problems that might come from outside groups visiting the trial."

18. This incident was presented by the prosecutors in the effort to deny Killen a bail bond in August 2005.

19. See Jerry Mitchell, "Court Told J.D. Killen Planned Hit on Judge," *Jackson Clarion-Ledger*, September 9, 2005, p. A1, for additional information.

20. Quoted in Watkins, "Judge for Killen."

21. Interview, Judge Gordon, June 23, 2005.

22. Quoted in Jerry Mitchell, "Judge Tough, but Has a 'Heart,'" *Jackson Clarion-Ledger*, June 24, 2005, p. A1.

23. Quoted in Mitchell, "Judge Tough." Slaughter-Harvey told Mitchell: "I've had judges not deserving to wear the robe, calling me a nigger, laughing when a witness used the word nigger."

24. Quoted in Laura Hipp, "Killen Judge," *Jackson Clarion-Ledger*, July 28, 2005, p. A1.

25. Quoted in Watkins, "Judge for Killen Case."

26. Interview, Judge Gordon, June 23, 2005.

27. Quoted in Watkins, "Judge for Killen Case."

28. The members of the seventeen-person jury cohort were:
Beddie Ruth Covington, WF, seventy-two, homemaker
Jacquelin Hearn, WF, fifty-five, registered nurse

Troy Savell, WM, forty, teacher and coach
Atlantia Griffin, BF, twenty-seven, automobile plant worker
Brenda Smith, WF, thirty-four, technical services librarian
Gregory Griffin, BM, thirty-six, chicken plant worker
Beverly Agent, WF, fifty, quality control plant worker
Shirley Vaughan, WF, fifty-six, office manager (jury forewoman)
John Miller, WM, thirty-six, teacher
Willis Lyon, BM, forty-two, bus driver and assistant teacher
Patricia Moore, BF, fifty-four, social worker
Jackie Wilson, WF, forty-six, chicken farmer
Norma Perdeye, WF, sixty-one, registered nurse
Thomas Pinter, WM, twenty-seven, automobile plant worker
Alice Clark, WF, forty-eight, casino games auditor
Karen Moody, WF, forty-four, teacher
Warren Paprocki, WM, fifty-four, engineer

29. Duncan quoted in an excellent interview conducted by Sid Salter. See Sid Salter, "Sunday Morning with Mark Duncan," *Jackson Clarion-Ledger*, July 3, 2005, p. G1.

30. Ibid.

31. Circuit Court of Neshoba County, Mississippi, *State of Mississippi vs. Edgar Ray Killen*, No. 05-CR-0006-NS-G, 2005 (Killen trial transcript; hereinafter cited as KTT), vol. 4, p. 874.

32. See, for example, Shaila Dewan, "Prosecution Completes Case in 1964 Civil Rights Killings," *New York Times*, June 19, 2005, p. A1.

33. Quoted in Salter, "Sunday Morning."

34. Quoted in Jerry Mitchell, "High Profile Case Puts Spotlight on Humble DA," *Jackson Clarion-Ledger*, June 15, 2005, p. A1.

35. Interview, Debbie Burt Myers, June 22, 2005, Philadelphia, Mississippi.

36. Debbie Burt Myers, "Duncan, the Gourmet DA," *Neshoba Democrat*, June 10, 2005, p. 1.

37. Ibid.

38. Quoted in Mitchell, "High Profile Case."

39. Quoted in Salter, "Sunday Morning."

40. Quoted in Steven G. Watson, "AG Eyeing Potential Witnesses," *Neshoba Democrat*, June 24, 2004, p. 1.

41. Telephone interview, Jim Hood, August 17, 2005.

42. Quoted in Jerry Mitchell, "As Crime Victim, Hood Understands Wanting Justice," *Jackson Clarion-Ledger*, January 9, 2005, p. A1.

43. Quoted in John Fuquay, "AG's Crime-Fighting Bent Ignited by Own Tragedies," *Jackson Clarion-Ledger*, June 16, 2005, p. A1.

44. Telephone interview, Wendy Moran, wife of Mitch Moran, September 26, 2005.

45. Mitchell, "Seeing 80-Year-Old in Jail Cell."

46. Ibid.

47. Ibid.

48. Ibid.

49. See http://inebriatedmule.blogspot.com/2005/06/mitch-moran-meth -case-looms.html. The story appeared in the *Kosciusko Star Herald*. A section of the story follows: "Mitch Moran, a well-known defense attorney in Leake County, was arrested for attempting to buy methamphetamine Wednesday night, just hours after losing a methamphetamine case in Attala County Circuit Court. Moran, who lives west of Carthage, is charged with a federal misdemeanor of attempting to possess of precursor chemicals to manufacture methamphetamine. The Drug Enforcement Agency worked with the Mississippi Bureau of Narcotics and the Leake County Sheriff's Department on the arrest. Outside agencies were called in by Leake County Sheriff Greg Waggoner. A DEA spokesman said that was to prevent local officers from looking as if they were out to get Moran, who often defends people they arrest." See http://www.starherald.net/articles/2003/09/18/news/news1.txt.

50. Telephone interview, Wendy Moran.

51. John F. Sugg, "Mississippi Lawyer: What's White Is Right," *Truthout/ Report*, June 17, 2005, at http://www.truthout.org/docs_2005/061705C.shtml.

52. Telephone interview, James McIntyre, taped, September 1, 2005.

53. Ibid.

54. Sugg, "Mississippi Lawyer."

55. Telephone interview, James McIntyre, taped, September 14, 2005.

56. Ibid.

57. Ibid.

58. Some of the following material is from a first-person essay I wrote as a special correspondent for the *Burlington Free Press*. See Howard Ball, "The Past Is Present in Mississippi," *Burlington Free Press*, June 16, 2005, p. 1. My goal was to convey to the readers the atmosphere surrounding the Killen trial, in and out of the courtroom.

59. This secrecy did not last very long. Because of suspicion that the twelve jurors were all white, the clerk told the press that the twelve jurors included nine whites and three blacks. The names of the jurors were not announced until after the concluding statements were made by counsel.

60. Julie Goodman, "Trial Reunited Civil Rights Workers," *Jackson Clarion-Ledger*, June 22, 2005, p. A1.

61. Judge Gordon to prospective jurors, KTT, vol. 1, p. 144.

62. See KTT, vol. 1, pp. 106–179; vol. 2, pp.180–509; vol. 3, pp. 510–520.

63. KTT, vol.1, p. 109.

64. KTT, vol. 1, pp. 110–141, passim.

65. The questionnaire was provided to me by fax, from Mark Duncan, District Attorney, 8th Circuit Court District, Philadelphia, Mississippi, September 14, 2005.

66. The information contained in the questionnaires was used by counsel to either ask for dismissal for cause or peremptory challenge, as well as to provide them with useful information for counsel when quizzing potential jurors.

67. See, generally, KTT, vol. 1, pp. 169–250, passim; vol. 2, pp. 251–509, passim; vol. 3, pp. 510–518, passim.

68. See KTT, vol. 2, pp. 481–500, passim; vol. 3, pp. 501–507, passim.

69. KTT, vol. 3, p. 520.

70. Quoted in Harriet Ryan, "In High Profile Murder Trial, Picking Jury Is a Small-Town Affair," Court TV, June 15, 2005, at http://www.courttv.com/trials/killen/061405_ctv.html.

71. Harriet Ryan, "Defense: Killen Was Klansman but Not Involved in 1964 Murders," Court TV, June 15, 2005, at http://www.courttv.com/trials/killen/061505_ctv.html.

72. KTT, vol. 1, pp. 145–146.

Chapter Six. The Murder Trial of Edgar Ray Killen, June 13–21, 2005: Testimony and Post-Trial Events

1. Quoted in Manuel Roig-Franzia, "Ex-Klan Leader Convicted in '64 Case," *Washington Post,* June 22, 2005, p. A1.

2. Quoted in http://www.nationalist.org.

3. Quoted on "Mississippi Justice," Court TV, September 14, 2004.

4. Circuit Court of Neshoba County, Mississippi, *State of Mississippi vs. Edgar Ray Killen,* No. 05-CR-0006-NS-G, 2005 (Killen trial transcript; hereinafter cited as KTT), vol. 3, pp. 521–535, passim.

5. Jerry Mitchell, "Dead Witnesses' Accounts Key to Prosecuting Killen," *Jackson Clarion-Ledger,* June 12, 2005, p. A1.

6. Bobby DeLaugher, a Hinds County assistant district attorney who successfully prosecuted Byron De La Beckwith in 1994, also used transcripts from De La Beckwith's 1964 trial. He rehearsed the transcript's words endlessly with staff in order to provide a sense of drama to the jurors. Unless the reading was done well, the evidence therein "would lose its feeling of being a murder trial. . . . I felt it was important to provide as much drama as attended to any other murder trial." Quoted in Mitchell, "Dead Witnesses' Accounts."

7. Killen took the stand in his defense in the 1975 trial, against his lawyer's protests. He argued that the voice on the tape threatening the private investigator (Mr. Ware) was not his. The jury did not believe him; neither did Killen's own lawyer.

8. KTT, vol. 3, p. 521.

9. Ibid., pp. 523–528, passim.

10. Ibid., p. 528.

11. Ibid., p. 529. "Now, Mr. Killen has denied in his own way of being involved in the Klan. For the sake of this trial, we are going to assume that he was in the Klan. Being a member of the Klan is not what's on trial here. What's on trial here is what the State of Mississippi has to prove, that Edgar Ray Killen intentionally killed the three Civil Rights workers."

12. Ibid., pp. 530, 532. Moran also told the jurors that the prosecutorial effort to paint Killen as a "godfather or the main perpetrator who called the shots was simply not true. . . . The evidence will show that he did not plan or orchestrate this killing."

13. Ibid., p. 532.

14. Ibid., pp. 532–533.

15. Ibid., pp. 560–574, passim., 571.

16. Ibid., p. 576.

17. Ibid., p. 577.

18. Ibid., p. 592.

19. Ibid., p. 616.

20. Ibid., pp. 620–632, passim.

21. Ibid., pp. 678–693, passim.

22. Ibid., pp. 693–708, passim.

23. Ibid., pp. 709–716, passim.

24. Ibid., pp. 718–728, passim.

25. Ibid., 734.

26. Ibid., pp. 736–748, passim.

27. KTT, vol. 4, p. 741.

28. Ibid., p. 780. "Killen told my grandfather, yes, and he was proud of it."

29. Ibid., pp. 775–791, passim.

30. Ibid., p. 795.

31. Ibid., p. 830.

32. Ibid., pp. 838–839.

33. Ibid., pp. 846–853, passim. "Oh, yeah. There were phone calls, throwing eggs on my house, shots [fired]. I couldn't get a job no more. The threatening got so bad, they said they'd put dynamite under my house and blow us to bits." (So frightening were these Klan threats that she and her young son, Ben, moved from

Neshoba County to New York. Five years ago, she moved to New Jersey, where she still resides.)

    34. Ibid., pp. 863–864, 869.

    35. Ibid., p. 871.

    36. Ibid., p. 873.

    37. Ibid., p. 874.

    38. Quoted in Shaila Dewan, "Prosecution Completes Case in 1964 Civil Rights Killings," *New York Times,* June 19, 2005, p. A1.

    39. KTT, vol. 4, p. 875.

    40. Ibid.

    41. KTT, vol. 4, p. 878–879.

    42. Ibid., p. 877.

    43. Ibid., pp. 903–905. Cross-examination by Duncan.

    44. Ibid., p. 900.

    45. Ibid., pp. 907–908.

    46. Ibid., p. 925.

    47. Ibid., p. 925.

    48. Ibid., pp. 925–927.

    49. Ibid., p. 933.

    50. Ibid., p. 936.

    51. Ibid., p. 941.

    52. Ibid., p. 943.

    53. Ibid., p. 946.

    54. Ibid., pp. 946, 953.

    55. Ibid., p. 952.

    56. Ibid., pp. 954–955.

    57. But, evidently, not loud enough to be transcribed by the court reporter. I was, however, in the first row, ten feet away from Killen. Even though my wife claims I'm hard of hearing, I clearly heard Killen's remark.

    58. KTT, vol. 4, p. 955.

    59. Ibid., p. 955, 956–957.

    60. Ibid., p. 958. "I would suggest to you that this is not a case to solve a crime. This is a case to pull back the curtain for the TV cameras."

    61. Ibid., p. 962.

    62. Ibid., p. 968.

    63. Ibid., p. 975.

    64. Ibid., p. 977.

    65. Ibid.

    66. Howard Ball, "A Diary of Mississippi Justice," *The View from the University of Vermont,* June 29, 2005. At http://www.uvm.edu/theview/article.php?id=1684.

67. See Warren Paprocki, "It Was about the Evidence," *Los Angeles Times,* July 8, 2005, p. 1.

68. Quoted in Shaila Dewan, "Jurors Keenly Aware of Trial's Significance and Symbolism," *New York Times,* June 29, 2005, p. A1.

69. Quoted in Jerry Mitchell, "Killen Jurors Outline Verdict," *Jackson Clarion-Ledger,* July 17, 2005, p. A1.

70. Quoted in Mitchell, "Killen Jurors."

71. Quoted in Shaila Dewan, "Former Klansman Found Guilty of Murder in 1964 Deaths," *New York Times,* June 22, 2005, p. 1A.

72. Interview, Mark Duncan, June 27, 2005, Philadelphia, Mississippi.

73. In my interview with Attorney General Hood, August 3, 2005, he acknowledged that the complaints of some jurors were valid and, again, spoke sadly about the deaths of two important witnesses, Price and Springer, and about frustration in not being able to introduce Price's proffer statement into evidence.

74. Quoted in Dewan, "Former Klansman Guilty."

75. Ibid.

76. KTT, vol. 4, p. 998.

77. Ibid., p. 1002.

78. Ibid., pp. 1002–1003.

79. Quoted in Jerry Mitchell, "Killen Remains Defiant Following Conviction," *Jackson Clarion-Ledger,* June 26, 2005, p. A1.

80. Some of the following paragraphs are from Howard Ball, "The Guilty Verdict Explained," *Jackson Free Press,* July 6, 2005, p. 8. I wrote this essay while in Mississippi because of the many questions raised surrounding Killen's manslaughter convictions.

81. See Attorney General Hood's concerns voiced in the documentary, "Mississippi Justice," Court TV, September 14, 2005.

82. Jerry Mitchell, "Ex-Klansman Convicted in 1964 Killings," *Jackson Clarion-Ledger,* June 22, 2005, p. A1.

83. Bender, Chaney, and Lewis quoted in Debbie Burt Myers, "Judge Gives Killen 60 Years," *Neshoba Democrat,* June 29, 2005, p. 1.

84. The student newspaper at the University of Mississippi.

85. KTT, vol. 4, pp. 1004–1019, passim.

86. Ibid., pp. 1019–1029.

87. Ibid., p. 1021.

88. Interview, Chris Epps, June 27, 2005, Philadelphia, Mississippi.

89. Ibid.

90. The defense argument reminds one of the classic definition of the Yiddish term "chutzpah": A man brutally and with premeditation kills his parents but then throws himself on the mercy of the court because he is an orphan!

91. The U.S. Supreme Court has total discretion on the cases it will hear each term. In any term, there will be about 9,000 petitions asking the Court to review the case on the merits. In any term, the Court will hear approximately eighty cases on the merits. See, generally, David O'Brien, *Storm Center,* 7th ed. (New York: Norton, 2003).

92. Mississippi Code of 1972, as amended, Sec. 99-35-115-Subsec. (1), 1997 amendment.

93. Ibid., Subsec. (2).

94. Ibid.

95. Chris Epps's office at the MDOC denied Killen's claims of improper care. "As far as I know," said Nic Lott, "he's received the best medical service that's possible out there."

96. Above quotes from Debbie Burt Myers, "Killen Released on $600,000 Bail," *Neshoba Democrat,* August 12, 2005, p. 1.

97. Quoted in Emily Wagster Pettus, "Judge Awards Killen $600,000 Bail," *Northeast Mississippi Daily Journal,* August 12, 2005, p. 1.

98. Quoted in Bill Nichols, "Mississippi Town Grapples with Killer's Release amid Appeal," *USA Today,* August 29, 2005, p. 2.

99. In addition, the Mississippi White Knights of the Ku Klux Klan in Petal, Mississippi, announced that it would hold a rally on November 12, 2005, to protest Killen's conviction. No rally took place.

100. Barrett quoted in Jerry Mitchell, "Supremacist Wants Day to Honor Killen," *Jackson Clarion-Ledger,* August 13, 2005, p. A1.

101. Quoted in Jerry Mitchell, "Permission Sought for Killen Tribute," *Jackson Clarion-Ledger,* August 18, 2005, p. A1. In the story, Mitchell revealed the contents of a letter Killen wrote while in prison in July 2005. It was sent to Travis Golie, an inmate in the Iowa State Penitentiary (serving time for robbery). "My Christian convictions is [*sic*] almost all I have left, but the liberal communist element will never take that away from me. I will go to my grave saying wake up America. You are too young to die. Please don't keep going the way of the foreigners, aliens, and most politicians of America."

102. Deputy Hampton quoted in Jerry Mitchell, "Killen Seen Walking on His Own without Wheelchair," *Jackson Clarion-Ledger,* September 3, 2005, p. A1.

103. Duncan quoted in Jerry Mitchell, "High Court Refuses Request in Killen Case," *Jackson Clarion-Ledger,* September 8, 2005, p. A1.

104. Letter posted on http://www.nationalist.org/news/archives/2005/letters.html.

105. Quoted in Leesha Faulkner, "Analysis: If Convicted, Killen's Chances for Appeal Seem Slim," *Northeast Mississippi Daily Journal,* June 21, 2005, p. 1.

106. Mark Beason, "Common Bond Age, Friendship, Not Color," *Neshoba Democrat*, June 29, 2005, p. 1.

107. Clyde Haberman, "Closure or Something Close Enough," *New York Times*, June 29, 2005, p. A16.

Chapter Seven. Beyond 2005: Truth, Reconciliation, and Change in Mississippi

1. Quoted in Jerry Mitchell, "Widow of Schwerner Says She Hopes Case a Beginning," *Jackson Clarion-Ledger*, June 22, 2005, p. A1.

2. Quoted in Billy Watkins, "Verdict Will Help Heal Mississippi, Some Say," *Jackson Clarion-Ledger*, June 22, 2005, p. A1.

3. Circuit Court of Neshoba County, Mississippi, *State of Mississippi vs. Edgar Ray Killen*, No. 05-CR-0006-NS-G, 2005, vol. 4, p. 925.

4. Quoted in Watkins, "Verdict Will Help Heal."

5. Quoted in Donna Ladd, "After Killen: What's Next for Mississippi," *Jackson Free Press*, June 22, 2005, p. 12.

6. McLemore and I chaired our political science departments at Jackson State University (a predominantly black institution) and at Mississippi State University. For six years, between 1976 and 1982, we worked, with our faculty and students, to create an interactive exchange of ideas and personnel between the two campuses. It was an exciting time for the discipline in Mississippi.

7. Quoted in Debbie Burt Myers, "Historian Sees Coalition's Efforts as a Model for the State," *Neshoba Democrat*, June 24, 2004, p. 1.

8. The material in the following paragraphs is from http://www.olemiss .edu/winterinstitute/outreach.htm.

9. For more information, visit http://www.outreach.olemiss.edu/Freedom _Riders/Home.html.

10. Download the resource book at http://www.olemiss.edu/winterinstitute/ resourceguide.

11. See, for example, Jeanetta Craigwell-Graham, "Revisiting Freedom Summer: An Intern's Perspective," *Wellspring* 2, 1 (May 2005): 2–3.

12. Quoted in Ladd, "After Killen."

13. Quoted in Watkins, "Verdict Will Help Heal."

14. Quoted in Lindsay, "Relations Calm," *Jackson Clarion-Ledger*, June 12, 2005, p. A1. A black Philadelphia businessman, Randy Gill, owns McClellan's Café and Grocery in Philadelphia. He told reporter Lindsay: "Years ago, relations used to be based on race. Now it's based on economics. The color of race relations is now green. . . . Everything's tied to the green."

15. See http://www.census.gov/1989. The data from 1968 showed an even higher poverty rate in Mississippi.

16. U.S. Census Bureau, *Income, Poverty, and Health Insurance Coverage in the United States: 2004* (Washington, D.C.: U.S. Department of Commerce, August 30, 2005).

17. Ibid.

18. Jonathan Alter, "The Other America," *Newsweek* 146, 12 (September 19, 2005), p. 22.

19. In Mississippi, 12 percent of children live in extreme poverty and nearly 24 percent live in poverty; 41 percent of black children live in poverty, while 10 percent of white children live in poverty. See National Center for Children in Poverty, "Child Poverty in States Hit by Hurricane Katrina," at http://www.nccp.org/pub_cpt05a.html. In Louisiana, 13 percent of children live in extreme poverty, while another 23 percent of children live in poverty; 44 percent of black children live in poverty, while 9 percent of white children live in poverty. In New Orleans, Louisiana, 38 percent of children live in poverty. See National Center for Children in Poverty, "Child Poverty in States Hit by Hurricane Katrina."

20. In addition to the WWIRR, the NAACP, the Medgar Evers Institute, the James Chaney Foundation, and some churches and synagogues are actively engaged in the process of encouraging reconciliation. The Reverend Dolphus Weary, the president of the Christian racial conciliation group Mission Mississippi, said that "I will visit some of the pastors in Philadelphia [and other towns] and say, 'What are we going to do now? What are we going to do to work on real healing? This [trial] was just an event. Healing takes place over a long time.'" Quoted in Watkins, "Verdict Will Help Heal."

21. Gary Younge, "Racism Rebooted," *Nation*, July 11, 2005, p. 11. When one visits Mississippi in 2005, he observed, one sees very clear racial disparities in health, education, employment, incarceration, and poverty.

22. E-mail to author, August 8, 2005. For further information: Art.Cosby@SSRC.MsState.edu.

23. See census data from 1960 to 2005 to note the changes in poverty over time, http://www.census.gov.

24. William Raspberry, "Racial Fairness Still a Dream, but There's Movement in Mississippi," *Jackson Clarion-Ledger*, June 22, 2005, p. A16.

25. Karl Fleming, "A Reporter Goes Home to a New South," *Los Angeles Times*, June 29, 2005, p. A1.

26. Ibid.

27. Raspberry, "Racial Fairness Still a Dream."

28. Quoted in Debbie Burt Myers, "Public Schools Statewide Can Teach Civil Rights History," *Neshoba Democrat*, March 22, 2006, p. 1.

Bibliography and Resources

Secondary Sources: Books and Articles

Allen, James, Hilton Als, John Lewis, and Leon F. Litwack. *Without Sanctuary: Lynching Photography in America.* Santa Fe, NM: Twin Palms, 2000.

Ball, Howard. "A Diary of Mississippi Justice." *The View from the University of Vermont,* June 29, 2005. http://www.uvm.edu/theview/article.php?id=1684.

———. *Hugo L. Black: Cold Steel Warrior.* New York: Oxford University Press, 1995.

———. *Murder in Mississippi.* Lawrence: University Press of Kansas, 2004.

———. *Prosecuting War Crimes and Genocide: The Twentieth-Century Experience.* Lawrence: University Press of Kansas, 1999.

Ballentine, James A. *Ballentine's Law Dictionary.* 3d. ed. Rochester, NY: Lawyers Co-operative Publishing Company, 1969.

Belfrage, Sally. *Freedom Summer.* New York: Viking, 1965.

Chaney, Ben. "Schwerner, Chaney, and Goodman: The Struggle for Justice," *Human Rights Magazine,* Spring 2000. http://www.abanet.org/irr/hr/spring00 humanrights/chaney.html.

Craigwell-Graham, Jeanetta. "Revisiting Freedom Summer: An Intern's Perspective." *Wellspring* 2, 1 (May 2005).

Durr, Virginia Foster. *Outside the Magic Circle.* Tuscaloosa: University of Alabama Press, 1990.

Glisson, Susan. "On Truth and Freedom." *Wellspring* 2, 1 (May 2005).

Hilberg, Raul. *Perpetrators, Victims, Bystanders: The Jewish Conspiracy, 1933–1945.* New York: HarperCollins, 1992.

Katagiri, Yasuhiro. *The Mississippi State Sovereignty Commission: Civil Rights and States' Rights.* Jackson: University Press of Mississippi, 2001.

Orr-Klopfer, M. Susan. *Where Rebels Roost: Mississippi Civil Rights Revisited.* 2005. http://www.lulu.com/content/135246.

Ladd, Donna. "Unfinished Business: Mississippi's Struggles with Racist Past and

Present," master's thesis, Columbia University School of Journalism, May 2000.

Mars, Florence. *Witness in Philadelphia.* Baton Rouge: University of Louisiana Press, 1977.

McMillan, Neil. *The Citizen's Council: Organizing Resistance to the Second Reconstruction.* Urbana: University of Illinois Press, 1971.

Nossiter, Adam. *Of Long Memory: Mississippi and the Murder of Emmett Till.* Cambridge, MA: Da Capo Press, 2002.

O'Brien, David. *Storm Center.* 7th ed. New York: Norton, 2003.

Philadelphia Coalition. "Roots of Struggle, Rewards of Freedom: African-American Heritage Driving Tour." http://www.neshobajustice.com/RootsofStruggle.pdf.

Rubin, Richard. "The Ghosts of Emmett Till." *New York Times Sunday Magazine,* July 31, 2005: 30–35.

Salmond, John A. *The Conscience of a Lawyer: Clifford J. Durr and American Civil Liberties, 1899–1975.* Tuscaloosa: University of Alabama Press, 1990.

Silver, James. *Mississippi: The Closed Society.* New York: Harcourt, Brace, and World, 1963.

U.S. Census Bureau. *Income, Poverty, and Health Insurance Coverage in the United States: 2004.* Washington, D.C.: U.S. Department of Commerce, August 30, 2005.

Younge, Gary. "Racism Rebooted." *Nation,* July 11, 2005: 10–16.

Interviews and Other Communications

Rita Schwerner Bender, widow of Michael Schwerner

Clyde Carter, *Neshoba Democrat* reporter/photographer

Ben Chaney, brother of James Chaney

Leroy Clemons, cochair, Philadelphia Coalition; president, Neshoba County NAACP

Drew Days III, assistant attorney general, civil rights division, Carter Administration

Stanley Dearman, former editor, *Neshoba Democrat;* member, Philadelphia Coalition

Fenton DeWeese, member, Philadelphia Coalition

Mark Duncan, district attorney, Neshoba County, Mississippi

Chris Epps, commissioner, Mississippi Department of Corrections

Jim Gilliland, office of Mississippi attorney general

Ann Amis Gilmer, court reporter, 8th District, Mississippi

Ruth Bader Ginsburg, associate justice, U.S. Supreme Court (letters)

Susan Glisson, director, William Winter Institute for Racial Reconciliation; special liaison, Philadelphia Coalition
Marcus D. Gordon, judge, 8th Judicial Circuit, Neshoba County, Mississippi
Jim Hood, Mississippi attorney general
Donna Ladd, executive editor, *Jackson Free Press*
Angela Lewis, daughter of James Chaney
James McIntyre, Killen defense counsel
Jewell McDonald, member, Philadelphia Coalition
Jerry Mitchell, reporter, *Jackson Clarion-Ledger*
Dick Molpus, former Mississippi secretary of state
Mitch Moran, Killen lead defense counsel (press conference)
Wendy Moran, wife of defense counsel Moran
Debbie Burt Myers, news reporter, *Neshoba Democrat*
Deborah Owens, member, Philadelphia Coalition
Deborah Posey, member, Philadelphia Coalition
Jim Prince III, editor, *Neshoba Democrat;* cochair, Philadelphia Coalition
Anne Pullin, waitress, Peggy's Restaurant
Jacob Ray, office of Mississippi attorney general
Sid Salter, features editor, *Jackson Clarion-Ledger*
James Shelton, jury expert for the prosecution
Jim Sugg, reporter, *Truthout*

Web Sites Cited

www.abanet.org
www.awkkkk.org
www.baptistfire.com
www.cbsnews.org
www.census.gov
www.cnn.com
www.cnn.com/law
www.courttv.com
www.doj.gov.za/trc/index.html
www.lib.usm.edu
www.msnbc.msn.com
www.nationalist.org
www.nccp.org
www.neshobademocrat.com
www.neshobajustice.com

www.olemiss.edu
www.pbs.org/newshour/
www.southernresearchgroup.com
www.splcenter.org
www.starherald.net
www.truthout.org
www.uvm.edu
www.voicesofcivilrights.com
www.workers.org
www.olemiss.edu/winterinstitute/

Documents

1870 Enforcement Act, 18 U.S. Section 241
Allen v. United States, 164 U.S. 492, 1896
Case Files, 2K 0076W. State of Mississippi, Office of the Attorney General, Public Integrity Division (interviews with seven surviving Klansmen involved in the murders of the three civil rights workers in 1964)
Grand Jury Report, 8th Judicial District, Neshoba County, Mississippi, October 1, 1964 Indictment, Edgar Ray Killen, State of Mississippi, Neshoba County, Mississippi, January 6, 2005
Mississippi Statutes, Mississippi Code of 1972, as Amended, Section 97-3-27, 1994
Mississippi Statutes, Mississippi Code of 1972, as Amended, Section 99-35-115 (1) (2), 1997
State of Mississippi v. Edgar Ray Killen, No. 05-CR-0006-NS-G, 2005.
U.S. DOJ, FBI "MIBURN" Files, 1964
United States v. Cecil Price, et al., 385 U.S. 787, 1967

Newspapers Cited

Arkansas Democrat-Gazette
Boston Globe
Burlington Free Press
Connecticut Post
Daily Mississippian
Jackson Clarion-Ledger
Jackson Free Press

Joplin Globe
Kosciusko Star Herald
Los Angeles Times
Mississippi Sun Herald
Neshoba Democrat
New York Times
Northeast Mississippi Daily Journal
Tallahassee Democrat
USA Today
Washington Post

Index